HERE and NOW II

HERE and NOW II

an approach to writing through perception

FRED MORGAN

HARCOURT BRACE JOVANOVICH, INC.

New York   Chicago   San Francisco   Atlanta

Cover photograph by Linda Lindroth.

ISBN: 0-15-535622-4

Library of Congress Catalog Card Number: 75-187527

Printed in the United States of America

to my mother

Florence H. Morgan

—a dedicated teacher

contents

3

getting the feel of action

4

perceiving emotional attitudes

5

observing a person

6

observing a scene

7

estimating a person

8

identifying with a person

9

identifying with a thing or an animal

10

evaluating a possession

11

examining a desire

12

analyzing an institution

13

looking back

14

taking a new perspective

preface

This book, like *Here and Now*, consists of fourteen units designed to improve the student's writing by developing his perception. Each unit takes up a specific area of perception, and each includes a short discussion of one aspect of writing, assignments that focus on relating writing to perception, examples from literature and art, and questions that help the student search out the meaning of the selections. By using the material provided in the units as a guide, the student may perceive and organize the data of his own experience and thus increase his writing skills. The selections offer examples of how accomplished writers have handled similar material.

Although *Here and Now II* contains all new material, it is based on the same premise as *Here and Now:* good writing grows organically out of good thinking, which in turn begins with the materials of sensory experience. An accurate and integrated perception of the self and the environment is primary. The writing assignments invite the student to examine his own experience systematically. The prose readings, poems, and works of art with their accompanying questions then show him how similar perceptions can be expanded and interpreted. In each case the examples have been chosen to show development and variation of the theme, rather than simply illustrations of that theme. The selections have been placed after the writing assignments for two reasons: first, to let more emphasis fall on the creative than on the interpretive processes; and second, to provide, through the assignments, analogous experiences derived from the student's involvement in the material.

Once more the author would like to thank those whose assistance was indispensable: Miss May Robbie of Merced College and Mr. William Speer of Imperial Valley College, who helped revise the manuscript; those instructors all over the country, too numerous to name individually, who responded to questionnaires or volunteered helpful letters; and the many students who have been candid critics. If *Here and Now II* is useful, credit is due these people.

FRED MORGAN

HERE and NOW II

Drawing by Giovannetti. © Punch, London

1

using

your

senses

The first step in learning to observe and write well is to sharpen your senses. All creative activity, as well as much of your pleasure in life, depends on your sensory awareness. Even your ability to absorb and use second-hand information depends on your ability to relate it to your own first-hand observations. Yet, constantly exposed to second-hand information, you may forget to use your senses and may become, to some degree, cut off from the world immediately around you.

keeping in touch

The senses are often listed as five—sight, hearing, smell, taste, and touch. There are two things wrong with this list. First, it is incomplete in that it leaves out at least three important kinds of sensory awareness: the sense of movement, such as you get when you shake your head, which we call the *kinesthetic* sense; the sense of what is going on inside your body, such as you get when you breathe; and the sense of heat and cold, which affects the whole body rather than just the skin. Second, this list of senses is in the wrong order. Touch should be first, because the others are based on it. A baby learns what things are by touching them, and recognizes them by sight or hearing only after he has touched them. A pillow "looks" soft because you have felt pillows and have found them soft. When a person behaves unrealistically, we say he is "out of touch": he is too far away from things to think soundly about them. In an age of telephones, television, and rapid transportation in various kinds of padded containers, you need to make a constant effort to "keep in touch."

enjoying your senses

Most of your vivid memories of childhood probably involve sensory awareness; children, who are less preoccupied with abstract thought than adults, are more open to sense impressions. In the following passage, Thomas Wolfe captures some of a child's pleasure in sensory experiences, especially those involving the sense of smell.

from Look Homeward, Angel

THOMAS WOLFE

He remembered yet the East India Tea House at the Fair, the sandalwood, the turbans, and the robes, the cool interior and the smell of India tea; and he had felt now the nostalgic thrill of dew-wet mornings in Spring, the cherry scent, the cool clarion earth, the wet loaminess of the garden, the pungent breakfast smells and the floating snow of blossoms. He knew the inchoate sharp excitement of hot dandelions in young Spring grass at noon; the smell of cellars, cobwebs, and built-on secret earth; in July, of watermelons bedded in sweet hay, inside a farmer's covered wagon; of cantaloupe and crated peaches; and the scent of orange rind, bitter-sweet, before a fire of coals. He knew the good male smell of his father's sitting-room; of the smooth worn leather sofa, with the gaping horse-hair rent; of the blistered varnished wood upon the hearth; of the heated calf-skin bindings; of the flat moist plug of apple tobacco, stuck with a red flag; of wood-smoke and burnt leaves in October; of the brown tired autumn earth; of honey-suckle at night; of warm nasturtiums; of a clean ruddy farmer who comes weekly with printed butter, eggs and milk; of fat limp underdone bacon and of coffee; of a bakery-oven in the wind; of large deep-hued stringbeans smoking-hot and seasoned well with salt and butter; of a room of old pine boards in which books and carpets have been stored, long closed; of Concord grapes in their long white baskets.

Yes, and the exciting smell of chalk and varnished desks; the smell of heavy bread-sandwiches of cold fried meat and butter; the smell of new leather in a saddler's shop, or of a warm leather chair; of honey and of unground coffee; of barrelled sweet-pickles and cheese and all the fragrant compost of the grocer's; the smell of stored apples in the cellar, and of orchard-apple smells, of pressed-cider pulp; of pears ripening on a sunny shelf, and of ripe cherries stewing with sugar on hot stoves before preserving; the smell of whittled wood, of all young lumber, of sawdust and shavings; of peaches stuck with cloves and pickled in brandy; of pine-sap, and green pine-needles; of a horse's pared hoof; of chestnuts roasting, of bowls of nuts and raisins; of hot cracklin, and of young roast pork; of butter and cinnamon melting on hot candied yams.

Yes, and of the rank slow river, and of tomatoes rotten on the vine; the smell of rain-wet plums and boiling quinces; of rotten lily-pads; and of foul weeds rotting in green marsh scum; and the exquisite smell of the South, clean but funky, like a big woman; of soaking trees and the earth after heavy rain.

Yes, and the smell of hot daisy-fields in the morning; of melted pud-dling iron in a foundry; the winter smell of horse-warm stables and smoking dung; of old oak and walnut; and the butcher's smell of meat, of strong slaughtered lamb, plump gouty liver, ground pasty sausages, and red beef; and of brown sugar melted with slivered bitter chocolate; and of crushed mint leaves, and of a wet lilac bush; of magnolia beneath the heavy moon, of dogwood and laurel; of an old caked pipe and Bourbon rye, aged in kegs of charred oak; the sharp smell of tobacco; of carbolic and nitric acids; the coarse true smell of a dog; of old imprisoned books; and the cool fern-smell near springs; of vanilla in cake-dough; and of cloven ponderous cheeses.

employing your senses

While random use of the senses for enjoyment can heighten your experience and improve your writing ability, you also need to focus your senses purposefully at times to gain knowledge. To observe something is to organize your sense impressions of it. In his autobiography, the geologist Nathaniel Shaler tells of his first lesson in observation. He had been fortunate enough to be accepted as a pupil and assistant to the famous naturalist Louis Agassiz, and describes what happened when he began to work in the laboratory.

from Autobiography

NATHANIEL SOUTHGATE SHALER

When I sat me down before my tin pan, Agassiz brought me a small fish, placing it before me with the rather stern requirement that I should study it, but should on no account talk to any one concerning it, nor read anything relating to fishes, until I had his permission so to do. To my inquiry "What shall I do?" he said in effect: "Find out what you can without damaging the specimen; when I think that you have done the work I will question you." In the course of an hour I thought I had compassed that fish; it was rather an unsavory object, giving forth the stench of old alcohol, then loathsome to me, though in time I came to like it. Many of the scales were loosened so that they fell off. It appeared to me to be a case for a summary report, which I was anxious to make and get on to the next stage of the business. But Agassiz, though always within call, concerned himself no further with me that day, nor the next, nor for a week. At first, this neglect was distressing; but I saw that it was a game, for he was, as I discerned rather than saw, covertly watching me. So I set my wits to work upon the thing, and in the course of a hundred hours or so thought I had done much—a hundred times as much as seemed possible at the start. I got interested in finding out how the scales went in series, their shape, the form and placement of the teeth, etc. Finally, I felt full of the subject and probably expressed it in my bearing; as for words about it then, there were none from my master except his cheery "Good morning." At length on the seventh day, came the question "Well?" and my disgorge of learning to him as he sat on the edge of my table puffing his cigar. At the end of the hour's telling, he swung off and away, saying, "That is not right." Here I began to think that after all perhaps the rules for scanning Latin verse were not the worst infliction in the world. Moreover, it was clear that he was playing a game with me to find if I were capable of doing hard, continuous work without the support of a teacher, and this stimulated me to labor. I went at the task anew, discarded my first notes, and in another week of ten hours a day labor I had results which astonished myself and satisfied him. Still there was no trace of praise in words or manner. He signified that it would do by placing before me about a half a peck of bones, telling me to see what I could make of them, with no further directions to guide me.

AUTOBIOGRAPHY from *The Autobiography of Nathaniel Southgate Shaler*. Copyright 1909 by Sophia P. Shaler, 1936 by Gabriella Shaler Webb. Reprinted by permission of the Estate of Gabriella Web.

class exercise

A piece of chalk might seem an object of little interest to anyone, except for its usefulness. For years you have handled chalk and seen it around you. Just because it seems such a simple and familiar thing, it may be worthwhile to examine it more closely and find out if you can gain a stronger sense of its reality.

Examine a small fragment of chalk as though you had never seen one before and try to describe it so that a person who has never seen a piece of chalk could get a clear idea of what it is.

1. Give your description in the order easiest to understand. Begin with the size, shape, and color; then go on to the more obvious details and, finally, to the less obvious ones. Whenever you can, go from large to small, the way you naturally see an object.
2. Be clear at all times. It is not enough to say, "It is broken off at one end." How does the break look? What is the break's shape, texture, color? What does the way it has broken tell us about the material?
3. Use all your senses. Feel the chalk, smell it, taste it, weigh it in your hand, rub it, test its hardness, listen to the sound it makes when you drop it, crumble it and feel the texture of the powder, wet it and smell it again, and so on: put it through every sensory test you can think of.
4. Try to find the best words for your description. If you can't find a good word to describe a quality, look for an *analogy*—something that it is *like*.
5. If there is time, try describing another common object, such as a pencil or a penny.

writing assignment

1. Select a simple, common object around the house. A kitchen match, a cigarette, an apple, or an egg might be good choices. Be sure that it is an object you can easily replace, since you will want to take it apart.
2. Inspect the object closely. Observe its size, shape, color, texture, weight, hardness, smell, taste, flexibility—all the qualities you can discover without destroying it. Write down notes of your observations as you make them.
3. Experiment with the object. Using all your senses, take it apart in a way that allows you to discover how it is made. Test it: hit it, drop it, squeeze it, bend it, scratch it, burn it, soak it—do anything you can think of that might tell you something about it. Write down a second list of observations.
4. Now rearrange your observations, putting them into a logical order that is easy to follow. You can start from large to small; then, perhaps, from end to end. Finally, when you are telling about your experiments, you

can use a time sequence, saying "First I did this and found out that; then I tried . . ." and so on.

5. Write your report on the object, following the order you set up. Always be sure your reader knows where you are; strive to be clear. At the conclusion, add a short paragraph summing up what you have learned about the object.

The following is a description of the kind you have been asked to write. Compare it with yours and test yours against it for clarity, completeness, and logical order.

the lemon

The lemon I hold in my hand is an oval, bright yellow fruit about the size and weight of a large egg. Its shape is about the shape an egg would be if it had two large ends, except that at each end there is a small bump, like a nipple, perhaps a quarter-inch high and a half-inch across.

Unlike the egg, the lemon is resilient: I can push a dent into it with my thumb, and when I remove my thumb the dent disappears. When I drop the lemon, it bounces a little, though not as much as a rubber ball. The sound it makes is a solid "thud." The surface is shiny but not smooth. It is pocked with tiny round dents about the size a dull pencil point might make. These dents are not arranged in any definite pattern, but cover the surface fairly evenly. The surface is slightly oily to the touch and seems to have no taste. It does have a smell, however, that I find hard to describe: a little like fresh leaves or grass, with a slightly acid tinge. By driving my thumbnail into it, I can make a small break into which a little clear, oily liquid oozes, followed by a much stronger, fruity smell.

Using my nail more strongly, I find I can tear up a bit of the skin, uncovering a spongy, white layer underneath. The outer, bright yellow layer is very thin; the second, white layer seems about a sixteenth of an inch thick and nearly dry. The little dents on the outside come through the yellow layer and into the white layer as small, circular cones that let the light through. The inside of the skin smells much stronger than the outside, with a sharp odor like lemon extract.

As I tear more of the skin away, I find that the inside of the lemon is ribbed with bulges about three-quarters of an inch across, running from end to end and hinting that the inside has a definite structure. In order to find out what that structure is, I slice the lemon straight across with a knife and find the inside so juicy that the knife blade comes out dripping. This juice is nearly clear, with a strong, fresh smell and a sour taste. It is not at all oily like the outer skin, and its smell makes my mouth water.

There is indeed a definite structure to the inside. The juice is held in ten sections separated by some sort of membrane or skin. These sections are shaped somewhat like brazil nuts, with the sharp edges toward the center of the lemon and the curved edges forming the bulges I first observed. Where these sections are cut across, they fit together like the slices of a pie. The small core of skin from which they radiate is hollow.

Since most of the juice has not run out of the lemon where I cut it but remains inside the halves, I guess that there must be smaller compartments within these wedge-shaped sections that are still holding it. As I examine the sliced surface more closely, I find that this is true; the juice is held in tiny pod-like sacs of transparent membrane. Only the juice in the sacs the knife cut through has run out. However, if I pick up half the lemon and squeeze it, more and more of these little sacs burst and more juice runs out. Holding it close to my ear as I do this, I can hear a kind of squeaking sound made by the bursting sacs.

On the inside of the wedges, next to the hollow core, are a few whitish seeds of different sizes, the largest about an eighth of an inch long. They are shaped like miniature lemons. They are not very hard and can be cut in two; they are solid and white, with a thin, greenish skin.

When I squeeze the juice from the lemon halves into a glass, I find it is somewhat pulpy, probably because the sacs have still smaller compartments inside them to hold the juice. The membrane dividing the lemon into sections remains in place inside the squeezed-out skin.

One of the nipples that was at either end of the lemon has a small green stem sticking out of it. When I pull this off, there seems to be a kind of spongy tube leading from it to the hollow core inside, hinting that water may get into the lemon by this route while it is growing. The opposite nipple is a solid, spongy white material like the second layer of skin, and probably serves as an anchor for that end of the tube.

I find that the juice in the glass, mixed with sugar, ice, and a large amount of water, makes a refreshing drink.

sketching assignment

Now that you have carefully described a fairly simple object, you may want to try a less complete description of a larger, more complex object. Outside your classroom, select a tree, building, basketball or tennis court, electrical transformer, or any large object that is nearby. Describe it rapidly but clearly, using the same kind of order you used for the smaller object. Give the general outlines; then fill in the larger details and, finally, the smaller ones. Use an order that suits the object, such as going from top to bottom or from side to side. Always let your reader know where you are so he won't get lost; be clear.

At the Gudgers'

JAMES AGEE

the supper

The biscuits are large and shapeless, not cut round, and are pale, not tanned, and are dusty with flour. They taste of flour and soda and damp salt and fill the mouth stickily. They are better with butter, and still better with butter and jam. The butter is pallid, soft, and unsalted, about the texture of cold-cream; it seems to taste delicately of wood and wet cloth; and it tastes 'weak.' The jam is loose, of little berries, full of light raspings of the tongue; it tastes a deep sweet purple tepidly watered, with a very faint sheen of a sourness as of iron. Field peas are olive-brown, the shape of lentils, about twice the size. Their taste is a cross between lentils and boiled beans; their broth is bright with seasoning of pork, and of this also they taste. The broth is soaked up in bread. The meat is a bacon, granular with salt, soaked in the grease of its frying: there is very little lean meat in it. What there is is nearly as tough as rind; the rest is pure salted stringy fat. The eggs taste of pork too. They are fried in it on both sides until none of the broken yolk runs, are heavily salted and peppered while they fry, so that they come to table nearly black, very heavy, rinded with crispness, nearly as dense as steaks. Of milk I hardly know how to say; it is skimmed, blue-lighted; to a city palate its warmth and odor are somehow dirty and at the same time vital, a little as if one were drinking blood. There is even in so clean a household as this an odor of pork, of sweat, so subtle it seems to get into the very metal of the cooking-pans beyond any removal of scrubbing, and to sweat itself out of newly washed cups; it is all over the house and all through your skin and clothing at all times, yet as you bring each piece of food to your mouth it is so much more noticeable, if you are not used to it, that a quiet little fight takes place on your palate and in the pit of your stomach; and it seems to be this odor, and a sort of wateriness and discouraged tepidity, which combine to make the food seem unclean, sticky, and sallow with some invisible sort of disease, yet this is the odor and consistency and temper and these are true tastes of home; I know this even of myself; and much as my reflexes are twitching in refusal of each mouthful a true homesick and simple fondness for it has so strong hold of me that in fact there is no fight to speak of and no faking of enjoyment at all

in the bedroom

Six sides of me, all pine: Floor supported; walls walled, stood vertical, joined at their four edges, at floor, at one another, and at roof: roof, above rafters, tilted tall, from eaves to crest. Between slats, the undersides of shingles. One wall is lapboard, that one which joins the other bedroom: the others, the skeleton and the inward surface of the outward skin of the house. A door to the bedroom: a door by my bed to the hallway: in the wall at the foot of my bed, a square window, shuttered; another in the wall next at right angles. On the floor beneath this window, a small trunk. To its left, stood across the corner, a bureau and mirror. To its right, stood across the corner, a sewing-machine:

I have told of these: But here, and now, I was first acquainting myself of this room in a silence of wonder to match the silence of sleeping in the next room. Its fragrance was everywhere; its plainness and coloring were beautiful to me. The furniture stood, where I have begun to see, sober and naked to me in the solemn light, and seemed as might the furnishing of a box-car, a barn. This barn and box-car resemblance I use, it occurred to me then and since, as an indication of the bonelike plainness and as if fragility of the place; but I would not mislead or miscolor: this was a room of a human house, of a sort stood up by the hundreds of thousands in the whole of a country; the sheltering and home of the love, hope, ruin, of the living of all of a family, and all the shelter it shall ever know, and since of itself it is so ordinary, so universal, there is no need to name it as a barn, or as a box-car.

But here, I would only suggest how thin-walled, skeletal, and beautiful it seemed in a particular time, as if it were a little boat in the darkness, floated upon the night, far out on the steadiness of a vacant sea, whose crew slept while I held needless watch, and felt the presence of the country round me and upon me. I looked along the walls, how things which were pretty were stuck and pinned to the wood; and at the wood: I should find it hard to tire of watching plain wood which is in some human image; of running my fingers upon it as it were skin; little tricks of glass and china, and of sewn cloths, which were created to be pretty, to be happy: the restings of furniture on the surface of the naked floor; various reflections of the room in the eaten mirror: the square, useless lamp which stood in the dark corner under the sewing-machine: the iron bed, whose sheets and coverlets Mrs. Gudger had drawn smooth for me, the mark of my butt on its edge, my shoes beside it, crazy with mud, worn out and sleeping as a pair of wrecked horses: how the shutters filled their squares of window and were held shut with strings and nails: crevices in the walls, stuffed with hemp, rags, newsprint, and raw cotton: large damp spots and rivulets on the floor, and on the walls, streams and crooked wetness; and a shivering, how chilly and wet the air is in this room: a shutting-off of these matters and mere 'touch' and listening, how the home was squared on us and beyond on all sides the billion sleeping of the natural earth: sitting, where the table blocks the fireplace, watching the lamp, how the light stands up and the wick sleeps in the glass, and meditating those who sleep just beyond this wall: it was in this first night that I found, on the bureau, a bible; very cheap; bound in a limp brown fake-leather which was almost slimily damp; a family bible. . . . I sat on the edge of the bed, turned out the lamp, and lay back along the outside of the covers. After a couple of minutes I got up, stripped, and slid in between the sheets. The bedding was saturated and full of chill as the air was, its lightness upon me nervous like a belt too loosely buckled. The sheets were at the same time coarse and almost slimily or stickily soft: much the same material floursacks are made of. There was a ridgy seam down the middle. I could feel the thinness and lumpiness of the mattress and the weakness of the springs. The mattress was rustlingly noisy if I turned or contracted my body. The pillow was hard, thin, and noisy, and smelled as of acid and new blood; the pillowcase seemed to crawl at my cheek. I touched it with my lips: it felt a little as if it would thaw like spun candy. There was an odor something like that of old moist stacks of newspaper. I tried to imagine intercourse in this bed; I managed to imagine it fairly well. I began to feel sharp little piercings and crawlings all along the surface of my body. I was not surprised; I had heard that pine is full of them anyhow. Then, too, for a while longer I thought it could be my own nerve-ends; I itch a good deal at best: but it was bugs all right. I felt places growing on me and scratched at them, and they became unmistakable bedbug bites. I lay awhile rolling and tightening against each new point of irritation, amused and curious how I had changed about bedbugs. In France I used to wake up and examine a new crop each morning, with no revulsion: now I was squeamish in spite of myself. To lie there naked feeling whole regiments of them tooling at me, knowing I must be imagining two out of three, became more unpleasant than I could stand. I struck a match and a half-dozen broke along my pillow: I caught two, killed them, and smelled their queer rankness. They were full of my blood. I struck another match and spread back the cover; they rambled off by dozens. I got out of bed, lighted the lamp, and scraped the palms of my hands all over my body, then went for the bed. I killed maybe a dozen in all; I couldn't find the rest; but I did find fleas, and, along the seams of the pillow and mattress, small gray translucent brittle insects which I suppose were lice. (I did all this very quietly, of course, very much aware I might wake those in the next room.) This going-over of the bed was only a matter of principle: I knew from the first I couldn't beat them. I might more wisely not have done so, for I shouldn't have discovered the 'lice.' The thought of their presence bothered me much more than the bedbugs. I unbuttoned the door by my bed and went out into the hallway; the dog woke and sidled toward me on his toenails sniffing and I put my hand on his head and he wagged from the middle of his spine on back. I was closely aware of all the bare wood of the house and of the boards under my bare feet, of the damp and deep gray night and of my stark nakedness. I went out to the porch and pissed off the edge, against the wall of the house, to be silent, and stood looking out. It was dark, and mist was standing up in streaks, and the woods along my left and at the bottom of the field in front of me were darkest of any part of the night. Down under the strongest streak of mist along my left, in the deep woods, there was a steady thrusting and spreading noise of water. There were a few stars through thin mist, and a wet gray light of darkness everywhere. I went down the steps and out into the yard, feeling the clay slippery and very cold on my feet, and turned round slowly to look at the house. The instant I was out under the sky, I felt much stronger than before, lawless and lustful to be naked, and at the same time weak. I watched the house and felt like a special sort of burglar; but still more I felt as if I trod water in a sea whose floor was drooped unthinkably deep beneath me, and I was unsafely far from the wall of the ship. I looked straight up into the sky, found myself nodding at whatever it was I saw, and came back and scraped my feet on the steps, rubbed them dry with my hands, and, with one more slow look out along the sunken landscape went back into the bedroom. I put on my coat, buttoned my pants outside it, put my socks on, got into bed, turned out the lamp, turned up my coat collar, wrapped my head in my shirt, stuck my hands under my coat at the chest, and tried to go to sleep. It did not work out well. They got in at the neck and along my face and at my ankles, and along the wrists and knuckles. I wanted if I could to keep my hands and face clear. I wasn't used to these bugs. Their bites would show, and it might be embarrassing whether questions or comments were placed or not. After a little while I worked it out all over, bandaging more tightly and carefully at every strategic joint of cloth. This time I put the socks on my hands and wrapped my feet in my shorts, and once I was set, took great care to lie still. But they got in as before, and along my back and up my belly too: through my stiff, starved dozing I could feel them crawling captured under the clothes, safe against my getting at them, pricking and munching away: so in time, I revised my attitude. I stripped once more, scratched and cleaned all over, shook out all my clothes, dressed again, lay down outside all the covers, and let them take their course while I attended as well as I could to other things; that is, to my surroundings, to whatever was on my mind, and to relaxing for sleep. This worked better. I felt them nibbling, but they were seldom in focus, and I lay smoking, using one shoe for an ashtray and looking up at the holes in the roof. Now and then I reached out and touched the rough wood of the wall just behind me and of the wall along my right: or felt the iron rods of the bed with my hands, my feet, and the crown of my head; or ran the fingertips of my left hand along the grain of the floor: or tilting my chin, I looked back beyond my forehead through the iron at the standing-up of the wall: all the while I would be rubbing and desperately scratching, but this had become mechanical by now. I don't exactly know why anyone should be 'happy' under these circumstances, but there's no use laboring the point: I was: outside the vermin, my senses were taking in nothing but a deep-night, unmeditatable consciousness of a world which was newly touched and beautiful to me, and I must admit that even in the vermin there was a certain amount of pleasure: and that, exhausted though I now was, it was the eagerness of my senses quite as fully as the bugs and the itching which made it impossible for me to sleep and, sickly as I now strained toward sleep, it was pleasurable to stay awake. I dozed off and on, but had no realization of deeper sleep. I must have been pretty far gone, though, for when Gudger came in barefooted to take up the lamp, I feigned sleeping, and lacked interest to look at the furniture which was now visible by a sort of sub-daylight: and heard the sounds of dressing and movements in the house, and saw the wall of their room slit with yellow light, only with a deep and gentle sorrow, in some memory out of childhood which seemed now restored like the ghost of one beloved and dead: and was taken out of full sleep by the sound, a little later, of his shoes on the floor, as he came to the side of the bed and spoke to me.

1. In the book from which this passage was taken, James Agee and Walker Evans (a photographer) tried to show us what it was like to live as a poor tenant farmer in the South. In the "The Supper," what parts of the description could be shown by a good color photograph? What parts could not?
2. How many senses does Agee use? Point out examples of each.
3. Kinesthetic sensations seem to be the ones least noted. Can you find sentences in which the feeling of movement is implied?
4. Can you think of anything in the two scenes that Agee might have noticed but did not?
5. Where does Agee use analogy to aid his description?
6. Near the end, Agee says that he is happy in spite of the bedbugs. Why is he?

Catalogue

ROSALIE MOORE

Cats sleep fat and walk thin.
Cats, when they sleep, slump;
When they wake, stretch and begin
Over, pulling their ribs in.
Cats walk thin.

Cats wait in a lump,
Jump in a streak.
Cats, when they jump, are sleek
As a grape slipping its skin—
They have technique.
Oh, cats don't creak.
They sneak.

Cats sleep fat.
They spread out comfort underneath them
Like a good mat,
As if they picked the place
And then sat;
You walk around one
As if he were the City Hall
After that.

If male,
A cat is apt to sing on a major scale;
This concert is for everybody, this
Is wholesale.
For a baton, he wields a tail.

(He is also found,
When happy, to resound
With an enclosed and private sound.)

A cat condenses.
He pulls in his tail to go under bridges,
And himself to go under fences.
Cats fit
In any size box or kit,
And if a large pumpkin grew under one,
He could arch over it.

When everyone else is just ready to go out,
The cat is just ready to come in.
He's not where he's been.
Cats sleep fat and walk thin.

---

1. What are some images in this poem that strongly suggest movement?
2. Besides movement, what other senses are brought into play?
3. What analogies are used?
4. Some of the observer's feelings toward the cat are implied. What are they and in what lines do you find them?

1. Like many Chinese landscape painters, T'ang Yin expects you to contemplate his picture, not merely look at it. This means you should let yourself enter the scene with all your senses turned on. Imagine yourself to be the man sitting on the end of the boat: what do you see? Smell? Feel? Hear?
2. The painting is done in a kind of shorthand, with little realistic detail. If there were too much detail, we might become too involved in only looking and neglect the other senses the painting appeals to. What are some things the painter has simplified or has not shown us in detail?
3. What effect does the massive rock cliff have on the scene? Does it affect the sounds? The temperature? The wind? The water? What sensations would you experience if you tried to climb it?
4. The waterfall is shown falling first into a deep cleft in the rock, then directly into the river. What sensations are evoked?
5. The Chinese painter is aware that a human being is a temporary expression of nature, like an ocean wave that takes form for a moment and then falls back into the whole. He understands that you are not essentially separate from the rocks, trees, and water around you, but that you are part of the same whole they are parts of. Therefore he makes his human figures small and anonymous, a part of the scene, so that you can identify not only with them, but with the entire scene. He hopes that you will be able to feel what it is to be the things around you, to identify with them. In Unit 9 you will have the chance to devote more time to this; meanwhile, experiment with your imagination. What might it feel like to be the tree in the picture? The water? The massive stone?

PLATE I SECLUDED FISHERMEN ON AN AUTUMN RIVER: T'ang Yin. Collection of The National Palace Museum, Taipei, Taiwan, Republic of China

2

being aware
of your
surroundings

We laugh at people who, like those in the cartoon, do not know where they are. But to some degree we all tend to wander through our surroundings without noticing them. We think about what happened yesterday or what we have to face tomorrow, instead of being aware of what is around us here and now. Being fully alive means being aware of the here and now as well as the past and the future.

We live in our immediate environment, day by day, second by second. It will help you to live more fully (and to think and write better) if you will remind yourself now and then to use your senses, to notice something you have not noticed before in the environment you thought was familiar to you. Every place is exciting to the person whose senses are "turned on."

class exercise

As you sit in your class, relax for a few minutes and let your senses receive data from around and inside you. For a while, close your eyes so that sight will not distract you from feeling, smelling, and hearing. Then write down some of the things you experience. Begin from within your own body and work outward; tell what you feel inside, what pressures and contacts your body feels against it, what you sense closest to you, and so on. Be as factual as you can: instead of saying, "I hear a pen writing," try to describe the sound.

writing assignment

1. Spend at least an hour in one place, writing sentences describing what you are aware of at each moment. An hour may seem a long time to do this, but if you concentrate on your sensations for this length of time, you may become aware of things that have not crossed the threshhold of your consciousness before.
2. Include sensations that come from your own body as well as those from outside.
3. Be as relaxed as you can. Don't look for sensations, but as you finish each sentence, just notice the next thing you are naturally aware of and write it down. Don't worry if you repeat yourself.
4. Do not revise. Simply keep noticing and writing until the hour is up.

unity

When you sat for an hour recording your sensations, you were having, in some respects, a unified experience. What made it unified? For one thing, the fact that it took place at one time and in one location. But perhaps you can find another, more significant kind of unity in the experience, an inner unity. Look at the list of things you were aware of during that hour and see if you can find some kind of pattern. What kinds of things do you seem to be most aware of? For example, some people might find themselves repeatedly recording their awareness of irritating noises; others might notice visual patterns or colors; and so on. See if you can find three or four sorts of sense impressions you were especially aware of during the hour.

When you have stated something a number of examples have in common, you have made a *generalization*. For instance, you might have seen a dozen cats, in different places and at different times, show enthusiasm for fish; you could *generalize*, then, that cats like fish. Let us say that during your hour you wrote, "I notice a bird flying overhead," "There is a man walking across the street," and "A tree branch is swaying in the wind." If you found such observations in the majority, you could generalize, "I seem to be aware of moving objects more than anything else." This generalization represents a kind of unity given to your experience by your own nature.

Very likely there are several kinds of things that you noticed. Your generalization might go something like this: "I seem to be aware of moving objects, loud or sharp sounds, feelings of things touching my skin, and sensations inside my body."

In order to write about an experience, you need to find the generalizations that give it unity, state them, and then give the specific examples that first led you to make these generalizations. In giving the examples, you are showing the reader why you think as you do.

class writing exercise

Organize your sensory observations, giving them as much unity as you can without adding to them. First, write two or three sentences explaining where you were when you made the observations, what time of day it was, what the conditions were, and so on. Then state your generalization in one sentence if possible.

Now, begin a new paragraph telling about the things you noticed most often. Try to remember more about them and how you noticed them, and write a sentence or two about each. Then in another paragraph tell about what you noticed next most often, and so on until you have included all the things you observed.

Finally, before you turn the paper in, look over these several kinds of observations and see if you can discover a generalization about them. Do all these things have something in common? If you can find this overall generalization, write it at the end as a summary; if not (and there may be nothing in common to be found), you may want to repeat your original generalization or make a statement about what you learned about yourself while doing the exercise.

Cliffrose and Bayonets

EDWARD ABBEY

May Day.

    A crimson sunrise streaked with gold flares out beyond Balanced Rock, beyond the arches and windows, beyond Grand Mesa in Colorado. Dawn winds are driving streamers of snow off the peaks of the Sierra La Sal and old man Tukuhnikivats, mightiest of mountains in the land of Moab, will soon be stripped bare to the granite if this wind doesn't stop. Blue scarves of snow flying in the wind twenty miles away—you wouldn't want to be up there now, as they say out here, 13,000 feet above the sea, with only your spurs on.

    In honor of the occasion I tack a scarlet bandanna to the ridgepole of the ramada, where my Chinese windbells also hang, jingling and jangling in the breeze. The red rag flutters brightly over the bells—poetry and revolution before breakfast. Afterwards I hoist the Stars and Stripes to the top of the flagpole up at the entrance station. Impartial and neutralist, taking no chances, I wish good fortune to both sides, good swill for all. Or conversely, depending on my mood of the moment, damn both houses and *pox vobiscum.* Swinish politics, our ball and chain.

    The gopher snake has deserted me, taking with him most of my mice, and the government trailerhouse is a lonely place this morning. Leaving the coffee to percolate slowly over the lowest possible flame, I take my cherry-wood and go for a walk before breakfast. The wind blows sand in my teeth but also brings the scent of flowering cliffrose and a hint of mountain snow, more than adequate compensation.

    Time to inspect the garden. I refer to the garden which lies all around me, extending from here to the mountains, from here to the Book Cliffs, from here to Robbers' Roost and Land's End—an area about the size of the Negev and, excepting me and the huddled Moabites, uninhabited.

    Inventory. Great big yellow mule-ear sunflowers are blooming along the dirt road, where the drainage from the road provides an extra margin of water, a slight but significant difference. Growing among the sunflowers and scattered more thinly over the rest of the desert are the others: yellow borage, Indian paintbrush, scarlet penstemon, skyrocket gilia, prickly pear, hedgehog cactus, purple locoweed, the coral-red globemallow, dockweed, sand verbena. Loveliest of all, however, gay and sweet as a pretty girl, with a fragrance like that of orange blossoms, is the cliffrose, *Cowania stansburiana*, also known—by the anesthetic—as buckbrush or quinine bush.

The cliffrose is a sturdy shrub with gnarled trunk and twisting branches, growing sometimes to twice a man's height. When not in bloom it might not catch your eye; but after the winter snows and a trace of rain in the spring it comes on suddenly and gloriously like a swan, like a maiden, and the shaggy limbs go out of sight behind dense clusters of flowers creamy white or pale yellow, like wild roses, each with its five perfect petals and a golden center.

There's a cliffrose standing near the shed behind the trailer, shaking in the wind, a dazzling mass of blossoms, and another coming up out of solid sandstone beside the ramada, ten feet tall and clothed in a fire of flowers. If Housman were here he'd alter those lines to

> Loveliest of shrubs the cliffrose now
> Is hung with bloom along the bough . . .

The word "shrub" presents a challenge, at least to such verse as this; but poetry is nothing if not exact. The poets lie too much, said Jeffers. Exactly. We insist on precision around here, though it bend the poesy a little out of shape.

The cliffrose is practical as well as pretty. Concealed by the flowers at this time are the leaves, small, tough, wax-coated, bitter on the tongue—thus the name quinine bush—but popular just the same among the deer as browse when nothing better is available—buckbrush. The Indians too, a practical people, once used the bark of this plant for sandals, mats and rope, and the Hopi medicine man is said, even today, to mash and cook the leaves as an emetic for his patients.

Because of its clouds of flowers the cliffrose is the showiest plant in the canyon country, but the most beautiful individual flower, most people would agree, is that of the cacti: the prickly pear, the hedgehog, the fishhook. Merely opinion, of course. But the various cactus flowers have earned the distinction claimed for them on the basis of their large size, their delicacy, their brilliance, and their transience—they bloom, many of them, for one day only in each year. Is that a fair criterion of beauty? I don't know. For myself I hold no preference among flowers, so long as they are wild, free, spontaneous. (Bricks to all greenhouses! Black thumb and cutworm to the potted plant!)

The cactus flowers are all much alike, varying only in color within and among the different species. The prickly pear, for example, produces a flower that may be violet, saffron, or red. It is cup-shaped, filled with golden stamens that respond with sensitive, one might almost say sensual, tenderness to the entrance of a bee. This flower is indeed irresistibly attractive to insects; I have yet to look into one and not find a honeybee or bumblebee wallowing drunkenly inside, powdered with pollen, glutting itself on what must be a marvelous nectar. You can't get them out of there—they won't go home. I've done my best to annoy them, poking and prodding with a stem of grass, but a bee in a cactus bloom will not be provoked; it stays until the flower wilts. Until closing time.

The true distinction of these flowers, I feel, is found in the contrast between the blossom and the plant which produces it. The cactus of the high desert is a small, grubby, obscure and humble vegetable associated with cattle dung and overgrazing, interesting only when you tangle with it in the wrong way. Yet from this nest of thorns, this snare of hooks and fiery spines, is born once each year a splendid flower. It is unpluckable and except to an insect almost unapproachable, yet soft, lovely, sweet, desirable, exemplifying better than the rose among thorns the unity of opposites.

Stepping carefully around the straggling prickly pear I come after a few paces over bare sandstone to a plant whose defensive weaponry makes the cactus seem relatively benign. This one is formed of a cluster of bayonetlike leaves pointing up and outward, each stiff green blade tipped with a point as intense and penetrating as a needle. Out of the core of this untouchable dagger's nest rises a slender stalk, waist-high, gracefully curved, which supports a heavy cluster of bell-shaped, cream-colored, wax-coated, exquisitely perfumed flowers. This plant, not a cactus but a member of the lily family, is a type of yucca called Spanish bayonet.

Despite its fierce defenses, or perhaps because of them, the yucca is as beautiful as it is strange, perfect in its place wherever that place may be—on the Dagger Flats of Big Bend, the high grasslands of southern New Mexico, the rim and interior of Grand Canyon or here in the Arches country, growing wide-spaced and solitaire from the red sands of Utah.

The yucca is bizarre not only in appearance but in its mode of reproduction. The flowers are pollinated not by bees or hummingbirds but exclusively by a moth of the genus *Pronuba* with which the yucca, aided by a liberal allowance of time, has worked out a symbiotic relationship beneficial and necessary to both. The moth lays its eggs at the proper time in the ovary of the yucca flower where the larvae, as they develop, feed on the growing seeds, eating enough of them to reach maturity but leaving enough in the pod to allow the plant, assisted by the desert winds, to sow next year's yucca crop. In return for this nursery care the moth performs an essential service for the yucca: in the process of entering the flower the moth—almost accidentally it might seem to us—transfers the flower's pollen from anther to pistil, thus accomplishing pollination. No more; but it is sufficient.

The wind will not stop. Gusts of sand swirl before me, stinging my face. But there is still too much to see and marvel at, the world very much alive in the bright light and wind, exultant with the fever of spring, the delight of morning. Strolling on, it seems to me that the strangeness and wonder of existence are emphasized here, in the desert, by the comparative sparsity of the flora and fauna: life not crowded upon life as in other places but scattered abroad in spareness and simplicity, with a generous gift of space for each herb and bush and tree, each stem of grass, so that the living organism stands out bold and brave and vivid against the lifeless sand and barren rock. The extreme clarity of the desert light is equaled by the extreme individuation of desert life-forms. Love flowers best in openness and freedom.

Patterns in the sand, tracks of tiger lizards, birds, kangaroo rats, beetles. Circles and semicircles on the red dune where the wind whips the compliant stems of the wild ricegrass back and forth, halfway around and back again. On the crest of the dune is a curving cornice from which flies a constant spray of fine sand. Crescent-shaped, the dune shelters on its leeward side a growth of sunflowers and scarlet penstemon. I lie on my belly on the edge of the dune, back to the wind, and study the world of the flowers from ground level, as a snake might see it. From below the flowers of the penstemon look like flying pennants; the sunflowers shake and creak from thick green hairy stalks that look, from a snake's viewpoint, like the trunks of trees.

I get up and start back to the trailer. A smell of burning coffee on the wind. On the way I pass a large anthill, the domed city of the harvester ants. Omniverous red devils with a vicious bite, they have denuded the ground surrounding their hill, destroying everything green and living within a radius of ten feet. I cannot resist the impulse to shove my walking stick into the bowels of their hive and rowel things up. Don't actually care for ants. Neurotic little pismires. Compared to ants the hairy scorpion is a beast of charm, dignity and tenderness.

My favorite juniper stands before me glittering shaggily in the sunrise, ragged roots clutching at the rock on which it feeds, rough dark boughs bedecked with a rash, with a shower of turquoise-colored berries. A female, this ancient grandmother of a tree may be three hundred years old; growing very slowly, the juniper seldom attains a height greater than fifteen or twenty feet even in favorable locations. My juniper, though still fruitful and full of vigor, is at the same time partly dead: one half of the divided trunk holds skyward a sapless claw, a branch without leaf or bark, baked by the sun and scoured by the wind to a silver finish, where magpies and ravens like to roost when I am not too close.

I've had this tree under surveillance ever since my arrival at Arches, hoping to learn something from it, to discover the significance in its form, to make a connection through its life with whatever falls beyond. Have failed. The essence of the juniper continues to elude me unless, as I presently suspect, its surface is also the essence. Two living things on the same earth, respiring in a common medium, we contact one another but without direct communication. Intuition, sympathy, empathy, all fail to guide me into the heart of this being—if it has a heart.

At times I am exasperated by the juniper's static pose; something in its stylized gesture of appeal, that dead claw against the sky, suggests catalepsy. Perhaps the tree is mad. The dull, painful creaking of the branches in the wind indicates, however, an internal effort at liberation.

The wind flows around us from the yellow haze in the east, a morning wind, a solar wind. We're in for a storm today, dust and sand and filthy air.

Without flowers as yet but bright and fresh, with leaves of a startling, living green in contrast to the usual desert olive drab, is a shrub known as singleleaf ash, one of the few true deciduous plants in the pinyon-juniper community. Most desert plants have only rudimentary leaves, or no leaves at all, the better to conserve moisture, and the singleleaf ash seems out of place here, anomalous, foredoomed to wither and die. (*Fraxinus anomala* is the botanical name.) But touch the leaves of this plant and you find them dry as paper, leathery in texture and therefore desert-resistant. The singleleaf ash in my garden stands alone along the path, a dwarf tree only three feet high but tough and enduring, clenched to the stone.

Sand sage or old man sage, a lustrous windblown blend of silver and blue and aquamarine, gleams in the distance, the feathery stems flowing like hair. Purple flowers no bigger than your fingernail are half-revealed, half-concealed by the shining leaves. *Purple* sage: crush the leaves between thumb and finger and you release that characteristic odor, pungent and bittersweet, which *means* canyon country, high lonesome mesaland, the winds that blow from far away.

Also worthy of praise is the local pinyon pine, growing hereabouts at isolated points, for its edible nuts that appear in good years, for its ragged raunchy piney good looks, for the superior qualities of its wood as fuel—burns clean and slow, little soot, little ash, and smells almost as good as juniper. Unfortunately, most of the pinyon pines in the area are dead or dying, victims of another kind of pine—the porcupine. This situation came about through the conscientious efforts of a federal agency known formerly as the Wildlife Service, which keeps its people busy in trapping, shooting and poisoning wildlife, particularly coyotes and mountain lions. Having nearly exterminated their natural enemies, the wildlife experts made it possible for the porcupines to multiply so fast and so far that they—the porcupines—have taken to gnawing the bark from pinyon pines in order to survive.

What else? Still within sight of the housetrailer, I can see the princess plume with its tall golden racemes; the green ephedra or Mormon tea, from which Indians and pioneers extracted a medicinal drink (contains ephedrine), the obnoxious Russian thistle, better known as tumbleweed, an exotic; pepper-weed, bladderweed, snakeweed, matchweed, skeleton weed—the last-named so delicately formed as to be almost invisible; the scrubby little wavyleaf oak, stabilizer of sand dunes; the Apache plume, poor cousin of the cliffrose; gray blackbrush, most ubiquitous and humble of desert plants, which will grow where all else has given up; more annuals—primrose, sourdock, yellow and purple beeplant, rockcress, wild buckwheat, grama grass, and five miles north across the floor of Salt Valley, acres and acres of the coral-colored globe-mallow.

Not quite within eyeshot but close by, in a shady dampish secret place, the sacred datura—moonflower, moonlily, thornapple—blooms in the night, soft white trumpet-shaped flowers that open only in darkness and close with the coming of the heat. The datura is sacred (to certain cultists) because of its content of atropine, a powerful narcotic of the alkaloid group capable of inducing visionary hallucinations, as the Indians discovered long before the psychedelic craze began. How they could have made such a discovery without poisoning themselves to death nobody knows; but then nobody knows how so-called primitive man made his many other discoveries. We must concede that science is nothing new, that research, empirical logic, the courage to experiment are as old as humanity.

Most of the plants I have named so far belong to what ecologists call the pinyon pine-juniper community, typical of the high, dry, sandy soils of the tablelands. Descend to the alkali flats of Salt Valley and you find an entirely different grouping: shadscale, four-winged saltbush, greasewood, spiny horse-brush, asters, milk vetch, budsage, galletagrass. Along the washes and the rare perennial streams you'll find a third community: the Fremont poplar or cottonwood tree, willow, tamarisk, rabbitbrush or *chamisa*, and a variety of sedges, tules, rushes, reeds, cattails. The fourth plant community, in the Arches area, is found by the springs and around the seeps on the canyon walls—the hanging gardens of fern, monkey-flower, death camas, columbine, helleborine orchid, bracken, panicgrass, bluestem, poison ivy, squawbush, and the endemic primrose *Primula specuiola*, found nowhere but in the canyonlands.

So much for the inventory. After such a lengthy listing of plant life the reader may now be visualizing Arches National Monument as more a jungle than a desert. Be reassured, it is not so. I have called it a garden, and it is—a *rock* garden. Despite the great variety of living things to be found here, most of the surface of the land, at least three-quarters of it, is sand or sandstone, naked, monolithic, austere and unadorned as the sculpture of the moon. It is undoubtedly a desert place, clean, pure, totally useless, quite unprofitable.

The sun is rising through a yellow, howling wind. Time for breakfast. Inside the trailer now, broiling bacon and frying eggs with good appetite, I hear the sand patter like rain against the metal walls and brush across the windowpanes. A fine silt accumulates beneath the door and on the window ledge. The trailer shakes in a sudden gust. All one to me—sandstorm or sunshine I am content, so long as I have something to eat, good health, the earth to take my stand on, and light behind the eyes to see by.

At eight o'clock I put on badge and ranger hat and go to work, checking in at headquarters by radio and taking my post at the entrance station to greet and orient whatever tourists may appear. None show. After an hour of waiting I climb in the government pickup and begin a patrol of the park, taking lunch and coffee with me. So far as I know there's no one camping in the park at this time, but it won't hurt to make sure.

The wind is coming from the north, much colder than before—we may have sleet or rain or snow or possibly all three before nightfall. Bad weather means that the park entrance road will be impassable; it is part of my job to inform campers and visitors of this danger so that they will have a chance to get out before it's too late.

Taking the Windows road first, I drive beneath the overhanging Balanced Rock, 3500 tons of seamless Entrada sandstone perched on a ridiculous, inadequate pedestal of the Carmel formation, soft and rotten stone eaten away by the wind, deformed by the weight above. One of these days that rock is going to fall—in ten, fifty, or five hundred years. I drive past more freestanding pinnacles, around the edge of outthrust ledges, in and out of the ravines that corrade the rolling terrain—wind-deposited, cross-bedded sand dunes laid down eons ago in the Mesozoic era and since compressed and petrified by overlying sediments. Everywhere the cliffrose is blooming, the yellow flowers shivering in the wind.

The heart-shaped prints of deer are plain in the dust of the road and I wonder where the deer are now and how they're doing and if they've got enough to eat. Like the porcupine the deer too become victims of human meddling with the natural scheme of things—not enough coyotes around and the mountain lions close to extinction, the deer have multiplied like rabbits and are eating themselves out of house and home, which means that many each year are condemned to a slow death by starvation. The deerslayers come by the thousands every autumn out of Salt Lake and California to harvest, as they like to say, the surplus deer. But they are not adequate for the task.

The road ends at the Double Arch campground. No one here. I check the garbage can for trapped chipmunks, pick up a few bottlecaps, and inspect the "sanitary facilities," where all appears to be in good order: roll of paper, can of lime, black widow spiders dangling in their usual strategic corners. On the inside of the door someone has written a cautionary note:

> Attention: Watch out for rattlesnakes, coral snakes, whip snakes, vinegaroons, centipedes, millipedes, ticks, mites, black widows, cone-nosed kissing bugs, solpugids, tarantulas, horned toads, Gila monsters, red ants, fire ants, Jerusalem crickets, chinch bugs and Giant Hairy Desert Scorpions before being seated.

I walk out the foot trail to Double Arch and the Windows. The wind moans a dreary tune under the overhanging coves, among the holes in the rock, and through the dead pinyon pines. The sky is obscure and yellow but the air in this relatively sheltered place among the rocks is still clear. A few birds dart about: black-throated sparrows, the cliff swallows, squawking magpies in their handsome academic dress of black and white. In the dust and on the sand dunes I can read the passage of other creatures, from the big track of a buck to the tiny prints of birds, mice, lizards, and insects. Hopefully I look for sign of bobcat or coyote but find none.

We need more predators. The sheepmen complain, it is true, that the coyotes eat some of their lambs. This is true but do they eat enough? I mean, enough lambs to keep the coyotes sleek, healthy and well fed. That is my concern. As for the sacrifice of an occasional lamb, that seems to me a small price to pay for the support of the coyote population. The lambs, accustomed by tradition to their role, do not complain; and the sheepmen, who run their hooved locusts on the public lands and are heavily subsidized, most of them as hog-rich as they are pigheaded, can easily afford these trifling losses.

We need more coyotes, more mountain lions, more wolves and foxes and wildcats, more owls, hawks and eagles. The livestock interests and their hired mercenaries from the Department of Agriculture have pursued all of these animals with unremitting ferocity and astonishing cruelty for nearly a century, utilizing in this campaign of extermination everything from the gun and trap to the airplane and the most ingenious devices of chemical and biological warfare. Not content with shooting coyotes from airplanes and hunting lions with dogs, these bounty hunters, self-styled sportsmen, and government agents like to plant poisoned meat all over the landscape, distribute tons of poisoned tallow balls by air, and hide baited cyanide guns in the ground and brush—a threat to humans as well as animals. Still not satisfied, they have developed and begun to use a biochemical compound which makes sterile any animal foolish enough to take the bait.

Absorbed in these thoughts, wind in my eyes, I round a corner of the cliff and there's a doe and her fawn not ten yards away, browsing on the cliffrose. Eating flowers. While she could not have heard or scented me, the doe sees me almost at once. But since I stopped abruptly and froze, she isn't sure that I am dangerous. Puzzled and suspicious, she and the fawn at her side, madonna and child, stare at me for several long seconds. I breathe out, making the slightest of movements, and the doe springs up and away as if bounced from a trampoline, followed by the fawn. Their sharp hooves clatter on the rock.

"Come back here!" I shout. "I want to talk to you."

But they're not talking and in another moment have vanished into the wind. I could follow if I wanted to, track them down across the dunes and through the open parks of juniper and cliffrose. But why should I disturb them further? Even if I found them and somehow succeeded in demonstrating my friendship and good will, why should I lead them to believe that anything manlike can be trusted? That is no office for a friend.

I come to the North Window, a great opening fifty feet high in a wall of rock, through which I see the clouded sky and the hazy mountains and feel the funneled rush of the wind. I climb up to it, walk through—like an ant crawling through the eyesocket of a skull—and down the other side a half-mile to a little spring at the head of a seldom-visited canyon. I am out of the wind for a change, can light up my pipe and look around without getting dust in my eyes; I can hear myself think.

Here I find the track of a coyote superimposed on the path of many deer. So there is at least one remaining in the area, perhaps the same coyote I heard two weeks ago wailing at the evening moon. His trail comes down off the sandstone from the west, passes over the sand under a juniper and up to the seep of dark green water in its circle of reeds. Under the juniper he has left two gray-green droppings knitted together with rabbit hair. With fingertip I write my own signature in the sand to let him know, to tip him off; I take a drink of water and leave.

Down below is Salt Creek Canyon, corraded through an anticline to the bed of the Colorado. If I were lucky I might find the trail of bighorn sheep, rumored still to lurk in these rimrock hideaways. In all these years of prowling on foot through the canyons and desert mountains of the Southwest I have yet to see, free and alive in the wild, either a lion or a bighorn. In part I can blame only my ignorance and incompetence, for I know they are out there, somewhere; I have seen their scat and their tracks.

As I am returning to the campground and the truck I see a young cottontail jump from the brush, scamper across the trail and freeze under a second bush. The rabbit huddles there, panting, ears back, one bright eye on me.

I am taken by the notion to experiment—on the rabbit. Suppose, I say to myself, you were out here hungry, starving, no weapon but your bare hands. What would you do? What *could* you do?

There are a few stones scattered along the trail. I pick up one that fits well in the hand, that seems to have the optimum feel and heft. I stare at the cottontail hunched in his illusory shelter under the bush. Blackbrush, I observe, the common variety, sprinkled with tightly rolled little green buds, ready to burst into bloom on short notice. Should I give the rabbit a sporting chance, that is, jump it again, try to hit it on the run? Or brain the little bastard where he is?

Notice the terminology. A sportsman is one who gives his quarry a chance to escape with its life. This is known as fair play, or sportsmanship.

Animals have no sense of sportsmanship. Some, like the mountain lion, are vicious—if attacked they defend themselves. Others, like the rabbit, run away, which is cowardly.

Well, I'm a scientist not a sportsman and we've got an important experiment under way here, for which the rabbit has been volunteered. I rear back and throw the stone with all I've got straight at his furry head.

To my amazement the stone flies true (as if guided by a Higher Power) and knocks the cottontail head over tincups, clear out from under the budding blackbush. He crumples, there's the usual gushing of blood, etc., a brief spasm, and then no more. The wicked rabbit is dead.

For a moment I am shocked by my deed; I stare at the quiet rabbit, his glazed eyes, his blood drying in the dust. Something vital is lacking. But shock is succeeded by a mild elation. Leaving my victim to the vultures and maggots, who will appreciate him more than I could—the flesh is probably infected with tularemia—I continue my walk with a new, augmented cheerfulness which is hard to understand but unmistakable. What the rabbit has lost in energy and spirit seems added, by processes too subtle to fathom, to my own soul. I try but cannot feel any sense of guilt. I examine my soul: white as snow. Check my hands: not a trace of blood. No longer do I feel so isolated from the sparse and furtive life around me, a stranger from another world. I have entered into this one. We are kindred all of us, killer and victim, predator and prey, me and the sly coyote, the soaring buzzard, the elegant gopher snake, the trembling cottontail, the foul worms that feed on our entrails, all of them, all of us. Long live diversity, long live the earth!

Rejoicing in my innocence and power I stride down the trail beneath the elephantine forms of melting sandstone, past the stark shadows of Double Arch. The experiment was a complete success; it will never be necessary to perform it again.

Back in the warm pickup I enjoy a well-earned sandwich and drink my coffee before driving on another six miles, through clouds of wind-driven dust and sand, to the old Turnbow Cabin and the beginning of the trail to Delicate Arch.

Once there was a man named Turnbow who lived in the grimy wastelands of an eastern city which we will not mention here—the name, though familiar to all the world, is not important. This Turnbow had consumption. His doctors gave him six months. Mr. Turnbow in his despair fled to the arid wilds, to this very spot, built the cabin, lived on and on for many years and died, many years ago.

The cabin stands on the banks of the unpotable waters of Salt Creek, a shallow stream on a bed of quicksand. Drinking water is available half a mile upstream at a tributary spring. Turnbow Cabin itself is a well-preserved ruin (nothing decays around here) made of juniper, pinyon and cottonwood logs, no two alike in shape or size. The crudity of the construction followed from the scarcity of wood, not lack of skill. The cracks between the unhewn logs were chinked with adobe; a few fragments still remain. The walls have a morbid greenish hue that matches the coloration of the nearby hills; this is dust from the Morrison formation, a loose friable shale containing copper oxides, agate, chert, and traces of vanadium and uranium. There is a doorway but no door, a single window and no glass. The floor consists of warped, odd-size planks. In one corner is a manger for horses, an addition made long after the death of Mr. Turnbow. Cobwebs complete with black widow spiders adorn the darker corners under the ceiling. In the center of the room is a massive post of juniper shoring up the ancient, sagging roof, which is a thatchwork affair of poles, mud and rock, very leaky. As shelter, the cabin cannot be recommended, except for its shade on a hot day.

Back of the cabin are the lonesome Morrison hills, utterly lifeless piles of clay and shale and broken rock, a dismal scene. In front are the walls of Dry Mesa and Salt Creek Canyon. It is a hot, sunken, desolate place, closed in and still, lacking even a view. As Genghis Khan said of India, "The water is bad and the heat makes men sick." A haunted place, in my opinion, haunted by the ghost of the lonely man who died here. Except for myself no one lives within thirty miles of Turnbow Cabin.

With relief I turn my back on this melancholy ruin and take the golden trail up the long ledge of Navajo sandstone which leads to Delicate Arch. I cross the swinging footbridge over Salt Creek, pestered on the way by a couple of yellow cowflies (cattlemen call them deerflies). The cowfly, or deerfly if you prefer, loves blood. Human blood especially. Persistent as a mosquito, it will keep attacking until either it samples your blood or you succeed in killing it, or both. The most artful among them like to land in your hair and attach themselves to the scalp, where they will not be noticed until too late. But they are home-loving insects; once over the bridge and away from the slimy little creek you leave them behind.

Many have made the climb to Delicate Arch, so many that the erosion of human feet is visible on the soft sandstone, a dim meandering path leading upward for a mile and a half into a queer region of knobs, domes, turrets and coves, all sculptured from a single solid mass of rock. What do the pilgrims see? The trail climbs and winds past isolate pinyons and solitary junipers to a vale of stone where nothing has happened for a thousand years, to judge from the quietude of the place, the sense of *waiting* that seems to hover in the air. From this vale you climb a second ledge blasted across the face of a cliff, round a corner at the end of the trail and Delicate Arch stands before you, a fragile ring of stone on the far side of a natural amphitheatre, set on its edge at the brink of a five hundred foot drop-off. Looking through the ring you see the rim of Dry Mesa and far beyond that the peaks of the La Sal Mountains.

There are several ways of looking at Delicate Arch. Depending on your preconceptions you may see the eroded remnant of a sandstone fin, a giant engagement ring cemented in rock, a bow-legged pair of petrified cowboy chaps, a triumphal arch for a procession of angels, an illogical geologic freak, a happening—a something that happened and will never happen quite that way again, a frame more significant than its picture, a simple monolith eaten away by weather and time and soon to disintegrate into a chaos of falling rock (not surprisingly there have been some, even in the Park Service, who advocate spraying Delicate Arch with a fixative of some sort—Elmer's Glue perhaps or Lady Clairol Spray-Net). There are the inevitable pious Midwesterners who climb a mile and a half under the desert sun to view Delicate Arch and find only God ("Gol-dangit Katherine where's my light meter, this glare is turrible"), and the equally inevitable students of geology who look at the arch and see only Lyell and the uniformity of nature. You may therefore find proof for or against His existence. Suit yourself. You may see a symbol, a sign, a fact, a thing without meaning or a meaning which includes all things.

Much the same could be said of the tamarisk down in the canyon, of the blue-black raven croaking on the cliff; of your own body. The beauty of Delicate Arch explains nothing, for each thing in its way, when true to its own character, is equally beautiful. (There is no beauty in nature, said Baudelaire. A place to throw empty beer cans on Sunday, said Mencken.) If Delicate Arch has any significance it lies, I will venture, in the power of the odd and unexpected to startle the senses and surprise the mind out of their ruts of habit, to compel us into a reawakened awareness of the wonderful—that which is full of wonder.

A weird, lovely, fantastic object out of nature like Delicate Arch has the curious ability to remind us—like rock and sunlight and wind and wilderness—that *out there* is a different world, older and greater and deeper by far than ours, a world which surrounds and sustains the little world of men as sea and sky surround and sustain a ship. The shock of the real. For a little while we are again able to see, as the child sees, a world of marvels. For a few moments we discover that nothing can be taken for granted, for if this ring of stone is marvelous then all which shaped it is marvelous, and our journey here on earth, able to see and touch and hear in the midst of tangible and mysterious things-in-themselves, is the most strange and daring of all adventures.

After Delicate Arch the others are anticlimactic but I go on to inspect them, as I'm paid to do. From Turnbow Cabin I drive northwesterly on a twisting road above Salt Valley past a labyrinth of fins and pinnacles toward the Devil's Garden. On the way I pass Skyline Arch, a big hole in the wall where something took place a few years ago which seems to bear out the hypotheses of geology: one November night in 1940 when no one was around to watch, a big chunk of rock fell out of this arch, enlarging the opening by half again its former size. The photographs, "Before & After," prove it. The event had doubtless been in preparation for hundreds maybe thousands of years—snow falling, melting, trickling into minute fissures, dissolving the cements which knit sandstone particles together, freezing and expanding, wedging apart the tiny cracks, undermining the base—but the cumulative result was a matter, probably, of only a few noisy and dusty minutes in which the mighty slabs cracked and grumbled, shook loose, dropped and slid and smashed upon the older slabs below, shattering the peace of ages. But none were there to see and hear except the local lizards, mice and ground squirrels, and perhaps a pair of outraged, astonished ravens.

I reach the end of the road and walk the deserted trail to Landscape Arch and Double-O Arch, picking up a few candy wrappers left from the weekend, straightening a trail sign which somebody had tried to remove, noting another girdled and bleeding pinyon pine, obliterating from a sandstone wall the pathetic scratchings of some imbeciles who had attempted to write their names across the face of the Mesozoic. (Where are you now, J. Soderlund? Alva T. Sarvis? Bob Riddle? Henry Lightcap? Malcom Brown?)

The wind blows, unrelenting, and flights of little gray birds whirl up and away like handfuls of confetti tossed in the air. The temperature is still falling, presaging snow. I am glad to return, several hours later, to the shelter and warmth of the housetrailer. I have not seen a soul anywhere in Arches National Monument today.

In the evening the wind stops. A low gray ceiling of clouds hangs over the desert from horizon to horizon, silent and still. One small opening remains in the west. The sun peers through as it goes down. For a few minutes the voodoo monuments burn with a golden light, then fade to rose and blue and violet as the sun winks out and drops. My private juniper stands alone, one dead claw reaching at the sky. The blossoms on the cliffrose are folding up, the scarlet penstemon and the bayonets of the yucca turn dull and vague in the twilight.

Something strange in the air. I go to the weather station and check the instruments—nothing much, actually, but a rain gauge, an anemometer or wind gauge, and a set of thermometers which record the lows and highs for the day. The little cups on the wind gauge are barely turning, but this breath of air, such as it is, comes from the southwest. The temperature is fifty-five or so, after a low this morning of thirty-eight. It is not going to snow after all. Balanced on a point of equilibrium, hesitating, the world of the high desert turns toward summer.

1. In a desert landscape where many tourists are bored, Edward Abbey spends an exciting day. What qualities has he developed that enable him to enjoy his surroundings so keenly?
2. What senses does he employ? Point out examples.
3. Abbey's enjoyment of his surroundings is not passive. What are some of the ways he actively participates in the scene?
4. What could you learn that would help you understand this description and participate in it more fully? Would this kind of knowledge help you enjoy other kinds of environments?

from Song of Myself

WALT WHITMAN

33. Space and Time! now I see it is true, what I guess'd at,
   What I guess'd when I loaf'd on the grass,
   What I guess'd while I lay alone in my bed,
   And again as I walk'd the beach under the paling stars of the morning.

   My ties and ballasts leave me, my elbows rest in sea-gaps,
   I skirt sierras, my palms cover continents,
   I am afoot with my vision.

   By the city's quadrangular houses—in log huts, camping with lumbermen,
   Along the ruts of the turnpike, along the dry gulch and rivulet bed,
   Weeding my onion-patch or hoeing rows of carrots and parsnips, crossing
      savannas, trailing in forests,
   Prospecting, gold-digging, girdling the trees of a new purchase,
   Scorch'd ankle-deep by the hot sand, hauling my boat down the shallow river,
   Where the panther walks to and fro on a limb overhead, where the buck turns
      furiously at the hunter,
   Where the rattlesnake suns his flabby length on a rock, where the otter is
      feeding on fish,
   Where the alligator in his tough pimples sleeps by the bayou,
   Where the black bear is searching for roots or honey, where the beaver pats the
      mud with his paddle-shaped tail;
   Over the growing sugar, over the yellow-flower'd cotton plant, over the rice in its
      low moist field,
   Over the sharp-peak'd farm house, with its scallop'd scum and slender shoots
      from the gutters,
   Over the western persimmon, over the long-leav'd corn, over the delicate
      blue-flower flax,
   Over the white and brown buckwheat, a hummer and buzzer there with the rest,
   Over the dusky green of the rye as it ripples and shades in the breeze;
   Scaling mountains, pulling myself cautiously up,
      holding on by low scragged limbs,

SONG OF MYSELF   Reprinted from the 1892 edition of *Leaves of Grass.*

Walking the path worn in the grass and beat through the leaves of the brush,
Where the quail is whistling betwixt the woods and the wheat lot,
Where the bat flies in the Seventh-month eve, where the great gold-bug drops
    through the dark,
Where the brook puts out of the roots of the old tree and flows to the meadow,
Where cattle stand and shake away flies with the tremulous shuddering of their
    hides,
Where the cheese-cloth hangs in the kitchen, where andirons straddle the
    hearth-slab, where cobwebs fall in festoons from the rafters;
Where trip-hammers crash, where the press is whirling its cylinders,
Wherever the human heart beats with terrible throes under its ribs,
Where the pear-shaped balloon is floating aloft,
    (floating in it myself and looking composedly down,)
Where the life-car is drawn on the slip-noose, where the heat hatches pale-green
    eggs in the dented sand,
Where the she-whale swims with her calf and never forsakes it,
Where the steam-ship trails hind-ways its long pennant of smoke,
Where the fin of the shark cuts like a black chip out of the water,
Where the half-burn'd brig is riding on unknown currents,
Where shells grow to her slimy deck, where the dead are corrupting below;
Where the dense-starr'd flag is borne at the head of the regiments,
Approaching Manhattan up by the long-stretching island,
Under Niagara, the cataract falling like a veil over my countenance,
Upon a door-step, upon the horse-block of hard wood outside,
Upon the race-course, or enjoying picnics or jigs or a good game of base-ball,
At he-festivals, with blackguard gibes, ironical license, bull-dances, drinking,
    laughter,
At the cider-mill tasting the sweets of the brown mash, sucking the juice through
    a straw,
At apple-peelings wanting kisses for all the red fruit I find,
At musters, beach-parties, friendly bees, huskings, house-raisings;
Where the mocking-bird sounds his delicious gurgles, cackles, screams, weeps,
Where the hay-rick stands in the barn-yard, where the dry-stalks are scatter'd,
    where the brood-cow waits in the hovel,
Where the bull advances to do his masculine work, where the stud to the mare,
    where the cock is treading the hen,
Where the heifers browse, where geese nip their food with short jerks,
Where sun-down shadows lengthen over the limitless and lonesome prairie,
Where herds of buffalo make a crawling spread of the square miles far and near,

Where the humming-bird shimmers, where the neck of the long-lived swan is
    curving and winding,
Where the laughing-gull scoots by the shore, where she laughs her near-human
    laugh,
Where bee-hives range on a gray bench in the garden
    half hid by the high weeds,
Where band-neck'd partridges roost in a ring on the ground
    with their heads out,
Where burial coaches enter the arch'd gates of a cemetery,
Where winter wolves bark amid wastes of snow and icicled trees,
Where the yellow-crown'd heron comes to the edge of the marsh at night and
    feeds upon small crabs,
Where the splash of swimmers and divers cools the warm noon,
Where the katy-did works her chromatic reed on the walnut-tree over the well,
Through patches of citrons and cucumbers with silver-wired leaves,
Through the salt-lick or orange glade, or under conical firs,
Through the gymnasium, through the curtain'd saloon,
    through the office or public hall;
Pleas'd with the native and pleas'd with the foreign,
    pleas'd with the new and old,
Pleas'd with the homely woman as well as the handsome,
Pleas'd with the quakeress as she puts off her bonnet and talks melodiously,
Pleas'd with the tune of the choir of the whitewash'd church,
Pleas'd with the earnest words of the sweating Methodist preacher, impress'd
    seriously at the camp-meeting;
Looking in at the shop-windows of Broadway the whole forenoon, flatting the
    flesh of my nose on the thick plate glass,
Wandering the same afternoon with my face turn'd up to the clouds, or down a
    lane or along the beach,
My right and left arms round the sides of two friends, and I in the middle;
Coming home with the silent and dark-cheek'd bush-boy,
    (behind me he rides at the drape of the day,)
Far from the settlements studying the print of animals' feet, or the moccasin print,
By the cot in the hospital reaching lemonade to a feverish patient,
Nigh the coffin'd corpse when all is still, examining with a candle;
Voyaging to every port to dicker and adventure,
Hurrying with the modern crowd as eager and fickle as any,
Hot toward one I hate, ready in my madness to knife him,
Solitary at midnight in my back yard, my thoughts gone from me a long while,
Walking the old hills of Judaea with the beautiful gentle God by my side,

Speeding through space, speeding through heaven and the stars,
Speeding amid the seven satellites and the broad ring,
   and the diameter of eighty thousand miles,
Speeding with tail'd meteors, throwing fire-balls like the rest,
Carrying the crescent child that carries its own full mother in its belly,
Storming, enjoying, planning, loving, cautioning,
Backing and filling, appearing and disappearing,
I tread day and night such roads.

---

1. In "Cliffrose and Bayonets," Edward Abbey concentrates on his immediate environment, the things he senses directly. Walt Whitman takes great pleasure in expanding his awareness to include things his senses are not experiencing at the moment but that he knows exist. What are some of the physical actions he enjoys imagining? What are some of the things he observes in his imagination?
2. Can you always distinguish between what he imagines *seeing* and what he imagines *doing*? Point out some lines in which both may be involved.
3. Some of the things Whitman describes are things he has actually seen or done himself; others he knows about only secondhand. Can you tell which ones are from his own experience and which are not? Point out examples.
4. Which senses does Whitman use most? Is there one he does not use at all in this selection?
5. Does he use analogy? Where?
6. Whitman first published "Song of Myself" in 1855. If you wrote a "Song of Myself" for your own times, in what ways would it have to be different from his?

1. Paintings like this one were popular in America a century ago. They are sometimes called *trompe l'oeil* paintings, done to fool the eye into thinking it is looking at real objects. Nothing was shown that was not familiar to everyone; some paintings were of such things as kitchen utensils, tools, houseflies, and even scraps of paper. People enjoyed them because of the artist's skill in making things look real, but a more lasting effect of such paintings was to make people more aware of ordinary objects around them. What qualities does this artist seem to take special pleasure in showing us?
2. What senses does he appeal to in addition to sight?
3. Unlike *Secluded Fishermen on an Autumn River*, in Unit 1, Peto's picture does not invite us to enter the scene and identify with the objects in it. What advantages does this quality have? What disadvantages?
4. Also unlike the Chinese painting, this one is contained within its borders, so that we do not think about what is outside its frame, as we do about the river flowing out of *Secluded Fishermen*. There is little sense of space in the painting, but do you find a sense of time? Does anything in the picture suggest the passing of time?
5. Which painting do you find more interesting? Why?

PLATE II

THE POOR MAN'S STORE: John Frederick Peto. Courtesy, Museum of Fine Arts, Boston; The M. and M. Karolik Collection

Drawing by Geo. Price; © 1940, 1968 The New Yorker Magazine, Inc.

3

getting
the feel
of action

We perceive action with our bodies as well as with our eyes and ears. Sport fans move as the players move. Your vocal chords move together with those of the singer you are listening to, even with the sounds of instruments; your hands or feet tap rhythms in time to the music you are hearing. Watching television, you feel the sensation of motion as the camera follows a car screeching around a curve or the hero dropping on the villain from a branch overhead.

Much of the fun of watching action is in feeling some of what the person doing it feels; and in describing action, you want to give your reader this feeling rather than an objective scientific account. The fact that kicking a football involves a sudden contraction of the *rectus femoris* muscle is of little interest to a person watching a game or reading about one. The reader has kicked a ball and enjoys being reminded of what it feels like to kick a ball.

How can you best communicate these kinesthetic feelings? Comic book artists draw bodies in exaggerated positions and add sounds like "pow!" and "ugh!" to suggest violence. Most writers, however, rely on clear, economical description of the action, trusting the reader to recall sensations from his own experience. This recall can be aided by the use of strong action verbs like "swing," "sway," "crouch," "jump," "lunge," "stride," "stretch," and hundreds of others. A few well-chosen words get action across better than many carelessly chosen ones.

Remember too that an action does not have to be violent to be interesting. The way a woman sets a plate on a table can tell us a great deal about her character and her mood.

class exercise

Most of us have been on a roller coaster or some other machine designed to give the excitement of movement. Try to describe how you feel on such a machine, or how you felt when you were a child on a swing, climbing a tree, or standing on your head. Use the present tense. Describe your feelings, not just the facts. Don't say, "The blood rushes to my head," but try to tell others what it feels like to have the blood rushing to your head.

writing assignment

1. Observe a person doing something: a child playing tetherball or climbing on bars; a woman sewing or washing dishes; a man digging or trimming a hedge; someone watering a lawn, making a bed, or shopping.
2. Watch the person's motions carefully and completely, taking notes. If a woman is washing dishes, for example, notice not only what her hands are doing, but also how her feet are moving, how she turns her body, how she moves her head, and so on. Record the sounds and smells that accompany the activity and note the person's reactions to things going on in the environment.
3. Try to find the best verbs to make the actions clear. Use analogy whenever it will help you.

coherence

Coherence is just what the word indicates: the quality of sticking together. In addition to being unified by subject, the parts of your writing should be connected with each other in such a way that the reader can always see how they are related. Here is an example that is unified but that lacks coherence:

Lucretia carries her purse different ways. She lets it hang like a suitcase on the street. When she is in a store, she tucks it under her arm or holds it behind her with both hands. She holds it with her hand when she is fumbling through it at the cash register. She curls her hand around the end and holds it along her arm when she is walking with a man. While talking with someone, she holds it cradled in both arms. She never drops it or leaves it behind.

Analyzing the paragraph, we find there are two elements consistent throughout: the ways she holds the purse and the situations that determine the way she holds it. To give coherence to the paragraph, we need (1) to restate the first sentence so that it reflects the main idea; (2) to express parallel ideas in parallel form; and (3) to make clear the relationship of the last sentence to the rest.

Lucretia carries her purse differently in different situations. When she walks down the street, she lets it hang like a suitcase. When she is shopping, she carries it under one arm or holds it behind her with both hands. When she is at the cash register, she grips it by the bottom with her left hand while she fumbles through it with her right. When she is walking with a man, she carries it resting along her left arm, with her hand curled around the end. Finally, when she is talking with someone, she holds it cradled in both arms. But though she carries it in all these different ways, she never drops her purse or leaves it behind in any situation.

In the next-to-last sentence, we have used a *transitional* expression, "finally," to let the reader know he is reaching the end of the series; and in the last sentence, we have repeated the expressions "different ways" and "situation" to pull the ideas together. The use of devices to achieve coherence has been exaggerated somewhat in this example, of course, but the point is, *always let your reader know where he is.* Don't surprise him with sentences that make him go back to see what on earth they have to do with the previous sentences.

class writing assignment

Look over the notes you took for the writing assignment and see if you can find a generalization that grows out of them naturally. Don't strain for something startling or original; you will probably come up with an idea like, "Making a bed is a complex activity." If such a simple statement doesn't seem to cover all you noticed, add another phrase, such as "involving many sensory and kinesthetic experiences." Begin your essay with your generalization and go on to support it by organizing the material in your notes into a clear description of the activity. Strive for coherence, always letting your reader know what you are doing, and clarity, letting him know exactly what is happening and where and when it is taking place.

from The Road to Wigan Pier

GEORGE ORWELL

When you go down a coal mine it is important to try and get to the coal face when the "fillers" are at work. This is not easy, because when the mine is working visitors are a nuisance and are not encouraged, but if you go at any other time, it is possible to come away with a totally wrong impression. On a Sunday, for instance, a mine seems almost peaceful. The time to go there is when the machines are roaring and the air is black with coal dust, and when you can actually see what the miners have to do. At those times the place is like hell, or at any rate like my own mental picture of hell. Most of the things one imagines in hell are there—heat, noise, confusion, darkness, foul air, and, above all, unbearably cramped space. Everything except the fire, for there is no fire down there except the feeble beams of Davy lamps and electric torches which scarcely penetrate the clouds of coal dust.

When you have finally got there—and getting there is a job in itself: I will explain that in a moment—you crawl through the last line of pit props and see opposite you a shiny black wall three or four feet high. This is the coal face. Overhead is the smooth ceiling made by the rock from which the coal has been cut; underneath is the rock again, so that the gallery you are in is only as high as the ledge of coal itself, probably not much more than a yard. The first impression of all, overmastering everything else for a while, is the frightful, deafening din from the conveyor belt which carries the coal away. You cannot see very far, because the fog of coal dust throws back the beam of your lamp, but you can see on either side of you the line of half-naked kneeling men, one to every four or five yards, driving their shovels under the fallen coal and flinging it swiftly over their left shoulders. They are feeding it on to the conveyor belt, a moving rubber belt a couple of feet wide which runs a yard or two behind them. Down this belt a glittering river of coal races constantly. In a big mine it is carrying away several tons of coal every minute. It bears it off to some place in the main roads where it is shot into tubs holding half a ton, and thence dragged to the cages and hoisted to the outer air.

It is impossible to watch the "fillers" at work without feeling a pang of envy for their toughness. It is a dreadful job that they do, an almost superhuman job by the standards of an ordinary person. For they are not only

From *The Road to Wigan Pier* by George Orwell. Reprinted by permission of Harcourt Brace Jovanovich, Inc.

shifting monstrous quantities of coal, they are also doing it in a position that doubles or trebles the work. They have got to remain kneeling all the while—they could hardly rise from their knees without hitting the ceiling— and you can easily see by trying it what a tremendous effort this means. Shoveling is comparatively easy when you are standing up, because you can use your knee and thigh to drive the shovel along; kneeling down, the whole of the strain is thrown upon your arm and belly muscles. And the other conditions do not exactly make things easier. There is the heat—it varies, but in some mines it is suffocating—and the coal dust that stuffs up your throat and nostrils and collects along your eyelids, and the unending rattle of the conveyor belt, which in that confined space is rather like the rattle of a machine gun. . . .

Probably you have to go down several coal mines before you can get much grasp of the processes that are going on round you. This is chiefly because the mere effort of getting from place to place makes it difficult to notice anything else. In some ways it is even disappointing, or at least is unlike what you have expected. You get into the cage, which is a steel box about as wide as a telephone box and two or three times as long. It holds ten men, but they pack it like pilchards in a tin, and a tall man cannot stand upright in it. The steel door shuts upon you, and somebody working the winding gear above drops you into the void. You have the usual momentary qualm in your belly and a bursting sensation in the ears, but not much sensation of movement till you get near the bottom, when the cage slows down so abruptly that you could swear it is going upward again. In the middle of the run the cage probably touches sixty miles an hour; in some of the deeper mines it touches even more. When you crawl out at the bottom you are perhaps four hundred yards under ground. That is to say you have a tolerable-sized mountain on top of you; hundreds of yards of solid rock, bones of extinct beasts, subsoil, flints, roots of growing things, green grass and cows grazing on it—all this suspended over your head and held back only by wooden props as thick as the calf of your leg. But because of the speed at which the cage has brought you down, and the complete blackness through which you have traveled, you hardly feel yourself deeper down than you would at the bottom of the Piccadilly tube.

What *is* surprising, on the other hand, is the immense horizontal distances that have to be traveled underground. Before I had been down a mine I had vaguely imagined the miner stepping out of the cage and getting to work on a ledge of coal a few yards away. I had not realized that before he even gets to his work he may have to creep through passages as long as from London Bridge to Oxford Circus. In the beginning, of course, a mine shaft is sunk somewhere near a seam of coal. But as that seam is worked out and fresh seams are followed up, the workings get farther and farther from the pit bottom. If it is a mile from the pit bottom to the coal face, that is probably an average distance; three miles is a fairly normal one; there are even said to be a few mines where it is as much as five miles. But these distances bear no relation to distances above ground. For in all that mile or three miles as it may be, there is hardly anywhere outside the main road, and not many places even there, where a man can stand upright.

You do not notice the effect of this till you have gone a few hundred yards. You start off, stooping slightly, down the dim-lit gallery, eight or ten feet wide and about five high, with the walls built up with slabs of shale, like the stone walls in Derbyshire. Every yard or two there are wooden props holding up the beams and girders; some of the girders have buckled into fantastic curves under which you have to duck. Usually it is bad going under-foot—thick dust or jagged chunks of shale, and in some mines where there is water it is as mucky as a farmyard. Also there is the track for the coal tubs, like a miniature railway track with sleepers a foot or two apart, which is tiresome to walk on. Everything is gray with shale dust; there is a dusty fiery smell which seems to be the same in all mines. You see mysterious machines of which you never learn the purpose, and bundles of tools slung together on wires, and sometimes mice darting away from the beam of the lamps. They are surprisingly common, especially in mines where there are or have been horses. It would be interesting to know how they got there in the first place; possibly by falling down the shaft—for they say a mouse can fall any distance uninjured, owing to its surface area being so large relative to its weight. You press yourself against the wall to make way for lines of tubs jolting slowly toward the shaft, drawn by an endless steel cable operated from the surface. You creep through sacking curtains and thick wooden doors which, when they are opened, let out fierce blasts of air. These doors are an important part of the ventilation system. The exhausted air is sucked out of one shaft by means of fans, and the fresh air enters the other of its own accord. But if left to itself the air will take the shortest way round, leaving the deeper workings unventilated; so all short-cuts have to be partitioned off.

At the start to walk stooping is rather a joke, but it is a joke that soon wears off. I am handicapped by being exceptionally tall, but when the roof falls to four feet or less it is a tough job for anybody except a dwarf or a child. You have not only got to bend double, you have also got to keep your head up all the while so as to see the beams and girders and dodge them when they come. You have, therefore, a constant crick in the neck, but this is nothing to the pain in your knees and thighs. After half a mile it becomes (I am not exaggerating) an unbearable agony. You begin to wonder whether you will ever get to the end—still more, how on earth you are going to get back. Your pace grows slower and slower. You come to a stretch of a couple of hundred yards where it is all exceptionally low and you have to work yourself along in a squatting position. Then suddenly the roof opens out to a mysterious height—scene of an old fall of rock, probably— and for twenty whole yards you can stand upright. The relief is overwhelming. But after this there is another low stretch of a hundred yards and then a succession of beams which you have to crawl under. You go down on all fours; even this is a relief after the squatting business. But when you come to the end of the beams and try to get up again, you find that your knees have temporarily struck work and refuse to lift you. You call a halt, ignominiously, and say that you would like to rest for a minute or two. Your guide (a miner) is sympathetic. He knows that your muscles are not the same as his. "Only another four hundred yards," he says encouragingly; you feel that he might as well say another four hundred miles. But finally you do somehow creep as far as the coal face. You have gone a mile and taken the best part of an hour; a miner would do it in not much more than twenty minutes. Having got there, you have to sprawl in the coal dust and get your strength back for several minutes before you can even watch the work in progress with any kind of intelligence.

Coming back is worse than going, not only because you are already tired out but because the journey back to the shaft is probably slightly uphill. You get through the low places at the speed of a tortoise, and you have no shame now about calling a halt when your knees give way. Even the lamp you are carrying becomes a nuisance and probably when you stumble you drop it; whereupon, if it is a Davy lamp, it goes out. Ducking the beams becomes more and more of an effort, and sometimes you forget to duck. You try walking head down as the miners do, and then you bang your backbone. Even the miners bang their backbones fairly often. This is the reason why in very hot mines, where it is necessary to go about half naked, most of the miners have what they call "buttons down the back"—that is, a permanent scab on each vertebra. When the track is downhill the miners sometimes fit their clogs, which are hollow underneath, on to the trolley rails and slide down. In mines where the "traveling" is very bad all the miners carry sticks about two and a half feet long, hollowed out below the handle. In normal places you keep your hand on top of the stick and in the low places you slide your hand down into the hollow. These sticks are a great help, and the wooden crash-helmets—a comparatively recent invention—are a godsend. They look like a French or Italian steel helmet, but they are made of some kind of pith and very light, and so strong that you can take a violent blow on the head without feeling it. When finally you get back to the surface you have been perhaps three hours underground and traveled two miles, and you are more exhausted than you would be by a twenty-five-mile walk above ground. For a week afterward your thighs are so stiff that coming downstairs is quite a difficult feat; you have to work your way down in a peculiar sidelong manner, without bending the knees. Your miner friends notice the stiffness of your walk and chaff you about it. ("How'd ta like to work down pit, eh?" etc.) Yet even a miner who has been long away from work—from illness, for instance—when he comes back to the pit, suffers badly for the first few days.

---

1. Orwell is telling us what it is like to go down a coal mine and, by implication, what it is like to be a coal miner. He does this by describing his own sensations and the actions of the miners. What are some of the sensations he experiences? Point out particular sentences.
2. How do the miners work at the coal face? From what you have read, what can you guess about how they feel?
3. Action cannot be described apart from the environment in which it takes place. What are some of the qualities of the environment that Orwell describes?
4. Which senses does this environment affect most?
5. Orwell uses "you" instead of "I" to describe his experiences. Why?
6. Orwell uses a good many action verbs, such as "crawl" and "kneel." What are some others?

The Base Stealer

ROBERT FRANCIS

Poised between going on and back, pulled
Both ways taut like a tightrope-walker,
Fingertips pointing the opposites,
Now bouncing tiptoe like a dropped ball
Or a kid skipping rope, come on, come on,
Running a scattering of steps sidewise,
How he teeters, skitters, tingles, teases,
Taunts them, hovers like an ecstatic bird,
He's only flirting, crowd him, crowd him,
Delicate, delicate, delicate, delicate—now!

---

1. The effect of this poem is based largely on the use of words that signify kinesthetic feelings. What are these words? (There are a dozen or more.)
2. What analogies are used? Are they good ones? Why or why not?
3. If you had never been down a coal mine, you could still understand most of Orwell's description of one. If you had never seen a baseball game, could you understand "The Base Stealer?"
4. What is the difference, then, between describing an action familiar to your reader and one that is not? What devices do you have to use in describing unfamiliar action?

1. What kinesthetic sensations are suggested in this picture? How has the artist communicated them?
2. Are any other kinds of sensations implied? What are they and how are they communicated?
3. Has the artist used exaggeration or distortion to help communicate sensation? Where?
4. The ceiling of the building is not shown. Does this omission contribute to the effect? How?
5. Daumier is saying more than is immediately apparent, and he is saying it, with humor, through an analogy. Can you spot the analogy? What does he seem to be saying? (The analogy is pointed up by the pair of carcasses and the pair of hams on both sides of the butcher.)

PLATE III

THE BUTCHER: Honoré Daumier. Courtesy, Fogg Art Museum, Harvard University;
bequest of Grenville L. Winthrop

Drawing by Chas. Addams; © 1941, 1969 The New Yorker Magazine, Inc.

4

perceiving
emotional
attitudes

Our interests and attitudes usually dictate how we see things. A lumberman sees a tree as board feet, a tired hiker sees it as shade from the sun, a conservationist sees it as a producer of the oxygen he breathes. These are reasonable perceptions in accord with the interest of the person looking at the tree. But many of our perceptions are conditioned by training or emotional association. We prefer a cat to a gopher snake, or a vase to a garbage can, largely because we have been taught to prefer them or because we associate them in our minds with more pleasant things.

Everyone has emotional attitudes he has never examined. These unexamined attitudes are called *prejudices* because they make us pre-judge something before we really know anything about it. A common example is the horror of insects that many people have. Such people fail to discriminate between harmful and beneficial insects and kill any insect they find. If you ask them why they dislike insects, you will not get a reasonable answer. They were probably conditioned by others who had the same attitude.

class exercise

Name a dislike you have which you suspect might be a prejudice. If you dislike oranges because they make you break out, this is obviously not a prejudice; but if you simply dislike them for no reason, it may be because of some conditioning or association in the past. Try to think of some experience that might have caused you to dislike this thing without good reason; let others in the class suggest possibilities.

Then move on to discuss qualities you dislike in people. Think of something a person does that causes you no real harm but that irritates you. Analyze your reaction; see if you can discover anything in yourself that makes you subject to the irritation.

writing assignment

1. With your pen and notebook, sit down wherever it is convenient to work for an hour: in a room, on a porch or step, or on a park bench.
2. Look at the various objects around you and choose three: (*a*) one that you like, (*b*) one that you dislike, and (*c*) one that you feel indifferent toward. Jot down the name of each and the feeling it arouses in you; for example, purple armchair—ugly.
3. Examine the reasons for your feeling toward each of these objects. Exactly what are the qualities of object *a* that you like, or do you like it because of some pleasant association? What makes you dislike object *b*? If you find it ugly, just what do you mean by "ugly"? What is lacking in object *c* so that it fails to arouse any feeling? Describe these qualities so that others can see what you see.
4. Write down three groups of thoughts, one about each object. If you really try to analyze your feelings and explain them clearly to others, you should have no difficulty doing this.

paragraphing

Like coherence, good paragraphing helps your reader to know what you are doing. When he reaches a sentence with the beginning indented, he knows that you are changing your subject or your approach, or that there is some sort of division in your thought. A paragraph is usually a unit of several sentences about the same thing. In the previous chapter, the description of how Lucretia carries her purse forms a paragraph; if we went on to tell what kinds of shoes she wears, the reader would expect a new paragraph. A paragraph break is like a pause in speaking before you go on to the next subject.

class writing assignment

The material you have collected for the writing assignment should naturally form three paragraphs: one about the object you like and your reasons for liking it; one about the one you dislike and your reasons for disliking it; and one about the object you are indifferent to and what it lacks. Begin with a brief introductory paragraph explaining where you are and what you are doing, and end with a concluding paragraph generalizing about your reasons for liking and disliking things. You will finish with a five paragraph essay. Unity is provided by your subject, but keep coherence in mind, and make your essay easy for the reader to follow.

The Cries of Love

PATRICIA HIGHSMITH

Hattie pulled the little chain of the reading lamp, drew the covers over her shoulders and lay tense, waiting for Alice's sniffs and coughs to subside.

"Alice?" she said.

No response. Yes, she was sleeping already, though she said she never closed an eye before the clock struck eleven.

Hattie eased herself to the edge of the bed and slowly put out a white-stockinged foot. She twisted round to look at Alice, of whom nothing was visible except a thin nose projecting between the ruffle of her nightcap and the sheet pulled over her mouth. She was quite still.

Hattie rose gently from the bed, her breath coming short with excitement. In the semi-darkness she could see the two sets of false teeth in their glasses of water on the bed table. She giggled, nervously.

Like a white ghost she made her way across the room, past the Victorian settle. She stopped at the sewing table, lifted the folding top and groped among the spools and pattern papers until she found the scissors. Then, holding them tightly, she crossed the room again. She had left the wardrobe door slightly ajar earlier in the evening, and it swung open noiselessly. Hattie reached a trembling hand into the blackness, felt the two woollen coats, a few dresses. Finally she touched a fuzzy thing, and lifted the hanger down. The scissors slipped out of her hand. There was a clatter, followed by her half-suppressed laughter. She peeked round the wardrobe door at Alice, motionless on the bed. Alice was rather hard of hearing.

With her white toes turned up stiffly, Hattie clumped to the easy chair by the window where a bar of moonlight slanted, and sat down with the scissors and the angora sweater in her lap. In the moonlight her face gleamed, toothless and demoniacal. She examined the sweater in the manner of a person who toys with a piece of steak before deciding where to put his knife.

It was really a lovely sweater. Alice had received it the week before from her niece as a birthday present. Alice would never have indulged herself in such a luxury. She was happy as a child with the sweater and had worn it every day over her dresses.

The scissors cut purringly up the soft wool sleeves, between the wristbands and the shoulders. She considered. There should be one more cut. The back, of course. But only about a foot long, so it wouldn't be immediately visible.

A few seconds later, she had put the scissors back into the table, hung the sweater in the wardrobe, and was lying under the covers. She heaved a tremendous sigh. She thought of the gaping sleeves, of Alice's face in the morning. The sweater was quite beyond repair, and she was immensely pleased with herself.

They were awakened at eight-thirty by the hotel maid. It was a ritual that never failed: three bony raps on the door and a bawling voice with a hint of insolence, "Eight-thirty! You can get breakfast now!" Then Hattie, who always woke first, would poke Alice's shoulder.

Mechanically they sat up on their respective sides of the bed and pulled their nightgowns over their heads, revealing clean white undergarments. They said nothing. Seven years of co-existence had pared their conversation to an economical core.

This morning, however, Hattie's mind was on the sweater. She felt self-conscious, but she could think of nothing to say or do to relieve the tension, so she spent more time than usual with her hair. She had a braid nearly two feet long that she wound around her head, and every morning she undid it for its hundred strokes. Her hair was her only vanity. Finally, she stood shifting uneasily, pretending to be fastening the snaps on her dress.

Alice seemed to take an age at the washbasin, gargling with her solution of tepid water and salt. She held stubbornly to water and salt in the mornings, despite Hattie's tempting bottle of red mouthwash sitting on the shelf.

"What are you giggling at now?" Alice turned from the basin, her face wet and smiling a little.

Hattie could say nothing, looked at the teeth in the glass on the bed table and giggled again. "Here's your teeth." She reached the glass awkwardly to Alice. "I thought you were going down to breakfast without them."

"Now when did I *ever* go off without my teeth, Hattie?"

Alice smiled to herself. It was going to be a good day, she thought. Mrs. Crumm and her sister were back from a weekend, and they could all play gin rummy together in the afternoon. She walked to the wardrobe in her stockinged feet.

Hattie watched as she took down the powder-blue dress, the one that went best with the beige angora sweater. She fastened all the little buttons in front. Then she took the sweater from the hanger and put one arm into a sleeve.

"Oh!" she breathed painfully. Then like a hurt child her eyes almost closed and her face twisted petulantly. Tears came quickly down her cheeks. "H-Hattie—"

Hattie smirked, uncomfortable yet enjoying herself thoroughly. "Well, I do know!" she exclaimed. "I wonder who could have done a trick like that!" She went to the bed and sat down, doubled up with laughter.

"Hattie, you did this," Alice declared in an unsteady voice. She clutched the sweater to her. "Hattie, you're just wicked!"

Lying across the bed, Hattie was almost hysterical. "You know I didn't now, Alice . . . hah-haw! . . . Why do you think I'd—" Her voice was choked off by incontrollable laughing.

Hattie lay there several minutes before she was calm enough to go down to breakfast. And when she left the room, Alice was sitting in the big chair by the window, sobbing, her face buried in the angora sweater.

Alice did not come down until she was called for lunch. She chatted at the table with Mrs. Crumm and her sister and took no notice of Hattie. Hattie sat opposite her, silent and restless, but not at all sorry for what she had done. She could have endured days of indifference on Alice's part without feeling the slightest remorse.

It was a beautiful day. After lunch, they went with Mrs. Crumm, her sister, and the hotel hostess, Mrs. Holland, and sat in Gramercy Park.

Alice pretended to be absorbed in her book. It was a detective story by her favorite author, borrowed from the hotel's circulating library. Mrs. Crumm and her sister did most of the talking. A weekend trip provided conversation for several afternoons, and Mrs. Crumm was able to remember every item of food she had eaten for days running.

The monotonous tones of the voices, the warmth of the sunshine, lulled Alice into half-sleep. The page was blurred to her eyes.

Earlier in the day, she had planned to adopt an attitude toward Hattie. She should be cool and aloof. It was not the first time Hattie had committed an outrage. There had been the ink spilt on her lace tablecloth months ago, the day before she was going to give it to her niece . . . And her missing volume of Tennyson that was bound in morocco. She was sure Hattie had it, somewhere. She decided that that evening she should calmly pack her bag, write Hattie a note, short but well worded, and leave the hotel. She would go to another hotel in the neighborhood, let it be known through Mrs. Crumm where she was, and have the satisfaction of Hattie's coming to her and apologizing. But the fact was, she was not at all sure Hattie would come to her, and this embarrassing possibility prevented her from taking such a dangerous course. What if she had to spend the rest of her life alone? It was much easier to stay where she was, to have a pleasant game of gin rummy in the afternoons, and to take out her revenge in little ways. It was also more ladylike, she consoled herself. She did not think beyond this, of the particular times she would say or do things calculated to hurt Hattie. The opportunities would just come of themselves.

Mrs. Holland nudged her. "We're going to get some ice cream now. Then we're going to play some gin rummy."

"I was just at the most exciting part of the book." But Alice rose with the others and was almost cheerful as they walked to the drugstore.

Alice won at gin rummy, and felt pleased with herself. Hattie, watching her uneasily all day, was much relieved when she decreed speaking terms again.

Nevertheless, the thought of the ruined sweater rankled in Alice's mind, and prodded her with a sense of injustice. Indeed, she was ashamed of herself for being able to take it as lightly as she did. It was letting Hattie walk over her. She wished she could muster a really strong hatred.

They were in their room reading at nine o'clock. Every vestige of Hattie's shyness or pretended contrition had vanished.

"Wasn't it a nice day?" Hattie ventured.

"Um-hm." Alice did not raise her head.

"Well," Hattie made the inevitable remark through the inevitable yawn, "I think I'll be going off to bed."

And a few minutes later they were both in bed, propped up by four pillows, Hattie with the newspaper and Alice with her detective story. They were silent for a while, then Hattie adjusted her pillows and lay down.

"Good night, Alice."

"Good night."

Soon Alice pulled out the light, and there was absolute silence in the room except for the soft ticking of the clock and the occasional purr of an automobile. The clock on the mantel whirred and began to strike ten.

Alice lay open-eyed. All day her tears had been restrained, and now she began to cry. But they were not the childish tears of the morning, she felt. She wiped her nose on the top of the sheet.

She raised herself on one elbow. The darkish braid of hair outlined Hattie's neck and shoulder against the white bedclothes. She felt very strong, strong enough to murder Hattie with her own hands. But the idea of murder passed from her mind as swiftly as it had entered. Her revenge had to be something that would last, that would hurt, something that Hattie must endure and that she herself could enjoy.

Then it came to her, and she was out of bed, walking boldly to the sewing table, as Hattie had done twenty-four hours before . . . and she was standing by the bed, bending over Hattie, peering at her placid, sleeping face through her tears and her shortsighted eyes. Two quick strokes of the scissors would cut through the braid, right near the head. But Alice lowered the scissors just a little, to where the braid was tighter. She squeezed the scissors with both hands, made them chew on the braid, as Hattie slowly awakened with the touch of cold metal on her neck. *Whack,* and it was done.

"What is it? . . . What—?" Hattie said.

The braid was off, lying like a dark gray snake on the bed cover.

"Alice!" Hattie said, and groped at her neck, felt the stiff ends of the braid's stump. "Alice!"

Alice stood a few feet away, staring at Hattie who was sitting up in bed, and suddenly Alice was overcome with mirth. She tittered, and at the same time tears started in her eyes. "You did it to me!" she said. "You cut my sweater!"

Alice's instant of self-defense was unnecessary, because Hattie was absolutely crumpled and stunned. She started to get out of bed, as if to go to the mirror, but sat back again, moaning and weeping, feeling of the horrid thing at the end of her hair. Then she lay down again, still moaning into her pillow. Alice stayed up, and sat finally in the easy chair. She was full of energy, not sleepy at all. But toward dawn, when Hattie slept, Alice crept between the covers.

Hattie did not speak to her in the morning, and did not look at her. Hattie put the braid away in a drawer. Then she tied a scarf around her head to go down to breakfast, and in the dining room, Hattie took another table from the one at which Alice and she usually sat. Alice saw Hattie speaking to Mrs. Holland after breakfast.

A few minutes later, Mrs. Holland came over to Alice, who was reading in a corner of the lounge.

"I think," Mrs. Holland said gently, "that you and your friend might be happier if you had separate rooms for a while, don't you?"

This took Alice by surprise, though at the same time she had been expecting something worse. Her prepared statement about the spilt ink, the missing Tennyson, and the ruined angora subsided in her, and she said quite briskly, "I do indeed, Mrs. Holland. I'm agreeable to anything Hattie wishes."

Alice offered to move out, but it was Hattie who did. She moved to a smaller room three doors down on the same floor.

That night, Alice could not sleep. It was not that she thought about Hattie particularly, or that she felt in the least sorry for what she had done— she decidedly didn't—but that things, the room, the darkness, even the clock's ticking, were so different because she was alone. A couple of times during the night, she heard a footstep outside the door, and thought it might be Hattie coming back, but it was only people visiting the W.C. at the end of the hall. It occurred to Alice that she could knock on Hattie's door and apologize but, she asked herself, why should she?

In the morning, Alice could tell from Hattie's appearance that she hadn't slept either. Again, they did not speak or look at each other all day, and during the gin rummy and tea at four, they managed to take different tables. Alice slept very badly that night also, and blamed it on the lamb stew at dinner, which she was having trouble digesting. Hattie would have the same trouble, perhaps, as Hattie's digestion was, if anything, worse.

Three more days and nights passed, and the ravages of Hattie's and Alice's sleepless nights became apparent on their faces. Mrs. Holland noticed, and offered Alice some sedatives, which Alice politely declined. She had her pride, she wasn't going to show anyone she was disturbed by Hattie's absence, and besides, she thought it was weak and self-indulgent to yield to sleeping pills—though perhaps Hattie would.

On the fifth day, at three in the afternoon, Hattie knocked on Alice's door. Her head was still swathed in a scarf, one of three that Hattie possessed, and this was one Alice had given her last Christmas.

"Alice, I want to say I'm sorry, if *you're* sorry," Hattie said, her lips twisting and pursing as she fought to keep back the tears.

This was or should have been a moment of triumph for Alice. It was, mainly, she felt, though something—she was not sure what—tarnished it a little, made it not quite pure victory. "I am sorry about your braid, if you're sorry about my sweater," Alice replied.

"I am," said Hattie.

"And about the ink stain on my tablecloth and . . . where is my volume of Alfred Lord Tennyson's poems?"

"I have not got it," Hattie said, still tremulous with tears.

"You haven't *got* it?"

"No," Hattie declared positively.

And in a flash, Alice knew what had really happened: Hattie had at some point in some place, destroyed it, so it was in a way true now that she hadn't "got" it. Alice knew, too, that she must not stick over this, that she ought to forgive and forget it, though neither emotionally nor intellectually did she come to this decision: she simply knew it, and behaved accordingly, saying, "Very well, Hattie. You may move back, if you wish."

Hattie then moved back, though at the card game at four-thirty they still sat at separate tables.

Hattie, having swallowed the biggest lump of pride she had ever swallowed in knocking on Alice's door and saying she was sorry, slept very much better back in the old arrangement, but suffered a lurking sense of unfairness. After all, a book of poems and a sweater could be replaced, but could her hair? Alice had got back at her all right, and then some. The score was not quite even.

After a few days, Hattie and Alice were back to normal, saying little to each other, but outwardly being congenial, taking meals and playing cards at the same table. Mrs. Holland seemed pleased.

It crossed Alice's mind to buy Hattie some expensive hair tonic she saw in a Madison Avenue window one day while on an outing with Mrs. Holland and the group. But Alice didn't. Neither did she buy a "special treatment" for hair which she saw advertised in the back of a magazine, guaranteed to make the hair grow thicker and faster, but Alice read every word of the advertisements.

　　Meanwhile, Hattie struggled in silence with her stump of braid, brushed her hair faithfully as usual, but only when Alice was having her bath or was out of the room, so Alice would not see it. Nothing in Alice's possession now seemed important enough for Hattie's vengeance. But Christmas was coming soon. Hattie determined to wait patiently and see what Alice got then.

---

1. What is the significance of the title, "The Giles of Love"?
2. Hattie and Alice do not seem to be conscious of their own motives. What makes them act the way they do?
3. Can you think of people you know who do things like these? Are their motives similar? Are there situations in the world at large that this story reflects?
4. Most of the story is told in terms of actions. What are some of the more revealing actions besides the main ones of cutting the sweater and the hair? What do they reveal?
5. What senses are used in telling the story? Point out particular sentences. What senses are neglected? Would their inclusion improve the story?

The Snare

JAMES STEPHENS

I hear a sudden cry of pain!
There is a rabbit in a snare:
Now I hear the cry again,
But I cannot tell from where.

But I cannot tell from where
He is calling out for aid!
Crying on the frightened air,
Making everything afraid!

Making everything afraid!
Wrinkling up his little face!
As he cries again for aid;
—And I cannot find the place!

And I cannot find the place
Where his paw is in the snare!
Little One! Oh, Little One!
I am searching everywhere!

---

1. Obviously, this poem is not about a man looking for a rabbit. What kind of subject is the poem about?
2. Who or what do you think is speaking the words of the poem? Is it the poet himself or not?
3. What kind of sensory data does the poem seem based on? What kind of total sensation does it leave you with?
4. Can you think of a reason for capitalizing "Little One"?
5. What emotional attitude does the poem express?

---

1. As Stephens tries to communicate the essence of a feeling in "The Snare," Picasso in the *Woman Weeping* gives us the image of a person crying without realistically depicting a person in tears. How has he given us the impression of crying?
2. Picasso could have painted a literal picture of a particular woman (his wife, for example) crying, as many artists have done. What advantage does he gain by avoiding this?
3. Crying, of course, is the outward expression of a common feeling. What kinds of emotional attitudes can bring about this feeling?
4. The painter himself seems to have a certain emotional attitude toward his subject. Can you define it? (It may help to imagine the painter's actual movements while painting the picture, as recorded in the lines he has made.)

PLATE IV
WOMAN WEEPING: Pablo Picasso. Penrose Collection, London

Drawing by Chas. Addams; © 1937, 1965 The New Yorker Magazine, Inc.

5

observing
a person

When we look at a person, we tend to take in a great deal at a glance and immediately jump to a conclusion about him. We glance at a man and say, "He looks like a banker," without noting each aspect of his appearance that leads to that conclusion.

At this point, we need to make the distinction between *fact* and *inference*. A *fact* is a direct observation that no one can dispute, such as, "He is wearing a white cap and overalls, is carrying a paintbrush, and has spots of paint all over his clothes." An *inference* is a conclusion that seems reasonable in light of the facts; for example, "He is probably a painter."

class exercise

Think of a person you know. Describe that person in factual terms, avoiding inferences; using only descriptive facts, see if you can lead others in the class to make correct inferences regarding his age, occupation, status, character, and so on. Do not say, for example, "He is about twenty years old": this is an inference. Describe the factual data that give the impression of his age. Work at keeping the distinction between fact and inference clear.

writing assignment

1. Taking a small notebook with you, go to some public place such as a bus station, railway station, airport terminal, city bus, crowded supermarket,

or dime store: a place busy enough for you to observe and take notes without attracting your subject's attention.

2. Pick out a person who looks interesting, preferably an older person. Observe him as closely as you can without letting him know he is being observed.

3. Take detailed notes about your subject. First write down a general description such as you might give to someone who was looking for him. Then do the detective work: catalogue every detail you can find from which some inference might be made about his occupation, financial status, family status, personal habits, home life, and so on. Watch for revealing actions as well as appearances.

4. Now, putting your material in the kind of order you used in the assignment in Unit 1, make up an intensive description of the person, including all your sound inferences and the evidence to support them.

emphasis

Emphasis is calling attention to important things you want your reader to remember; it is making certain parts stand out. If an artist wants to emphasize something, he puts it in the center of the picture, colors it more brightly, or makes it stand out through contrast.

Poor writers overuse such obvious emphasis devices as underlining, exclamation points, and words like "very," "only," "absolutely," and "awfully." Such words can serve a purpose if they are used sparingly, but there are better methods of achieving emphasis. To emphasize something you can:

1. make short, flat statements. In the first paragraph above, "it is making certain parts stand out" is such a statement.

2. place what is most important at the beginning or end of a sentence, paragraph, or essay. First and last things get attention; things in the middle get lost.

3. give a larger proportion of your writing to what is more important. When you describe a person, for example, write most about the things that tell us what kind of person he is, and cover the other necessary details briefly.

class writing assignment

Rewrite the material you have collected for the writing assignment, organizing it into paragraphs, each one based on a *generalization*. Begin with a paragraph of general description. The generalization that begins this introductory paragraph should reflect the impression the person gives at first glance; for example, "He is a tall, neatly dressed man who probably works indoors." Then round out the paragraph with the simple physical facts that support this generalization, such as height, weight, complexion, and kind of clothes.

Then, using your inferences as generalizations, write two or three more paragraphs about such matters as details of dress and appearance, movements and facial expressions, and reactions to things around him. Unify each paragraph by putting in only material that supports the generalization at the head of it, and try to give full and convincing evidence for each of these inferences.

Generalizations on which paragraphs and essays are based are often called *topic sentences* because they represent the topic, or subject, of the paragraph or essay.

At the end of your description, add a brief paragraph in which you summarize the inferences you have made about the person. This will help to emphasize the point of your essay.

Floyd Patterson

GAY TALESE

At the foot of a mountain in upstate New York, about sixty miles from Manhattan, there is an abandoned country clubhouse with a dusty dance floor, upturned barstools, and an untuned piano; and the only sounds heard around the place at night come from the big white house behind it—the clanging sounds of garbage cans being toppled by raccoons, skunks, and stray cats making their nocturnal raids down from the mountain.

The white house seems deserted, too; but occasionally, when the animals become too clamorous, a light will flash on, a window will open, and a Coke bottle will come flying through the darkness and smash against the cans. But mostly the animals are undisturbed until daybreak, when the rear door of the white house swings open and a broad-shouldered Negro appears in gray sweat clothes with a white towel around his neck.

He runs down the steps, quickly passes the garbage cans and proceeds at a trot down the dirt road beyond the country club toward the highway. Sometimes he stops along the road and throws a flurry of punches at imaginary foes, each jab punctuated by hard gasps of his breathing—"hegh-hegh-hegh-hegh"—and then, reaching the highway, he turns and soon disappears up the mountain.

At this time of morning farm trucks are on the road, and the drivers wave at the runner. And later in the morning other motorists see him, and a few stop suddenly at the curb and ask: "Say, aren't *you* Floyd Patterson?"

"No," says Floyd Patterson. "I'm his brother, Raymond."

The motorists move on, but recently a man on foot, a disheveled man who seemed to have spent the night outdoors, staggered behind the runner along the road and yelled, "Hey, Floyd Patterson!"

"No, I'm his brother, Raymond."

"Don't tell *me* you're not Floyd Patterson. I know what Floyd Patterson looks like."

"Okay," Patterson said, shrugging, "if you want me to be Floyd Patterson, I'll be Floyd Patterson."

"So let me have your autograph," said the man, handing him a rumpled piece of paper and a pencil.

He signed it—"Raymond Patterson."

One hour later Floyd Patterson was jogging his way back down the dirt path toward the white house, the towel over his head absorbing the sweat from his brow. He lives alone in a two-room apartment in the rear of the house, and has remained there in almost complete seclusion since getting knocked out a second time by Sonny Liston.

In the smaller room is a large bed he makes up himself, several record albums he rarely plays, a telephone that seldom rings. The larger room has a kitchen on one side and on the other, adjacent to a sofa, is a fireplace from which are hung boxing trunks and T-shirts to dry, and a photograph of him when he was the champion, and also a television set. The set is usually on except when Patterson is sleeping, or when he is sparring across the road inside the clubhouse (the ring is rigged over what was once the dance floor), or when, in a rare moment of painful honesty, he reveals to a visitor what it is like to be the loser.

"Oh, I would give up anything to just be able to work with Liston, to box with him somewhere where nobody would see us, and to see if I could get past three minutes with him," Patterson was saying, wiping his face with the towel, pacing slowly around the room near the sofa. "I *know* I can do better. . . . Oh, I'm not talking about a rematch. Who would pay a nickel for another Patterson-Liston match? I know *I* wouldn't. . . . But all I want to do is get past the first round."

Then he said, "You have no idea how it is in the first round. You're out there with all those people around you, and those cameras, and the whole world looking in, and all that movement, that excitement, and 'The Star-Spangled Banner,' and the whole nation hoping you'll win, including President Kennedy. And do you know what this all does? It blinds you, just blinds you. And then the bell rings, and you go at Liston and he's coming at you, and you're not even aware that there's a referee in the ring with you.

". . . Then you can't remember much of the rest, because you don't want to. . . . All you recall is, all of a sudden, you're getting up, and the referee is saying, 'You all right?' and you say, 'Of *course* I'm all right,' and he says, 'What's your name?' and you say 'Patterson.'

"And then, suddenly, with all this screaming around you, you're down again, and know you have to get up, but you're extremely groggy, and the referee is pushing you back, and your trainer is in there with a towel, and people are all standing up, and your eyes focus directly at no one person— you're sort of floating.

"It's not a *bad* feeling when you're knocked out," he said. "It's a *good* feeling, actually. It's not painful, just a sharp grogginess. You don't see angels or stars; you're on a pleasant cloud. After Liston hit me in Nevada, I felt, for about four or five seconds, that everybody in the arena was actually in the ring with me, circled around me like a family, and you feel warmth toward all the people in the arena after you're knocked out. You feel lovable to all the people. And you want to reach out and kiss everybody—men and women—and after the Liston fight somebody told me I actually blew a kiss to the crowd from the ring. I don't remember that. But I guess it's true because that's the way you feel during the four or five seconds after a knockout. . . .

"But then," Patterson went on, still pacing, "this good feeling leaves you. You realize where you are, and what you're doing there, and what has just happened to you. And what follows is a hurt, a confused hurt—not a physical hurt—it's a hurt combined with anger; it's a what-will-people-think hurt; it's an ashamed-of-my-own-ability hurt . . . and all you want then is a hatch door in the middle of the ring—a hatch door that will open and let you fall through and land in your dressing room instead of having to get out of the ring and face those people. The worst thing about losing is having to walk out of the ring and face those people. . . ."

Then Patterson walked over to the stove and put on the kettle for tea. He remained silent for a few moments. Through the walls could be heard the footsteps and voices of the sparring partners and the trainer, who live in the front of the house. Soon they would be in the country club getting things ready should Patterson wish to spar.

Patterson wants to continue as a prizefighter but his wife, whom he rarely sees any more, and most of his friends think he should quit. They point out that he does not need the money. Even he admits that from investments alone on his $8,000,000 gross earnings he should have an annual income of about $35,000 for the next twenty-five years. But Patterson, who is only twenty-eight years old and barely scratched, cannot believe that he is finished. He cannot help but think that it was something more than Liston that destroyed him—a strange, psychological force was also involved—and unless he can fully understand what it was, and learn to deal with it in the boxing ring, he may never be able to live peacefully anywhere but under this mountain. Nor will he ever be able to discard the false whiskers and mustache that, ever since Johansson beat him in 1959, he has carried with him in a small attaché case into each fight so he can slip out of the stadium unrecognized should he lose.

"I often wonder what other fighters feel, and what goes through their minds when they lose," Patterson said, placing the cups of tea on the table. "I've wanted so much to talk to another fighter about all this, to compare thoughts, to see if he feels some of the same things I've felt. But who can you talk to? Most fighters don't talk much anyway. And I can't even look another fighter in the eye at a weigh-in, for some reason.

"At the Liston weigh-in, the sportswriters noticed this, and said it showed I was afraid. But that's not it. I can never look *any* fighter in the eye because . . . well, because we're going to fight, which isn't a nice thing, and because . . . well, once I actually did look a fighter in the eye. It was a long, long time ago. I must have been in the amateurs then. . . . And when I looked at this fighter, I saw he had such a nice face. . . . And then he looked at *me* . . . and *smiled* at me . . . and *I* smiled back! . . . It was strange, very strange. When a guy can look at another guy and smile like that, I don't think they have any business fighting.

"I don't remember what happened in that fight, and I don't remember what the guy's name was. I only remember that, ever since, I have never looked another fighter in the eye. . . ."

The telephone rang in the bedroom. Patterson got up to answer it. It was his wife, Sandra. So he excused himself, shutting the bedroom door behind him.

Sandra Patterson and their four children live in a $100,000 home in an upper-middle-class white neighborhood in Scarsdale, New York. Floyd Patterson feels uncomfortable in this home surrounded by a manicured lawn and stuffed with soft furniture, and, since losing his title to Liston, he has preferred living full time at his camp, which his children have come to know as "Daddy's house." The children, the eldest of whom is a six-year-old daughter named Jeannie, do not know exactly what their father does for a living. But Jeannie, who watched the last Liston-Patterson fight on closed-circuit television, accepted the explanation that her father performs in a kind of game where the men take turns pushing one another down; he had his turn pushing them down, and now it is their turn.

The bedroom door opened again, and Floyd Patterson, shaking his head, was very angry and nervous.

"I'm not going to work out today," he said. "I'm going to fly down to Scarsdale. Those boys are picking on Jeannie again. She's the only Negro in this school, and the older kids give her a rough time, and some of the older boys tease her and lift up her dress all the time. Yesterday she went home crying, and so today I'm going down there and plan to wait outside the school for those boys to come out, and . . ."

"How old are they?" he was asked.

"Teenagers," he said. "Old enough for a left hook."

Patterson telephoned his pilot friend, Ted Hanson, who stays at the camp and does public relations work for him, and has helped teach Patterson to fly. Five minutes later Hanson, a lean white man with a crewcut and glasses, was knocking on the door; and ten minutes later both were in the car that Patterson was driving almost recklessly over the narrow, winding country roads toward the airport, about six miles from the camp.

"Sandra is afraid I'll cause trouble; she's worried about what I'll do to those boys; she doesn't want trouble!" Patterson snapped, swerving around a hill and giving his car more gas. "She's just not firm enough! She's afraid. . . . She was afraid to tell me about that grocery man who's been making passes at her. It took her a long time before she told me about that dishwasher repairman who comes over and calls her '*baby*.' They all know I'm away so much. And that dishwasher repairman's been to my home about four, five times this month already. That machine breaks down every week. I guess he fixes it so it breaks down every week. Last time, I laid a trap. I waited forty-five minutes for him to come, but then he didn't show up. I was going to grab him and say, 'How would you like it if I called *your* wife *"baby"*? You'd feel like punching me in the nose, wouldn't you? Well, that's what I'm going to do—if you ever call her *"baby"* again. You call her Mrs. Patterson; or Sandra, if you know her. But you don't know her, so call her Mrs. Patterson.' . . . And then I told Sandra that these men, this type of white man, he just wants to have some fun with colored women. He'll never marry a colored woman, just wants to have some fun. . . ."

Now he was driving into the airport's parking lot. Directly ahead, roped to the grass air strip, was the single-engine, green Cessna that Patterson bought and learned to fly in Denver before the second Liston fight. Flying was a thing Patterson had always feared—a fear shared by, maybe inherited from, his manager, Cus D'Amato, who still will not fly.

D'Amato, who began training Patterson when the fighter was fourteen years old and exerted a tremendous influence over his psyche, is a strange but fascinating man of fifty-six who is addicted to spartanism and self-denial and is possessed by suspicion and fear: he avoids subways because he fears someone might push him onto the tracks; never has married because he believes a wife might be duped by his enemies; never reveals his home address because he suspects snipers.

"I must keep my enemies confused," D'Amato once explained. "When they are confused, then I can do a job for my fighters. What I do not want in life, however, is a sense of security; the moment a person knows security, his senses are dulled—and he begins to die. I also do not want many pleasures in life; I believe the more pleasures you get out of living, the more fear you have of dying."

Until a few years ago, D'Amato did most of Patterson's talking, and ran things like an Italian *padrone*. But later Patterson, the maturing son, rebelled against the Father Image. After losing to Sonny Liston the first time—a fight D'Amato had urged Patterson to resist—Patterson took flying lessons. And before the second Liston fight Patterson had conquered his fear of height, was master at the controls, was filled with renewed confidence—and knew, too, that even if he lost he at least possessed a vehicle that could get him out of town, fast.

But it didn't. After the flight, the little Cessna, weighed down by too much luggage, became overheated ninety miles outside of Las Vegas. Patterson and his pilot companion, having no choice but to turn back, radioed the airfield and arranged for the rental of a larger plane. When they landed, the Vegas air terminal was filled with people leaving town after the fight. Patterson hid in the shadows behind a hangar. His beard was packed in the trunk. But nobody saw him.

Later the pilot flew Patterson's Cessna back to New York alone. And

Patterson flew in the larger, rented plane. He was accompanied on this flight by Ted Hanson, a friendly forty-two-year-old, thrice-divorced Californian, who once was a crop duster, a bartender, and a cabaret hoofer; later he became a pilot instructor in Las Vegas, and it was there that he met Patterson. The two became good friends. And, when Patterson asked Hanson to help fly the rented plane back to New York, Hanson did not hesitate, even though he had a slight hangover that night—partly due to being depressed by Liston's victory, partly to being slugged in a bar by a drunk after objecting to some unflattering things the drunk had said about the fight.

Once in the airplane, however, Ted Hanson became very alert. He had to be because, after the plane had cruised awhile at ten thousand feet, Floyd Patterson's mind seemed to wander back to the ring, and the plane would drift off course, and Hanson would say, "Floyd, Floyd, how's about getting back on course?" and then Patterson's head would snap up and his eyes would flash toward the dials. And everything would be all right for a while. But then he was back in the arena, reliving the fight, hardly believing that it had really happened. . . .

". . . And I kept thinking, as I flew out of Vegas that night, of all those months of training before the fight, all the roadwork, all the sparring, all the months away from Sandra . . . thinking of the time in camp when I wanted to stay up until 11:15 p.m. to watch a certain movie on the Late Show, but I didn't because I had roadwork the next morning. . . .

"And I was thinking about how good I'd felt before the fight, as I lay on the table in the dressing room. . . . I remember thinking, 'You're in excellent physical condition, you're in good mental condition—but are you vicious?' But you tell yourself, 'Viciousness is not important now, don't think about it now; a championship fight's at stake, and that's important enough and, who knows? maybe you'll get vicious once the bell rings.'

"And so you lay there trying to get a little sleep . . . but you're only in a twilight zone, half-asleep, and you're interrupted every once in a while by voices out in the hall, some guy's yelling, 'Hey, Jack,' or 'Hey, Al,' or, 'Hey, get those four-rounders into the ring.' And when you hear that you think, 'They're not ready for you yet.' So you lay there . . . and wonder, 'Where will I be tomorrow?' 'Where will I be three hours from now?' . . . Oh, you think all kinds of thoughts, some thoughts completely unrelated to the fight . . . you wonder whether you ever paid your mother-in-law back for all those stamps she bought a year ago . . . and you remember that time at 2 a.m. when Sandra tripped on the steps while bringing a bottle up to the baby . . . and then you get mad and ask: 'WHAT AM I THINKING ABOUT THESE THINGS FOR?' . . . and you try to sleep . . . but then the door opens and somebody says to somebody else, 'Hey, is somebody gonna go to Liston's dressing room to watch 'em bandage up?'

"And so then you know it's about time to get ready. . . . You open your eyes. You get off the table. You glove up, you loosen up. Then Liston's trainer walks in. He looks at you, he smiles. He feels the bandages and later he says, 'Good luck, Floyd,' and you think, 'He didn't have to say that; he must be a nice guy.'

"And then you go out, and it's the long walk, always a long walk, and you think, 'What am I gonna be when I come back this way?' Then you climb into the ring. You notice Billy Eckstine at ringside leaning over to talk to somebody, and you see the reporters—some you like, some you don't like—and then it's 'The Star-Spangled Banner,' and the cameras are rolling, and the bell rings. . . .

"How could the same thing happen twice? How? That's all I kept thinking after the knockout. . . . Was I fooling these people all these years? . . . Was I ever the champion? . . . And then they lead you out of the ring . . . and up the aisle you go, past those people, and all you want is to get to your dressing room, fast . . . but the trouble was in Las Vegas they made a wrong turn along the aisle, and when we got to the end, there was no dressing room there . . . and we had to walk all the way back down the aisle, past the same people, and they must have been thinking, 'Patterson's not only knocked out, but he can't even find his dressing room.' . . .

"In the dressing room I had a headache. Liston didn't hurt me physically—a few days later I only felt a twitching nerve in my teeth—it was nothing like some fights I've had: like that Dick Wagner fight in '54 when he beat my body so bad I was urinating blood for days. . . . After the Liston fight, I just went into the bathroom, shut the door behind me, and looked at myself in the mirror. I just looked at myself, and asked, 'What happened?' and then they started pounding on the door, and saying, 'C'm'on out, Floyd, c'm'on out; the press is here, Cus is here, c'm'on out, Floyd.' . . .

"And so I went out, and they asked questions, but what can you say? . . . What you're thinking about is all those months of training, all the conditioning, all the depriving; and you think, 'I didn't have to run that extra mile, didn't have to spar that day, *I could have stayed up that night in camp and watched the Late Show. . . . I could have fought this fight tonight in no condition.' . . .*"

"Floyd, Floyd," Hanson had said, "let's get back on course. . . ."

Again Patterson would snap out of his reverie, and refocus on the Omnirange, and get his flying under control. After landing in New Mexico, and then in Ohio, Floyd Patterson and Ted Hanson brought the little plane into the New York air strip near the fight camp. The green Cessna that had been flown back by the other pilot was already there, roped to the grass at precisely the same spot it was on this day five months later, on this day when Floyd Patterson was planning to fly it toward perhaps another fight—a fight with some schoolboys in Scarsdale who had been lifting up his six-year-old daughter's dress.

Patterson and Ted Hanson untied the plane, and Patterson got a rag and wiped from the windshield the splotches of insects. Then he walked around behind the plane, inspected the tail, checked under the fuselage, then peered down between the wing and the flaps to make sure all the screws were tight. He seemed suspicious of something. D'Amato would have been pleased.

"If a guy wants to get rid of you," Patterson explained, "all he has to do is remove these little screws here. Then, when you try to come in for a landing, the flaps fall off, and you crash."

Then Patterson got into the cockpit and started the engine. A few moments later, with Hanson beside him, Patterson was racing the little plane over the grassy field, then soaring over the weeds, then flying high above the gentle hills and trees. It was a nice take-off.

Since it was only a forty-minute flight to the Westchester airport, where Sandra Patterson would be waiting with a car, Floyd Patterson did all the flying. The trip was uneventful until, suddenly behind a cloud, he flew into heavy smoke that hovered above a forest fire. His visibility gone, he was forced to the instruments. And at this precise moment a fly that had been buzzing in the back of the cockpit flew up front and landed on the instrument panel in front of Patterson. He glared at the fly, watched it crawl slowly up the windshield, then shot a quick smash with his palm against the glass. He missed. The fly buzzed safely past Patterson's ear, bounced off the back of the cockpit, circled around.

"This smoke won't keep up," Hanson assured. "You can level off."

Patterson leveled off.

He flew easily for a few moments. Then the fly buzzed to the front again, zigzagging before Patterson's face, then landed and proceeded to crawl across the panel. Patterson watched it, squinted. Then he slammed down at it with a quick right hand. Missed.

Ten minutes later, his nerves still on edge, Patterson began the descent. He picked up the radio microphone—"Westchester tower . . . Cessna 2729 uniform . . . three miles northwest . . . land in one-six on final. . . ." And then, after an easy landing, he climbed quickly out of the cockpit and strode toward his wife's station wagon outside the terminal.

But along the way a small man smoking a cigar turned toward Patterson, waved at him, and said, "Say, excuse me, but aren't you . . . aren't you . . . Sonny Liston?"

Patterson stopped. He glared at the man, bewildered. He wasn't sure whether it was a joke or an insult, and he really did not know what to do.

"Aren't you Sonny Liston?" the man repeated, quite serious.

"No," Patterson said, quickly passing by the man, "I'm his brother."

When he reached Mrs. Patterson's car, he asked, "How much time till school lets out?"

"About fifteen minutes," she said, starting up the engine. Then she said, "Oh, Floyd, I just should have told Sister, I shouldn't have . . ."

"*You* tell Sister; *I'll* tell the boys. . . ."

Mrs. Patterson drove as quickly as she could into Scarsdale, with Patterson shaking his head and telling Ted Hanson in the back, "Really can't understand these school kids. This is a religious school, and they want $20,000 for a glass window—and yet, some of them carry these racial prejudices, and it's mostly the Jews who are shoulder-to-shoulder with us, and . . ."

"Oh, Floyd," cried his wife, "Floyd, *I* have to get along here. *You're* not here, *you* don't live here, *I* . . ."

She arrived at the school just as the bell began to ring.

It was a modern building at the top of a hill, and on the lawn was the statue of a saint and, behind it, a large white cross.

"There's Jeannie," said Mrs. Patterson.

"Hurry, call her over here," Patterson said.

"Jeannie! Come over here, honey."

The little girl, wearing a blue school uniform and cap, and clasping books in front of her, came running down the path toward the station wagon.

"Jeannie," Floyd Patterson said, rolling down his window, "point out the boys who lifted your dress."

Jeannie turned and watched as several students came down the path; then she pointed to a tall, thin curly-haired boy walking with four other boys, all about twelve to fourteen years of age.

"Hey," Patterson called to him, "can I see you for a minute?"

All five boys came to the side of the car. They looked Patterson directly in the eye. They seemed not at all intimidated by him.

"You the one that's been lifting up my daughter's dress?" Patterson asked the boy who had been singled out.

"Nope," the boy said, casually.

"Nope?" Patterson said, caught off guard by the reply.

"Wasn't him, Mister," said another boy. "Probably was his little brother, Dennis."

Patterson looked at Jeannie. But she was speechless, uncertain. The five boys remained there, waiting for Patterson to do something.

"Well, er, where's Dennis?" Patterson asked.

"Hey, Dennis!" one of the boys yelled. "Dennis come over here."

Dennis walked toward them. He resembled his older brother; he had freckles on his small, upturned nose, had blue eyes, dark curly hair and, as he approached the station wagon, he seemed equally unintimidated by Patterson.

"You been lifting up my daughter's dress?"

"Nope," said Dennis.

"*Nope!*" Patterson repeated, frustrated.

"Nope, I wasn't lifting it," Dennis said. "I was just touching it a little . . ."

The other boys stood around the car looking down at Patterson, and other students crowded behind them, and nearby Patterson saw several white parents standing next to their parked cars; he became self-conscious, began to tap nervously with his fingers against the dashboard. He could not raise his voice without creating an unpleasant scene, yet could not retreat gracefully; so his voice went soft, and he said, finally, "Look, Dennis, I want you to stop it. I won't tell your mother—that might get you in trouble—but don't do it again, okay?"

"Okay."

The boys calmly turned and walked, in a group, up the street.

Sandra Patterson said nothing. Jeannie opened the door, sat in the front seat next to her father, and took out a small blue piece of paper that a nun had given her and handed it across to Mrs. Patterson. But Floyd Patterson snatched it. He read it. Then he paused, put the paper down, and quietly announced, dragging out the words, *"She didn't do her religion."*

Patterson now wanted to get out of Scarsdale. He wanted to return to camp.

After stopping at the Patterson home in Scarsdale and picking up Floyd Patterson, Jr., who is three, Mrs. Patterson drove them all back to the airport. Jeannie and Floyd, Jr., were seated in the back of the plane, and then Mrs. Patterson drove the station wagon alone up to camp, planning to return to Scarsdale that evening with the children.

It was 4 p.m. when Floyd Patterson got back to the camp, and the shadows were falling on the country club, and on the tennis court routed by weeds, and on the big white house in front of which not a single automobile was parked. All was deserted and quiet; it was a loser's camp.

The children ran to play inside the country club; Patterson walked slowly toward his apartment to dress for the workout.

"What could I do with those schoolboys?" he asked. "What can you do to kids of that age?"

It still seemed to bother him—the effrontery of the boys, the realization that he had somehow failed, the probability that, had those same boys heckled someone in Liston's family, the school yard would have been littered with limbs.

While Patterson and Liston both are products of the slum, and while both began as thieves, Patterson had been tamed in a special school with help from a gentle spinster; later he became a Catholic convert, and learned not to hate. Still later he bought a dictionary, adding to his vocabulary such words as "vicissitude" and "enigma." And when he regained his championship from Johansson, he became the great black hope of the Urban League.

He proved that it is not only possible to rise out of a Negro slum and succeed as a sportsman, but also to develop into an intelligent, sensitive, law-abiding citizen. In proving this, however, and in taking pride in it,

Patterson seemed to lose part of himself. He lost part of his hunger, his anger—and as he walked up the steps into his apartment, he was saying, "I became the good guy. . . . After Liston won the title, I kept hoping that he would change into a good guy, too. That would have relieved me of the responsibility, and maybe I could have been more of the bad guy. But he didn't. . . . It's okay to be the good guy when you're winning. But when you're losing, it is no good being the good guy. . . ."

Patterson took off his shirt and trousers and, moving some books on the bureau to one side, put down his watch, his cufflinks and a clip of bills.

"Do you do much reading?" he was asked.

"No," he said. "In fact, you know I've never finished reading a book in my whole life? I don't know why. I just feel that no writer today has anything for me; I mean, none of them has felt any more deeply than I have, and I have nothing to learn from them. Although Baldwin to me seems different from the rest. What's Baldwin doing these days?"

"He's writing a play. Anthony Quinn is supposed to have a part in it."

"Quinn?" Patterson asked.

"Yes."

"Quinn doesn't like me."

"Why?"

"I read or heard it somewhere; Quinn had been quoted as saying that my fight was disgraceful against Liston, and Quinn said something to the effect that he could have done better. People often say that—*they* could have done better! Well, I think that if *they* had to fight, *they* couldn't even go through the experience of waiting for the fight to begin. They'd be up the whole night before, and would be drinking, or taking drugs. They'd probably get a heart attack. I'm sure that if I was in the ring with Anthony Quinn I could wear him out without even touching him. I would do nothing but pressure him, I'd stalk him, I'd stand close to him. I wouldn't touch him, but I'd wear him out and he'd collapse. But Anthony Quinn's an old man, isn't he?"

"In his forties."

"Well, anyway," Patterson said, "getting back to Baldwin, he seems like a wonderful guy. I've seen him on television and, before the Liston fight in Chicago, he came by my camp. You meet Baldwin on the street and you say, 'Who's this poor slob?'—he seems just like another guy; and this is the same impression *I* give people when they don't know me. But I think Baldwin and me, we have much in common, and someday I'd just like to sit somewhere for a long time and talk to him. . . ."

Patterson, his trunks and sweat pants on, bent over to tie his shoelaces, and then, from a bureau drawer, took out a T-shirt across which was printed *The Deauville*. He has several T-shirts bearing the same name. He takes good care of them. They are souvenirs from the high point of his life. They are from the Deauville Hotel in Miami Beach, which is where he trained for the third Ingemar Johansson match in March of 1961.

Never was Floyd Patterson more popular, more admired than during that winter. He had visited President Kennedy; he had been given a $25,000 jeweled crown by his manager; his greatness was conceded by sportswriters— and nobody had any idea that Patterson, secretly, was in possession of a false mustache and dark glasses that he intended to wear out of Miami Beach should he lose the third fight to Johansson.

It was after being knocked out by Johansson in their first fight that Patterson, deep in depression, hiding in humiliation for months in a remote Connecticut lodge, decided he could not face the public again if he lost. So he bought false whiskers and a mustache, and planned to wear them out of his dressing room after a defeat. He had also planned, in leaving his dressing room, to linger momentarily within the crowd and perhaps complain out loud about the fight. Then he would slip undiscovered through the night and into a waiting automobile.

Although there proved to be no need to bring the disguise into the second or third Johansson fights, or into a subsequent bout in Toronto against an obscure heavyweight named Tom McNeeley, Patterson brought it anyway; and, after the first Liston fight, he not only wore it during his forty-eight-hour automobile ride from Chicago to New York, but he also wore it while in an airliner bound for Spain.

"As I got onto this plane, you'd never have recognized me," he said. "I had on this beard, mustache, glasses, and hat—and I also limped, to make myself look older. I was alone. I didn't care what plane I boarded; I just looked up and saw this sign at the terminal reading 'Madrid,' and so I got on that flight after buying a ticket.

"When I got to Madrid I registered at a hotel under the name 'Aaron Watson.' I stayed in Madrid about four or five days. In the daytime I wandered around to the poorer sections of the city, limping, looking at the people, and the people stared back at me and must have thought I was crazy because I was moving so slow and looked the way I did. I ate food in my hotel room. Although once I went to a restaurant and ordered soup. I hate soup. But I thought it was what old people would order. So I ate it. And, after a week of this, I began to actually think I was somebody else. I began to believe it. . . . And it is nice, every once in a while, being somebody else. . . ."

Patterson would not elaborate on how he managed to register under a name that did not correspond to his passport; he merely explained, "With money, you can do anything."

Now, walking slowly around the room, his black silk robe over his sweat clothes, Patterson said, "You must wonder what makes a man do things like this. Well, I wonder too. And the answer is, I don't know . . . but I think that within me, within every human being, there is a certain weakness. It is a weakness that exposes itself more when you're alone. And I have figured out that part of the reason I do the things I do, and cannot seem to conquer that one word—*myself*— is because . . . is because . . . I am a coward. . . ."

He stopped. He stood very still in the middle of the room, thinking about what he had just said, probably wondering whether he should have said it.

"I am a coward," he then repeated, softly. "My fighting has little to do with that fact, too. I mean you can be a fighter—and a *winning* fighter—and still be a coward. I was probably a coward on the night I won the championship back from Ingemar. And I remember another night, long ago, back when I was in the amateurs, fighting this big, tremendous man named Julius Griffin. I was only 153 pounds. I was petrified. It was all I could do to cross the ring. And then he came at me, and moved close to me . . . and from then on I don't know anything, I have no idea what happened. Only thing I know is, I saw him on the floor. And later somebody said, 'Man, I never saw anything like it. You just jumped up in the air, and threw thirty different punches.'. . ."

"When did you first think you were a coward?" he was asked.

"It was after the first Ingemar fight."

"How does one see this cowardice you speak of?"

"You see it when a fighter loses. Ingemar, for instance, is not a coward. When he lost the third fight in Miami, he was at a party later at the Fontainebleau. Had I lost, I couldn't have gone to that party. And I don't see how he did. . . ."

"Have you no hate left?"

"I have hated only one fighter," Patterson said. "And that was Ingemar in the second fight. I had been hating him for a whole year before that—not because he beat me in the first fight, but because of what he did after. It was all that boasting in public, and his showing off his right-hand punch on television, his thundering right, his 'toonder and lightning.' And I'd be home watching him on television, and *hating* him. It is a miserable feeling, hate. When a man hates, he can't have any peace of mind. And for one solid year I hated him because, after he took everything away from me, deprived me of everything I was, he *rubbed it in.* On the night of the second fight, in the dressing room, I couldn't wait until I got into the ring. When he was a little late getting into the ring, I thought, "He's holding me up; he's trying to unsettle me—well, I'll get him!'"

"Why couldn't you hate Liston in the second match?"

Patterson thought for a moment, then said, "Look, if Sonny Liston walked into this room now and slapped me in the face, then you'd see a fight. You'd see the fight of your life because, then, a principle would be involved. I'd forget he was a human being. I'd forget I was a human being. And I'd fight accordingly."

"Could it be, Floyd, that you made a mistake in becoming a prizefighter?"

"What do you mean?"

"Well, you say you're a coward; you say you have little capacity for hate; and you seemed to lose your nerve against those schoolboys in Scarsdale this afternoon. Don't you think you might have been better suited for some other kind of work? Perhaps a social worker, or . . ."

"Are you asking why I continue to fight?"

"Yes."

"Well," he said, not irritated by the question, "first of all, I love boxing. Boxing has been good to me. And I might just as well ask you the question: 'Why do you write?' Or, 'Do you retire from writing every time you write a bad story?' . . . And as to whether I should have become a fighter in the first place, well, let's see how I can explain it. . . . Look, let's say you're a man who has been in an empty room for days and days without food . . . and then they take you out of that room and put you into another room where there's food hanging all over the place . . . and the first thing you reach for, you eat. When you're hungry, you're not choosy, and so I chose the thing that was closest to me. That was boxing. One day I just wandered into a gymnasium and boxed a boy. And I beat him. Then I boxed another boy. I beat him, too. Then I kept boxing. And winning. And I said, 'Here, finally, is something I can do!'

"Now I wasn't a sadist," he quickly added. "But I liked beating people because it was the only thing I could do. And whether boxing was a sport or not, I wanted to make it a sport because it was a thing I could succeed at. And what were the requirements? Sacrifice. That's all. To anybody who comes from Bedford-Stuyvesant in Brooklyn, sacrifice comes easy. And so I kept fighting, and one day I became heavyweight champion, and I got to know people like you. And you wonder how I can sacrifice, how I can deprive myself so much. You just don't realize where I've come from. You don't understand where I was when it began for me.

"In those days, when I was about eight years old, everything I got I stole. I stole to survive, and I did survive, but I seemed to hate myself. Even when I was younger, my mother told me I used to point to a photograph of myself hanging in the bedroom and would say, 'I don't like that boy!' One day my mother found three large X's scratched with a nail or something over that photograph of me. I don't remember doing it. But I do remember feeling like a parasite at home. I remember how awful I used to feel at night when my father, a longshoreman, would come home so tired that, as my mother fixed food for him, he would fall asleep at the table because he was that tired. I would always take his shoes off and clean his feet. That was my job. And I felt so bad because here I was, not going to school, doing nothing, just watching my father come home; and on Friday nights it was even worse. He would come home with his pay, and he'd put every nickel of it on the table so my mother could buy food for all the children. I never wanted to be around to see that. I'd run and hide. And then I decided to leave home and start stealing—and I did. And I would never come home unless I brought something that I had stolen. Once I remember I broke into a dress store and stole a whole mound of dresses, at 2 a.m., and here I was, this little kid, carrying all those dresses over the wall, thinking they were all the same size, my mother's size, and thinking the cops would never notice me walking down the street with all those dresses piled over my head. They did, of course. . . . I went to the Youth House. . . ."

Floyd Patterson's children, who had been playing outside all this time around the country club, now became restless and began to call him, and Jeannie started to pound on his door. So Patterson picked up his leather bag, which contained his gloves, his mouthpiece, and adhesive tape, and walked with the children across the path toward the club.

He flicked on the light switches behind the stage near the piano. Beams of amber streaked through the dimly-lit room and flashed onto the ring. Then he walked to one side of the room, outside the ring. He took off his robe, shuffled his feet in the rosin, skipped rope, and then began to shadowbox in front of a spit-stained mirror, throwing out quick combinations of lefts, rights, lefts, rights, each jab followed by a *"hegh-hegh-hegh-hegh."* Then, his gloves on, he moved to the punching bag in the far corner, and soon the room reverberated to his rhythmic beat against the bobbling bag—rat-tat-tat-*tetteta*, rat-tat-tat-*tetteta*, rat-tat-tat-*tetteta*, rat-tat-tat-*tetteta!*

The children, sitting on pink leather chairs, moved from the bar to the fringe of the ring, watched him in awe, sometimes flinching at the force of his pounding against the leather bag.

And this is how they would probably remember him years from now: a dark, solitary, glistening figure punching in the corner of a forlorn spot at the bottom of a mountain where people once came to have fun—until the country club became unfashionable, the paint began to peel, and Negroes were allowed in.

As Floyd Patterson continued to bang away with lefts and rights, his gloves a brown blur against the bag, his daughter slipped quietly off her chair and wandered past the ring into the other room. There, on the other side of the bar and beyond a dozen round tables, was the stage. She climbed onto the stage and stood behind a microphone, long dead, and cried out, imitating a ring announcer, "Ladieeees and gentlemen . . . tonight we present . . ."

She looked around, puzzled. Then, seeing that her little brother had followed her, she waved him up to the stage and began again: "Ladiees and gentlemen . . . tonight we present . . . Floydie Patterson . . ."

Suddenly, the pounding against the bag in the other room stopped. There was silence for a moment. Then Jeannie, still behind the microphone and looking down at her brother, said, "Floydie, come up here!"

"No," he said.

"Oh, come up here!"

"NO," he cried.

Then Floyd Patterson's voice, from the other room, called: "Cut it out. . . . I'll take you for a walk in a minute."

He resumed punching—rat-tat-tat-*tetteta*—and they returned to his side. But Jeannie interrupted, asking, "Daddy, how come you sweating?"

"Water fell on me," he said, still pounding.

"Daddy," asked Floyd, Jr., "how come you spit water on the floor before?"

"To get it out of my mouth."

He was about to move over to the heavier punching bag—but just then the sound of Mrs. Patterson's station wagon could be heard moving up the road.

Soon she was in Patterson's apartment cleaning up a bit, patting the pillows, washing the teacups that had been left in the sink. One hour later the family was having dinner together. They were together for two more hours; then, at 10 p.m., Mrs. Patterson washed and dried all the dishes, and put the garbage out in the can—where it would remain until the raccoons and skunks got to it.

And then, after helping the children with their coats and walking out to the station wagon and kissing her husband good-bye, Mrs. Patterson began the drive down the dirt road toward the highway. Patterson waved once, and stood for a moment watching the tail lights go, and then he turned and walked slowly back toward the house.

---

1. For the most part, Talese describes the facts of Patterson's surroundings and actions or lets him speak for himself. But now and then he makes inferences. What are some of them? Why do you think his description needs these comments? Could he have left them out?
2. Talese doesn't give us a physical description of Patterson. Why not?
3. What are some of the details of Patterson's surroundings? What do they tell us about him?
4. What episodes and facts does Talese emphasize most? Which technique of emphasis does he use? Judging from this emphasis, what do you think he wants us to know about his subject?
5. If you review a short list of those facts that usually tell us most about a person, you will find that Talese has left out one of the most obvious. Which one? Do you think it should have been included?

Pigeon Woman

MAY SWENSON

Slate, or dirty-marble-colored,
or rusty-iron-colored, the pigeons
on the flagstones in front of the
Public Library make a sharp lake

into which the pigeon woman wades
at exactly 1:30. She wears a
plastic pink raincoat with a round
collar (looking like a little

girl, so gay) and flat gym shoes,
her hair square-cut, orange.
Wide-apart feet carefully enter
the spinning, crooning waves

(as if she'd just learned how
to walk, each step conscious,
an accomplishment); blue knots in the
calves of her bare legs (uglied marble),

age in angled cords of jaw
and neck, her pimento-colored hair,
hanging in thin tassles, is gray
around a balding crown.

The day-old bread drops down
from her veined hand dipping out
of a paper sack. Choppy, shadowy ripples,
the pigeons strike around her legs.

Sack empty, she squats and seems to rinse
her hands in them—the rainy greens and
oily purples of their necks. Almost
they let her wet her thirsty fingertips—

but drain away in an untouchable tide.
A make-believe trade
she has come to, in her lostness
or illness or age—to treat the motley

city pigeons at 1:30 every day, in all
weathers. It is for them she colors
her own feathers. Ruddy-footed
on the lime-stained paving,

purling to meet her when she comes,
they are a lake of love. Retreating
from her hands as soon as empty,
they are the flints of love.

---

1. Separate the facts about the woman from the imagery and the inferences. What does each fact tell us about her?
2. What inferences does the poet make? Would you make the same ones?
3. One image is emphasized by being placed at the beginning of the
   poem and again at the end. What is the image? What does it mean?
   Where else in the poem does it appear?
4. From the facts emphasized and from the images used, can you make
   an inference about what the poet is trying to say?

1. A painting cannot tell us as much about a person as a long article like "Floyd Patterson," but if it is good it can tell us a great deal. What things can you infer about the woman pictured? (The picture was painted in 1934, so of course allowance should be made for changes in style.)
2. What positions of various parts of the body communicate character and feeling? What does each tell us?
3. What do you infer from her clothing and her way of wearing it? Explain clearly.
4. What is her attitude toward the man watching her? What leads you to infer this?
5. How would this painting differ from a photograph of the same woman?

PLATE V

HIGH YALLER: Reginald Marsh. Collection of Mr. and Mrs. Alfred Easton Poor

Drawing by Peter Arno; © 1943, 1971 The New Yorker Magazine, Inc.

observing

a scene

When you first enter a room where a lively party is going on, your impression is one of noise and confusion. Chances are that you soon become involved yourself and most of the activity around you recedes into the background. But if you were invisible and observed carefully, the confusion would resolve itself into patterns of understandable action which you could describe. Of course you could not describe everything that was going on, but you could give your reader or listener an idea of what the scene was like and what kind of people were involved.

If you were to write a description of such a scene, your main problem would be continuity. To make clear where and when everything was happening, you would have to keep in mind the geography of the place and the sequence of time, using such expressions as "over near the fireplace" and "meanwhile, at the kitchen door." Always remember that your reader is not present; he has only your words to guide him.

When writing, be clear but economical. You will be describing both people and actions, but you will not want to slow your reader down with too much detail. Keep things moving. You might want to use "Laundromat" in this unit as a guide.

Here are some suggestions of places where you might find lively activity to observe and describe:

> a party
> a bargain basement sale
> a garage sale
> a busy bus or train station

a crowded city bus
an auction
a monkey cage at the zoo

One caution: sports will not work well for this assignment. The action is organized according to rules, and we tend to see it only in relation to the pattern we have been conditioned to expect.

class exercise

Variations of the following experiment are sometimes used in psychology classes, with interesting results:

Two volunteers from the class leave the room for a few minutes and plan a brief series of rapid actions, such as a mock pursuit and fight or a bewildering exchange of objects from hand to hand (a pile of books will do). They reenter the room without warning, go through the actions (for no more than ten seconds), and leave quickly. Then, members of the class try to agree on what they saw.

writing assignment

1. Find a place, such as one of those suggested above, where a number of people are engaged in various activities. Carry your notebook or clipboard and pen.
2. Take notes on what people are doing and what their relationships are with each other. Be sure to note briefly all the following:
   a. *Where* each person is and what position he is in (sitting, standing straight, bending over, walking rapidly, and so on).
   b. *How* the person looks (age, dress, expression, and so on).
   c. *When* the person is acting (meanwhile, a moment later, afterwards, and so on).
   d. *What* the person is doing at that moment (pointing, looking behind him, and so on).
3. Remain for a short time, not more than fifteen or twenty minutes. Don't try to write everything down; trust your memory for many of the details, but write down enough clues so that you won't forget them.
4. As soon as possible, sit down and organize your description of the scene, adding the details you haven't written down. Describe the setting briefly; then tell what you saw in a time sequence, from beginning to end.
5. Use as many of the senses as you can; include sounds and smells as well as sights.

economy

Economy means getting the same amount of information into fewer words. This does not mean cutting out words that give an easy flow to your writing, but it means, in many cases, rewriting two or three sentences into one. The where, how, when, and what of an action can often be put into one sentence; for example: "Meanwhile, bent over the lingerie counter, a red-faced old woman in a gray coat is grabbing a petticoat out of the hands of the girl across from her." Use judgment in making your information more compact. No one wants to read sentences with many adjectives in them, nor will the reader appreciate sentences that are too complicated to be clear.

class writing assignment

Rewrite your description of a scene for economy. Try to reduce the number of words by a third or so without omitting any of the information in your original version.

Laundromat

SUSAN SHEEHAN

It is one-forty-five on a cold, winter-gray Friday afternoon. There are about a dozen people inside the Apthorp Self-Service Laundromat, between Seventy-seventh and Seventy-eighth Streets on the west side of Broadway. The laundromat is a long, narrow room with seventeen Wascomat washing machines—twelve of them the size that takes two quarters, five of them the size that takes three—lined up on one side of the room, and nine dryers on the other. At the back of the alleylike room, four vending machines dispense an assortment of laundry supplies, which cost ten cents an item, to the younger customers; the older customers (more cost-conscious? more farsighted?) bring their own soap powders or liquids from home in small boxes or plastic bottles. On the laundromat's drab painted walls are a clock and a few signs: "No Tintex Allowed," "Last Wash: 10 P.M.," "Not Responsible for Personal Property," "Pack As Full As You Want." On the drab linoleum floor are two trash cans (filled to the brim), a wooden bench, three shabby chairs (occupied), and a

---

table, on which a pretty young black girl is folding clothes, and at which a dour, heavyset black woman in her sixties is eating lunch out of a grease-stained brown paper bag. The heavyset woman has brought no clothes with her to the laundromat. The regular patrons believe she has nowhere else to go that is warm, and accept her presence. On a previous visit, she had tossed a chicken bone at someone, wordlessly, and the gesture had been accepted, too, as a reasonable protest against the miserableness of her life.

Half the people in the laundromat have two washing machines going at once. The machines keep them busy inserting coins, stuffing in clothes, and adding detergents, bleaches, and fabric softeners at various stages of the cycle (twenty-five minutes). The newly washed clothes are retrieved from the washing machines and transferred, in a swooping motion, across the narrow corridor to the dryers. No one dares leave the laundromat to attend to other errands while his clothes are drying (at the rate of ten cents for ten minutes, with most things requiring twenty or thirty minutes), because it is known that clothes that have been left to their own devices in the dryers have disappeared in a matter of five minutes.

A middle-aged man whose clothes are in a small washing machine is standing in front of it reading a sports column in the *News,* but most of the other patrons who are between putting-in and taking-out chores seem to be mesmerized by the kaleidoscopic activity inside the machines. In one washing machine, a few striped sheets and pillowcases are spinning, creating a dizzying optical effect. In another, a lively clothes dance is taking place—three or four white shirts jitterbugging with six or eight pairs of gray socks. In a third, the clothes, temporarily obscured by a flurry of soapsuds, still cast a spell over their owner, who doesn't take her eyes off the round glass window in the front of the machine. The clothes in the dryers—here a few towels, there some men's work pants—seem to be free-falling, like sky divers drifting down to earth. The laundromat smells of a sweet mixture of soap and heat, and is noisy with the hum and whir of the machines. There is little conversation, but a woman suddenly tells her teen-age daughter (why isn't she in school at this hour?) that she takes the family's clothes to the self-service laundromat, rather than to the service laundromat right next door to it, where clothes can be dropped off in the morning and fetched in the evening, because everything at the service laundromat is washed in very hot water, which shrinks clothes that have a tendency to shrink. "Here you're supposed to be able to regulate the temperature of the water, but sometimes I punch the warm button and the water comes out ice-cold," she says. "Oh, well, you sort of have to expect things like that. The owner is very nice. He does the best he can."

A middle-aged man wearing a trenchcoat takes a load of children's clothes out of a large washing machine, folds them neatly, and runs out of the laundromat with the damp pile of girls' school dresses and boys' polo shirts and bluejeans over one arm. (What is his hurry? Will the children's clothes be hung up to dry on a rack at home?) A young Japanese boy, who is holding a book covered with a glossy Columbia University jacket, takes a few clothes out of a dryer. They include a lacy slip and a ruffled pale-pink nightgown with deep-pink rosebuds on it. (His girl's? His bride's? Or only his sister's? Is the nightgown's owner at work, putting him through school, or has she become a Liberated Woman and declined to go to the laundromat?) Two little children run down the narrow center aisle playing tag, chanting in Spanish, tripping over laundry carts, and meeting with scowls from the grownups. A washing machine goes on the blink. Someone goes next door to the service laundromat to summon the proprietor, who comes over immediately, climbs on top of the broken machine, reaches behind it, and restores it to working order in no time. He apologizes, in a Polish accent, to one of his regular customers for the scruffiness of the three chairs on the premises. "Six months ago, I brought in here three first-class chairs," he says. "Fifty-dollar chairs. The next day, they were gone."

People come and go, but the population inside the laundromat remains constant at about a dozen. The majority of the customers are blacks and Puerto Ricans who live in nearby tenements and welfare hotels. Most of the whites in the neighborhood live in apartment houses, and have washing machines and dryers in their apartments or in the basements of their buildings, or send their clothes out to local Chinese laundries. One white woman, a blonde in her fifties, says, to no one in particular, that she comes to the laundromat because the laundry room in the basement of her apartment building is not safe. "There have been incidents there," she says meaningfully. "I would love to have my own washing machine, but the landlord says he has to pay for the water, so he won't allow it. I hate coming here and wasting an hour in this depressing place. I wash everything I can by hand at home; that way, I only have to come here with the big things every two weeks, instead of every week. I dream of having my own washing machine and dryer. If I had my own machines, I could fix myself a cup of coffee and a bun, turn on the TV, and sit down in my easy chair; meanwhile, the clothes would all be getting done. It would be heaven."

---

1. No one has explained satisfactorily why we enjoy reading about things we are already familiar with, but we do, just as we enjoy looking at pictures of familiar scenes. Susan Sheehan knows we have seen laundromats. She keeps her description brief and economical to evoke the feel of the scene: if she were writing for people who had never been in laundromats, what details and explanations would she have to add?

2. What senses does she appeal to? Could she have used any others to advantage?
3. What action verbs does she use?
4. How does she organize her description so it is easy to follow? (You may want to go back to Unit 1 for suggestions.)
5. What words and phrases help you to know where things are and where and when actions occur?

Auto Wreck

KARL SHAPIRO

Its quick soft silver bell beating, beating,
And down the dark one ruby flare
Pulsing out red light like an artery,
The ambulance at top speed floating down
Past beacons and illuminated clocks
Wings in a heavy curve, dips down,
And brakes speed, entering the crowd.
The doors leap open, emptying light;
Stretchers are laid out, the mangled lifted
And stowed into the little hospital.
Then the bell, breaking the hush, tolls once,
And the ambulance with its terrible cargo
Rocking, slightly rocking, moves away,
As the doors, an afterthought, are closed.

We are deranged, walking among the cops
Who sweep glass and are large and composed.
One is still making notes under the light.
One with a bucket douches ponds of blood
Into the street and gutter.
One hangs lanterns on the wrecks that cling,
Empty husks of locusts, to iron poles.

Our throats were tight as tourniquets,
Our feet were bound with splints, but now,
Like convalescents intimate and gauche,

We speak through sickly smiles and warn
With the stubborn saw of common sense,
The grim joke and the banal resolution.
The traffic moves around with care,
But we remain, touching a wound
That opens to our richest horror.
Already old, the question Who shall die?
Becomes unspoken Who is innocent?
For death in war is done by hands;
Suicide has cause and stillbirth, logic;
And cancer, simple as a flower, blooms.

But this invites the occult mind,
Cancels our physics with a sneer,
And spatters all we knew of denouement
Across the expedient and wicked stones.

---

1. "Auto Wreck" is a description of a scene, a description of the observers' reactions to the scene, and a number of comments. Can you separate the three elements?
2. Note the analogies used: "like an artery," "tight as tourniquets," "bound with splints," and so on. Why are these particular analogies used?
3. What lines convey especially vivid visual images? What lines communicate through other senses?
4. Three kinds of organization help to keep the scene clear in our minds. What are they?
5. What general theme, or meaning, binds the whole poem together?

1. This painting is a *satire:* that is, exaggeration and distortion are used to convey the painter's critical attitude toward his subject, as in a cartoon. What are some of the distortions that make the painting quite different from a photograph?
2. What does the painter seem to be criticizing?
3. In spite of the close-packed confusion, what each person is doing seems clear. How has the painter organized his picture to achieve this clarity? What devices has he used? Are they similar to those of a good writer?
4. As a class exercise, try to describe clearly the physical events shown and the space and time relationships among them.
5. As a humorous device, Cadmus has shown a number of things happening that in a few seconds will cause other things to happen in a chain of cause and effect. What are some of these?

PLATE VI

CONEY ISLAND: Paul Cadmus. Owned jointly by The Los Angeles County Museum of Art and Mr. Peter Paanakker

Drawing by W. Miller; © 1970 The New Yorker Magazine, Inc.

7

estimating
a person

Many of our troubles arise from under-estimating or overestimating people or failing to understand what to expect from them. Sometimes we come up against a strong prejudice we did not suspect was there; at other times we reject a person who might otherwise have been a good friend because we do not understand something he does or says. In such cases, we often realize later that the evidence we needed was there and we overlooked it. Like the reader of a detective story, we were taken by surprise because we failed to see the clues.

Many of the clues are inside ourselves. People are basically alike but differ in the experiences they have had and in the situations in which they find themselves. One way of estimating a person is to try to put yourself in his place, to imagine how you might act if you were in the same situation with his background. Or to put it another way, ask yourself, "If I did that, why would I be doing it?" By making an effort to understand others, we may make our own world more pleasant to live in.

class discussion

Think of a person you prefer to avoid because of some quality or habit of his that annoys you. Describe this habit or quality to the class. Let others suggest possible interpretations of his behavior. What does he mean by it? What are the motives behind it?

writing assignment

1. Choose the person you have the least liking for of all those around you.
2. Write a full paragraph in which you give as many concrete examples as you can of the qualities that make you dislike this person. Exaggerate a little if you wish.
3. Write a second paragraph in which you suggest possible motives for each of these qualities. If you had these qualities, why would you have them?
4. Now write a third paragraph about all the good qualities of the same person. Don't make them up, find them. Write about the person as though you were very fond of him. This may be difficult, but give it a good try.

contrast

When you are going to contrast two things, such as the good and bad qualities of the person you are writing about, you have a choice of two ways to organize your essay. If you prefer, you can put all the bad qualities into one paragraph and all the good ones into a second, being sure that each time you bring up one of the good ones, you relate it to one of the bad ones. Or you can deal with the good and bad qualities sentence by sentence, something like this: "Joe is slovenly in his personal habits; he chews tobacco, seldom shaves, and almost never combs his hair. On the other hand, he keeps his shop neat, with everything always in its place." If you choose the latter method, your overall organization will be determined by categories, such as personal habits, social behavior, and business ethics, with a paragraph devoted to each. Whatever organization and categories you use, remember that they should grow naturally out of your material. Don't impose too fixed an organization and then try to force your material into it. Be conscious of the need for organization, but don't be rigid.

class writing assignment

Look over the material you have from the writing assignment.

1. Decide which form of contrast organization will suit your material best.
2. Decide how you want to fit in the comments you have made about the person's motives. You may want to discuss his motives as you go along, or you may want to collect the comments into one paragraph; if so, decide where that paragraph should be.

3. Plan an introductory paragraph explaining who the person is and what your relationship with him is, and a concluding paragraph summing up your qualified opinion of the person.

Jot these items down in the form of a brief, informal outline so that you can remember what to do next while you are writing. Then write your essay.

The Catbird Seat

JAMES THURBER

Mr. Martin bought the pack of Camels on Monday night in the most crowded cigar store on Broadway. It was theater time and seven or eight men were buying cigarettes. The clerk didn't even glance at Mr. Martin, who put the pack in his overcoat pocket and went out. If any of the staff at F & S had seen him buy the cigarettes, they would have been astonished, for it was generally known that Mr. Martin did not smoke, and never had. No one saw him.

It was just a week to the day since Mr. Martin had decided to rub out Mrs. Ulgine Barrows. The term "rub out" pleased him because it suggested nothing more than the correction of an error—in this case an error of Mr. Fitweiler. Mr. Martin had spent each night of the past week working out his plan and examining it. As he walked home now he went over it again. For the hundredth time he resented the element of imprecision, the margin of guesswork that entered into the business. The project as he had worked it out was casual and bold, the risks were considerable. Something might go wrong anywhere along the line. And therein lay the cunning of his scheme. No one would ever see in it the cautious, painstaking hand of Erwin Martin, head of the filing department at F & S, of whom Mr. Fitweiler had once said, "Man is fallible but Martin isn't." No one would see his hand, that is, unless it were caught in the act.

Sitting in his apartment, drinking a glass of milk, Mr. Martin reviewed his case against Mrs. Ulgine Barrows, as he had every night for seven nights. He began at the beginning. Her quacking voice and braying laugh had first profaned the halls of F & S on March 7, 1941 (Mr. Martin had a head for dates). Old Roberts, the personnel chief, had introduced her as the newly appointed special adviser to the president of the firm, Mr. Fitweiler. The woman had appalled Mr. Martin instantly, but he hadn't shown it. He had given her his dry hand, a look of studious concentration, and a faint smile. "Well," she had said, looking at the papers on his desk, "are you lifting the oxcart out of the ditch?" As Mr. Martin recalled that moment, over his milk, he squirmed slightly. He must keep his mind on her crimes as a special adviser, not on her peccadillos as a personality. This he found difficult to do, in spite of entering an objection and sustaining it. The faults of the woman as a woman kept chattering on in his mind like an unruly witness. She had, for almost two years now, baited him. In the halls, in the elevator, even in his own office, into which she romped now and then like a circus horse, she was constantly shouting these silly questions at him. "Are you lifting the oxcart out of the ditch? Are you tearing up the pea patch? Are you hollering down the rain barrel? Are you scraping around the bottom of the pickle barrel? Are you sitting in the catbird seat?"

It was Joey Hart, one of Mr. Martin's two assistants, who had explained what the gibberish meant. "She must be a Dodger fan," he had said. "Red Barber announces the Dodger games over the radio and he uses those expressions—picked 'em up down South." Joey had gone on to explain one or two. "Tearing up the pea patch" meant going on a rampage; "sitting in the catbird seat" meant sitting pretty, like a batter with three balls and no strikes on him. Mr. Martin dismissed all this with an effort. It had been annoying, it had driven him near to distraction, but he was too solid a man to be moved to murder by anything so childish. It was fortunate, he reflected as he passed on to the important charges against Mrs. Barrows, that he had stood up under it so well. He had maintained always an outward appearance of polite tolerance. "Why, I even believe you like the woman," Miss Paird, his other assistant, had once said to him. He had simply smiled.

A gavel rapped in Mr. Martin's mind and the case proper was resumed. Mrs. Ulgine Barrows stood charged with willful, blatant, and persistent attempts to destroy the efficiency and system of F & S. It was competent, material, and relevant to review her advent and rise to power. Mr. Martin had got the story from Miss Paird, who seemed always able to find things out. According to her, Mrs. Barrows had met Mr. Fitweiler at a party, where she had rescued him from the embraces of a powerfully built drunken man who had mistaken the president of F & S for a famous retired Middle Western football coach. She had led him to a sofa and somehow worked upon him a monstrous magic. The aging gentleman had jumped to the conclusion there and then that this was a woman of singular attainments, equipped to bring out the best in him and in the firm. A week later he had introduced her into F & S as his special adviser. On that day confusion got its foot in the door. After Miss Tyson, Mr. Brundage, and Mr. Bartlett had been fired and Mr.

Munson had taken his hat and stalked out, mailing in his resignation later, old Roberts had been emboldened to speak to Mr. Fitweiler. He mentioned that Mr. Munson's department had been "a little disrupted" and hadn't they perhaps better resume the old system there? Mr. Fitweiler had said certainly not. He had the greatest faith in Mrs. Barrows' ideas. "They require a little seasoning, a little seasoning, is all," he had added. Mr. Roberts had given it up. Mr. Martin reviewed in detail all the changes wrought by Mrs. Barrows. She had begun chipping at the cornices of the firm's edifice and now she was swinging at the foundation stones with a pickaxe.

Mr. Martin came now, in his summing up, to the afternoon of Monday, November 2, 1942—just one week ago. On that day, at 3 P.M., Mrs. Barrows had bounced into his office. "Boo!" she had yelled. "Are you scraping around the bottom of the pickle barrel?" Mr. Martin had looked at her from under his green eyeshade, saying nothing. She had begun to wander about the office, taking it in with her great, popping eyes. "Do you really need *all* these filing cabinets?" she had demanded suddenly. Mr. Martin's heart had jumped. "Each of these files," he had said, keeping his voice even, "plays an indispensable part in the system of F & S." She had brayed at him, "Well, don't tear up the pea patch!" and gone to the door. From there she had bawled, "But you sure have got a lot of fine scrap in here!" Mr. Martin could no longer doubt that the finger was on his beloved department. Her pickaxe was on the upswing, poised for the first blow. It had not come yet; he had received no blue memo from the enchanted Mr. Fitweiler bearing nonsensical instructions deriving from the obscene woman. But there was no doubt in Mr. Martin's mind that one would be forthcoming. He must act quickly. Already a precious week had gone by. Mr. Martin stood up in his living room, still holding his milk glass. "Gentlemen of the jury," he said to himself, "I demand the death penalty for this horrible person."

The next day Mr. Martin followed his routine, as usual. He polished his glasses more often and once sharpened an already sharp pencil, but not even Miss Paird noticed. Only once did he catch sight of his victim; she swept past him in the hall with a patronizing "Hi!" At five-thirty he walked home, as usual, and had a glass of milk, as usual. He had never drunk anything stronger in his life—unless you could count ginger ale. The late Sam Schlosser, the S of F & S, had praised Mr. Martin at a staff meeting several years before for his temperate habits. "Our most efficient worker neither drinks nor smokes," he had said. "The results speak for themselves." Mr. Fitweiler had sat by, nodding approval.

Mr. Martin was still thinking about that red-letter day as he walked over to the Schrafft's on Fifth Avenue near Forty-sixth Street. He got there, as he always did, at eight o'clock. He finished his dinner and the financial page of the *Sun* at a quarter to nine, as he always did. It was his custom after dinner to take a walk. This time he walked down Fifth Avenue at a casual pace. His gloved hands felt moist and warm, his forehead cold. He transferred the Camels from his overcoat to a jacket pocket. He wondered, as he did so, if they did not represent an unnecessary note of strain. Mrs. Barrows smoked only Luckies. It was his idea to puff a few puffs on a Camel (after the rubbing-out), stub it out in the ashtray holding her lipstick-stained Luckies, and thus drag a small red herring across the trail. Perhaps it was not a good idea. It would take time. He might even choke, too loudly.

Mr. Martin had never seen the house on West Twelfth Street where Mrs. Barrows lived, but he had a clear enough picture of it. Fortunately, she had bragged to everybody about her ducky first-floor apartment in the perfectly darling three-story red-brick. There would be no doorman or other attendants; just the tenants of the second and third floors. As he walked along, Mr. Martin realized that he would get there before nine-thirty. He had considered walking north on Fifth Avenue from Schrafft's to a point from which it would take him until ten o'clock to reach the house. At that hour people were less likely to be coming in or going out. But the procedure would have made an awkward loop in the straight thread of his casualness, and he had abandoned it. It was impossible to figure when people would be entering or leaving the house, anyway. There was a great risk at any hour. If he ran into anybody, he would simply have to place the rubbing-out of Ulgine Barrows in the inactive file forever. The same thing would hold true if there were someone in her apartment. In that case he would just say that he had been passing by, recognized her charming house and thought to drop in.

It was eighteen minutes after nine when Mr. Martin turned into Twelfth Street. A man passed him, and a man and a woman, talking. There was no one within fifty paces when he came to the house, halfway down the block. He was up the steps and in the small vestibule in no time, pressing the bell under the card that said "Mrs. Ulgine Barrows." When the clicking in the lock started, he jumped forward against the door. He got inside fast, closing the door behind him. A bulb in a lantern hung from the hall ceiling on a chain seemed to give a monstrously bright light. There was nobody on the stair, which went up ahead of him along the left wall. A door opened down the hall in the wall on the right. He went toward it swiftly, on tiptoe.

"Well, for God's sake, look who's here!" bawled Mrs. Barrows, and her braying laugh rang out like the report of a shotgun. He rushed past her like a football tackle, bumping her. "Hey, quit shoving!" she said, closing the door behind them. They were in her living room, which seemed to Mr. Martin to be lighted by a hundred lamps. "What's after you?" she said. "You're as jumpy as a goat." He found he was unable to speak. His heart was wheezing in his throat. "I—yes," he finally brought out. She was jabbering and laughing as she started to help him off with his coat. "No, no," he said. "I'll put it here." He took it off and put it on a chair near the door. "Your hat and gloves, too," she said. "You're in a lady's house." He put his hat on top of the coat.

Mrs. Barrows seemed larger than he had thought. He kept his gloves on. "I was passing by," he said. "I recognized—is there anyone here?" She laughed louder than ever. "No," she said, "we're all alone. You're as white as a sheet, you funny man. Whatever *has* come over you? I'll mix you a toddy." She started toward a door across the room. "Scotch-and-soda be all right? But say, you don't drink, do you?" She turned and gave him her amused look. Mr. Martin pulled himself together. "Scotch-and-soda will be all right," he heard himself say. He could hear her laughing in the kitchen.

Mr. Martin looked quickly around the living room for the weapon. He had counted on finding one there. There were andirons and a poker and something in a corner that looked like an Indian club. None of them would do. It couldn't be that way. He began to pace around. He came to a desk. On it lay a metal paper knife with an ornate handle. Would it be sharp enough? He reached for it and knocked over a small brass jar. Stamps spilled out of it and it fell to the floor with a clatter. "Hey," Mrs. Barrows yelled from the kitchen, "are you tearing up the pea patch?" Mr. Martin gave a strange laugh. Picking up the knife, he tried its point against his left wrist. It was blunt. It wouldn't do.

When Mrs. Barrows reappeared, carrying two highballs, Mr. Martin, standing there with his gloves on, became acutely conscious of the fantasy he had wrought. Cigarettes in his pocket, a drink prepared for him—it was all too grossly improbable. It was more than that; it was impossible. Somewhere in the back of his mind a vague idea stirred, sprouted. "For heaven's sake, take off those gloves," said Mrs. Barrows. "I always wear them in the house," said Mr. Martin. The idea began to bloom, strange and wonderful. She put the glasses on a coffee table in front of a sofa and sat on the sofa. "Come over here, you odd little man," she said. Mr. Martin went over and sat beside her. It was difficult getting a cigarette out of the pack of Camels, but he managed it. She held a match for him, laughing. "Well," she said, handing him his drink, "this is perfectly marvelous. You with a drink and a cigarette."

Mr. Martin puffed, not too awkwardly, and took a gulp of the highball. "I drink and smoke all the time," he said. He clinked his glass against hers. "Here's nuts to that old windbag, Fitweiler," he said, and gulped again. The stuff tasted awful, but he made no grimace. "Really, Mr. Martin," she said, her voice and posture changing, "you are insulting our employer." Mrs. Barrows was now all special adviser to the president. "I am preparing a bomb," said Mr. Martin, "which will blow the old goat higher than hell." He had only had a little of the drink, which was not strong. It couldn't be that. "Do you take dope or something?" Mrs. Barrows asked coldly. "Heroin," said Mr. Martin. "I'll be coked to the gills when I bump that old buzzard off." "Mr. Martin!" she shouted, getting to her feet. "That will be all of that. You must go at once." Mr. Martin took another swallow of his drink. He tapped his cigarette out in the ashtray and put the pack of Camels on the coffee table. Then he got up. She stood glaring at him. He walked over and put on his hat and coat. "Not a word about this," he said, and laid an index finger against his lips. All Mrs. Barrows could bring out was "Really!" Mr. Martin put his hand on the doorknob. "I'm sitting in the catbird seat," he said. He stuck his tongue out at her and left. Nobody saw him go.

Mr. Martin got to his apartment, walking, well before eleven. No one saw him go in. He had two glasses of milk after brushing his teeth, and he felt elated. It wasn't tipsiness, because he hadn't been tipsy. Anyway, the walk had worn off all effects of the whisky. He got in bed and read a magazine for a while. He was asleep before midnight.

Mr. Martin got to the office at eight-thirty the next morning, as usual. At a quarter to nine, Ulgine Barrows, who had never before arrived at work before ten, swept into his office. "I'm reporting to Mr. Fitweiler now!" she shouted. "If he turns you over to the police, it's no more than you deserve!" Mr. Martin gave her a look of shocked surprise. "I beg your pardon?" he said. Mrs. Barrows snorted and bounced out of the room, leaving Miss Paird and Joey Hart staring after her. "What's the matter with that old devil now?" asked Miss Paird. "I have no idea," said Mr. Martin, resuming his work. The other two looked at him and then at each other. Miss Paird got up and went out. She walked slowly past the closed door of Mr. Fitweiler's office. Mrs. Barrows was yelling inside, but she was not braying. Miss Paird could not hear what the woman was saying. She went back to her desk.

Forty-five minutes later, Mrs. Barrows left the president's office and went into her own, shutting the door. It wasn't until half an hour later that Mr. Fitweiler sent for Mr. Martin. The head of the filing department, neat, quiet, attentive, stood in front of the old man's desk. Mr. Fitweiler was pale and nervous. He took his glasses off and twiddled them. He made a small, bruffing sound in his throat. "Martin," he said, "you have been with us more than twenty years." "Twenty-two, sir," said Mr. Martin. "In that time," pursued the president, "your work and your—uh—manner have been exemplary." "I trust so, sir," said Mr. Martin. "I have understood, Martin," said Mr. Fitweiler, "that you have never taken a drink or smoked." "That is correct, sir," said Mr. Martin. "Ah, yes." Mr. Fitweiler polished his glasses. "You may describe what you did after leaving the office yesterday, Martin," he said. Mr. Martin allowed less than a second for his bewildered pause. "Certainly, sir," he said. "I walked home. Then I went to Schrafft's for dinner. Afterward I walked home again. I went to bed early, sir, and read a magazine for a while. I was asleep before eleven." "Ah, yes," said Mr. Fitweiler again. He was silent for a moment, searching for the proper words to say to the head of the filing department. "Mrs. Barrows," he said finally, "Mrs. Barrows has worked hard, Martin, very hard. It grieves me to report that she has suffered a severe breakdown. It has taken the form of a persecution complex accompanied by distressing hallucinations." "I am very sorry, sir," said Mr. Martin. "Mrs. Barrows is under the delusion," continued Mr. Fitweiler, "that you visited her last evening and behaved yourself in an—uh—unseemly manner." He raised his hand to silence Mr. Martin's little pained outcry. "It is the nature of these psychological diseases," Mr. Fitweiler said, "to fix upon the least likely and most innocent party as the—uh—source of persecution. These matters are not for the lay mind to grasp, Martin. I've just had my psychiatrist, Dr. Fitch, on the phone. He would not, of course, commit himself, but he made enough generalizations to substantiate my suspicions. I suggested to Mrs. Barrows when she had completed her—uh—story to me this morning, that she visit Dr. Fitch, for I suspected a condition at once. She flew, I regret to say, into a rage, and demanded—uh—requested that I call you on the carpet. You may not know, Martin, but Mrs. Barrows had planned a reorganization of your department—subject to my approval, of course, subject to my approval. This brought you, rather than anyone else, to her mind—but again that is a phenomenon for Dr. Fitch and not for us. So, Martin, I am afraid Mrs. Barrows' usefulness here is at an end." "I am dreadfully sorry, sir," said Mr. Martin.

It was at this point that the door to the office blew open with the suddenness of a gas-main explosion and Mrs. Barrows catapulted through it. "Is the little rat denying it?" she screamed. "He can't get away with that!" Mr. Martin got up and moved discreetly to a point beside Mr. Fitweiler's chair. "You drank and smoked at my apartment," she bawled at Mr. Martin, "and you know it! You called Mr. Fitweiler an old windbag and said you were going to blow him up when you got coked to the gills on your heroin!" She stopped yelling to catch her breath and a new glint came into her popping eyes. "If you weren't such a drab, ordinary little man," she said, "I'd think you'd planned it all. Sticking your tongue out, saying you were sitting in the catbird seat, because you thought no one would believe me when I told it! My God, it's really too perfect!" She brayed loudly and hysterically, and the fury was on her again. She glared at Mr. Fitweiler. "Can't you see how he has tricked us, you old fool? Can't you see his little game?" But Mr. Fitweiler had been surreptitiously pressing all the buttons under the top of his desk and employees of F & S began pouring into the room. "Stockton," said Mr. Fitweiler, "you and Fishbein will take Mrs. Barrows to her home. Mrs. Powell, you will go with them." Stockton, who had played a little football in high school, blocked Mrs. Barrows as she made for Mr. Martin. It took him and Fishbein together to force her out of the door into the hall, crowded with stenographers and office boys. She was still screaming imprecations at Mr. Martin, tangled and contradictory imprecations. The hubbub finally died out down the corridor.

"I regret that this has happened," said Mr. Fitweiler. "I shall ask you to dismiss it from your mind, Martin." "Yes, sir," said Mr. Martin, anticipating his chief's "That will be all" by moving to the door. "I will dismiss it." He went out and shut the door, and his step was light and quick in the hall. When he entered his department he had slowed down to his customary gait, and he walked quietly across the room to the W20 file, wearing a look of studious concentration.

1. Like the painting *Coney Island,* this story is a satire. But all satire is based on at least a grain of truth. What truth is in the theme of the story?
2. Why does Ulgine Barrows underestimate Mr. Martin?
3. If she had been better at sizing up people, what would she have found out about Mr. Martin? What clues would she have observed?
4. Some people assume that people are quiet and inconspicuous because they are cowardly or incompetent in dealing with life. What is Mr. Martin's motive for being inconspicuous?

Richard Cory

EDWIN ARLINGTON ROBINSON

Whenever Richard Cory went down town,
We people on the pavement looked at him:
He was a gentleman from sole to crown,
Clean favored, and imperially slim.

And he was always quietly arrayed,
And he was always human when he talked;
But still he fluttered pulses when he said,
"Good-morning," and he glittered when he walked.

And he was rich—yes, richer than a king—
And admirably schooled in every grace:
In fine, we thought that he was everything
To make us wish that we were in his place.

So on we worked, and waited for the light,
And went without the meat, and cursed the bread;
And Richard Cory, one calm summer night,
Went home and put a bullet through his head.

1. What did people assume about Richard Cory? Why did they assume it?
2. Was Cory "putting on an act"?
3. Apparently Cory's fellow townsmen knew very little about him. Can you think of possible reasons for this?
4. Often when someone has committed an act of spectacular violence (such as shooting down people at random from a university tower), the papers are full of comments about what a nice, polite boy he was and how he obeyed his teachers, respected his parents, and helped old ladies across the street. Discuss why such a person might commit a violent act.

RICHARD CORY   is reprinted by permission of Charles Scribner's Sons from *The Children of the Night* by Edwin Arlington Robinson (1897).

1. How would you evaluate this man if you were standing before him? What are your clues?
2. Nearly all people believe they have good reasons for the things they do. Cardinal Niño was Grand Inquisitor toward the end of the sixteenth century and must have condemned men to torture and death because they did not conform to Church beliefs. How do you think he may have felt about this?
3. Cardinal Niño wears red vestments, white lace, and four rings. Would you interpret this as vanity?
4. What evaluation do you think the painter El Greco makes of Cardinal Niño? Are there any clues in the way he has represented him?
5. Cardinal Niño commissioned the portrait and presumably approved of it, since it still exists. Does this fact incline you to revise your estimate of him or the artist's opinion of him?

PLATE VII

CARDINAL DON FERNANDO NIÑO de GUEVARA (1541–1609): El Greco. The
Metropolitan Museum of Art; bequest of Mrs. H. O. Havemeyer, 1929. The H. O.
Havemeyer Collection

Drawing by Ton Smits

8

identifying
with
a person

One important way of using your imagination is in identifying with another person, imagining for a time that you are that person. This is only a step beyond estimating, but it is a big step and requires some effort. Of course it is impossible to identify entirely with another person: you have not had his background, and the images in his mind are not yours. Nevertheless you can use things you know about yourself, combined with clues from his behavior, to gain a little insight into what it is like to be him. When you know something about the things he is interested in, you know something about him.

class discussion

Turn to the drawing *Peasant Resting* at the end of this unit. Put yourself in the place of the man pictured. How do you feel? (Use "I," not "he.") Go beyond simply saying, "I feel tired." Be specific. Describe the feelings in your body and mind. What do you want most? What is your attitude toward the passing of time? Toward your own future? What do you remember from the past? What is your home life like? Discuss any thoughts or feelings you have.

writing assignment

1. Return to the person you used for the previous writing assignment, the person you like least among those around you. Write a full account—several pages—of ten or fifteen minutes in the life of that person as though you

were he. Look for clues in the person's speech, actions, dress, and appearance. What does he talk about most? This may be a clue to the obsessions that run through his mind. How does he move about? What does he do with his hands, eyes, mouth? Does he dress to impress others? If so, what impression does he seem to want to make? What does he do with his hair? What kinds of facial expressions does he confront others with? Most importantly, as you answer each question try to imagine, "What would my motive be if I did that?"

2. Use *I* throughout, but do not insert your personality in place of his; try to figure out what his thoughts and feelings are.
3. Focus especially on the thoughts of the person as he appears in the situations where you usually see him. What does he think about others, including yourself? How does he justify his attitudes to himself? Get inside his skin and mind.

qualification

People who are looking for a fight or who just want to express their own emotions tend to make blanket statements in strong language, like, "Women are lousy drivers." People who are searching for truth or who want to find a common ground for constructive action *qualify* their statements of opinion. A man who impartially reviewed his own experience might say, "While I have seen some women drivers do foolish things, I also know several who are very skillful." Or a man who took the trouble to inform himself of insurance company statistics might say, "Women drivers tend to have more minor accidents than men, but not nearly as many serious ones; and their insurance rates are lower." These are *qualified* opinions, closely reflecting the facts on which they are based. They are stated in such a way as to be useful rather than inflammatory.

To state an unqualified opinion is, in many situations, to commit an act of aggression, which can only incite others to behave aggressively. The first step toward peace and constructive social action is to learn to qualify opinion.

class exercise

Now that you have tried to estimate a person fairly and have tried to identify with this same person, see if you can formulate a qualified opinion about this person, one that will reflect objectively both his virtues and shortcomings. Take a few minutes to work out such a statement and write it down; then submit it to the class for comments and suggestions.

The Beginning of Grief

L. WOIWODE

From the way his five children gathered around him at the dinner table Stanion could tell something was wrong. He put his silverware down beside his plate, leaving untouched the food he had prepared and heaped there, and leaned his forehead on clasped hands as if to say grace. He was reaching his limit. Beneath his closed eyelids, inflamed by lime burns and bits of sand, he saw pulsing networks, as though his vessels were of neon, and then the substance and strength of his muscles and long limbs seemed to move upward, pulsing, and he felt weak, out of touch with the big bulk of his body, reduced to less than he was, less than he'd ever been, trapped within the small sphere of his eye. The size of his world now.

He would quit work late, drive from whatever part of the county his job, plastering, had taken him to that day, back to Minneapolis, and pick up the little ones, the two girls, at the babysitter's, and then drive back home, to the outskirts of St. Paul, and cook dinner and call the three boys in to the table—now that it was summer, they spent the day at home alone—only to see in their attitudes that they were trying to conceal something. Then another circuit, familiar as the first, began. He would have to travel through the events of their day, prying his way into them, find out what the trouble was, find out who had caused it, and set right the one who was at fault, or, if there had been fighting, punish him. He hated it. It was difficult for him to pass judgment on anyone, much less his own children, and even harder for him to see them hurt. His wife had always handled the discipline.

She was prudent and judicious, and had no patience with any kind of wrongdoing. For years she tried to persuade him to give up his job, because she felt his employers were taking advantage of him. They went on long vacations and left the business in his hands. They showed up for work irregularly, at their leisure, knowing that he would keep things in order, and never increased his wages. But they were well-meaning and young, and he stayed on with them, in spite of her disapproval, because he liked them and knew that without him they wouldn't have a business. The memory of it, along with a thousand other memories, tormented him now. A year ago she died. The torment was more than grief. It grew, linking one memory to another, linking networks of them together, and would not let her go.

"Dad? Are you all right?"

He let his arms drop beside his plate. "Yes. Just tired."

She was at the periphery of everything, closing around his vision, his mind, his actions, like a second conscience. His ideas, before he could speak them, were observed by her and he gave them up. The sheen of her hair was in the hair of the older girl, who was only five, and to run his hand over the girl's hair was excruciating, almost a sin. Her indignation was in his voice when he began arguing bitterly with his employers and when, ten months ago, he gave them final notice. He mortgaged the house, sold the car, hired a laborer, and started a business of his own. *Wm Stanion & Sons, Plastering,* he hand-painted on the doors and tailgate of an old pickup he bought.

All they had for transportation was the pickup. In winter and when it was raining, the six of them rode in the cab, the boys holding the girls on their laps, an acrid smell of rubber and gasoline enwrapping them, the bags of plaster color breaking and spilling and staining the floorboards, then merging into a muddy gray. In good weather the boys rode in the bed of the truck, and at first they liked it so much that they sang and shouted, they stood and made wings like birds, they held their arms like Superman, and he had to keep knocking on the rear window and signalling them to sit. But lately when they went anywhere the boys huddled down with their backs against the cab, and Stanion could see, as they climbed out over the tailgate at their destination, her gestures and her averted eyes when she was suffering silent humiliation.

He would have taken his life just to end the torment, just to be at peace, and maybe to be with her (who could say?), if it hadn't been for the children. And when they were bad or unhappy he felt there was no use. He looked across the table at his middle son, Kevin, aged ten, who sat with his elbows on the tabletop and his eyes lowered, forking food into his mouth as fast as he could. Kevin's large skull had a bluish tint to it. A few days ago, for some unaccountable reason, he had taken out the electric razor and shaved off all his hair.

"Well, what kind of trouble did you cause today?" Stanion asked, and his words made him feel weary and resentful. He was being unjust. He couldn't help it. It seemed Kevin was always the guilty one. He had a bad temper, a savage energy, and was unpredictable. When she was alive, she seemed to favor Kevin, yet he was the only one she lost her temper with. Once she caught him striking matches along the foundation of the house and came up behind him, grabbed him by the arm, grabbed up a bundle of the matches, set the matches ablaze, and held them under his hand until he understood what it felt like to be burned.

Kevin couldn't stand to lose. When the simplest game or argument didn't go in his favor, he started a fight, and if he was left alone with the younger ones he set up strict rules, such as no singing or talking, no TV, no dinner, or he made them march in unison around the room, and if they violated the rules or disobeyed his commands he hit them or shoved them into a closet and held the door shut.

Kevin looked up, gave an impatient scowl, and said, "What did I *do?* Nothing." His gray eyes looked even larger now that he had no hair, and his long eyelashes, catching the light of the bare bulb overhead, sparkled as he blinked several times. He was also a practiced liar.

"*Nothing?* Then what's the matter? Why do you act so guilty? Why are you all so quiet?"

"We're eating," Kevin said.

Stanion turned to his eldest son, who sat next to Kevin, and said in a restrained and altered tone, as though speaking to an arbiter, "Carl, what is this?" Carl was twelve but could be left alone with the girls, the youngest of whom was only three, in complete trust. He understood them, sensed their needs, anticipated their whims, was gentle, and so could care for them better than most adults. He was straightforward and truthful unless he was protecting one of the others, in which case, with his intelligence, he could make himself a blank.

"Carl," Stanion said, placing both fists, broad as saucers, on the table-top. "I asked you a question. What's been going on here?"

"I don't know."

"You don't know?"

"I don't think I really saw it."

"Saw what?"

"Anything that happened."

"Then something did happen."

"I don't know."

"You just said it did."

"I didn't see it."

"Ach!"

It was futile. The two girls, sitting along the side of the table to his left, their wide eyes fastened on him, went pale at the sound of his voice. It angered him to keep at it this way, to give it such importance, but his interrogating and lecturing were becoming harder to control, obsessive, and more involved and emotional. He rarely lifted a hand against the children, as she sometimes had; he felt it was unnecessary and wrong, and, besides, he feared the strength of an adult against a child, especially his own strength. He stared for a long time at the open lime burns on his knuckles, clenching his fists, angered even more by his indecisiveness, and then reached for his fork. He stopped. His youngest son, Jim, who sat across from the girls, alone at that side of the table, looked anxiously at Stanion, then at his brothers, and then at his food, which he had hardly touched.

This boy, changed so by her death, had become Stanion's favorite. He was no longer exuberant and cheerful. He woke at night and wandered through the bedrooms trailing a blanket, saying her name, and if his wanderings and the sound of his voice didn't wake Stanion so that he could take the boy into bed with him, he searched through all the rooms of the house, went out the door into the back yard, went to the plot where she had had her garden, and lay down there and slept until morning. He was old enough to know his mother as his sisters would never know her, but too young to be a companion to his brothers, who became close after her death. When he approached them, shy and ill at ease, they sent him to play with the girls. For a while he had quietly accepted this. But since he started school he had been bringing home his own playmates—a procession of the most reticent, underfed, tattered, backward boys in his class. He invited them in for meals, offered them the pick of his toys, and attached himself to them, feeding off their presence, praising them, devoting himself to them, until they became bored with his passive reverence and worshipful stare and stopped coming to the house. Now the boy's eyes, light green, large and seductive, were travelling around the table with a harried look.

With his lime-burned hand, Stanion reached out and touched the boy's shoulder. "You didn't do anything, did you, Jim?" he asked, and the boy, shrugging off Stanion's hand, turned clear around and took hold of the back of his chair and broke into tears.

"Carl! What's this about? Answer me!"

"I don't know how to," Carl said, and looked aside at Kevin, who was still eating as fast as he could.

"Did he hurt Jim?" Stanion demanded. "Is Kevin the cause of this?"

Carl lowered his eyes.

"Jim, you can tell me," Stanion said. "You don't have to be afraid now."

"I'm done," Kevin said, and scraped back his chair. "I'm going out."

"You sit right where you are till I'm through with you."

Kevin sat, piled more food on his plate, and started eating again.

"And if we have to sit here all night till I find out what's been going on," Stanion said, "we will."

Jim shifted his weight restlessly, his eyes made an anxious circuit of the table, and then, shrinking back in his chair, he cried out, "He kicked Marvin!"

"Who did?"

"Kevin!"

"*Kicked* him?"

"Then Marvin went home! He was crying!" Marvin, a frail boy who had just moved up from Kentucky, was Jim's most recent and most enduring friend.

"What is this? Carl!"

Carl kept his eyes down, picking at his food, then murmured, "We were having a track meet over at the school and Marvin was on Kevin's side. Jim and I were on the other. Marvin got tired toward the end and didn't want to run, so maybe Kevin did something. I don't know. I didn't see it. I was running."

Realizing that Carl had said all he was going to say, Stanion moved his eyes to Kevin. "Is this true?"

"No."

"Don't lie to me."

"Marvin just started crying and wanted to go home, that's all. He's a baby."

"Quit eating and look at me when I speak to you. Now nobody just starts crying for no reason—I know that and you know it too."

"I told him to play right. He wasn't playing right."

"Wasn't playing 'right.' What's right?"

Sensing he had exposed himself, brought out something that had caused trouble in the past, Kevin's face lost its color and he seemed breathless, as though he were running again, circling something dangerous. "We were way ahead in points," he said, "and then Marvin faked like he was tired. He wouldn't do anything anymore. Then when we were all running the mile he just walked along. He could have got second or third, at least, and we score 5, 3, 1. He didn't care whether we got those last points. We needed them."

"You mean you hurt him just because you were worried about losing?"

"Who says I hurt him?"

"Jim said you kicked him."

"If I had to run every race, Marvin could run at least one. He was just in the field events."

"How could you do such a thing?"

"What?"

"Whatever you did."

"Well, what would you do if you were all tired out and came around the track about the third time and there your teammate was, just walking along just like an old lady."

"So you kicked him."

"I brushed against him. Maybe I nicked him with my foot."

"Can't you leave other people alone? Don't you realize he's one of the few friends Jim's got? Let him run or walk or crawl or sit on his can or do what he wants, dammit!" Silverware jumped as Stanion hit the tabletop. "What's the matter with you? What makes you think you're a judge of others?"

"I know I was running and he wasn't."

"He's not you. He's—"

"He was on my side!"

"Will you *listen* to me!"

Stanion started to rise, and his belt caught on the edge of the table, upsetting his coffee and a carton of milk. Kevin pushed himself back from the table and tipped over his chair, and the slap that was meant for him carried past and struck the youngest girl. She went back off her stool neatly as a bundle and dropped to the floor. When she realized where she was, she started wailing, and her sister joined in.

"Now look! Look what you made me do," Stanion said, and started around the table with all the galling details—the girl on the floor, the puddle of coffee and milk beside her, Jim with his hands over his face—streaming along the edge of his vision, sharpening his outrage. Kevin hadn't got to his feet, and was maneuvering around among the chairs on his hands and knees, trying to make it to a safe spot, his rump raised. Stanion came up behind him and kicked hard and struck bone, and Kevin, his limbs splaying out, hit flat on his stomach. Stanion lifted him to his feet. "Now get upstairs," he said. "Get upstairs before something worse happens."

Kevin gave him a furious going over with his eyes before he turned and ran up the steps. And then, as Kevin disappeared around the corner, Stanion realized what he had done and started trembling. He sent Jim and Carl outside, took the girls, one in each arm, and carried them into the bedroom and tried to comfort them. Their eyes were wide with terror, and the youngest girl didn't want to be touched.

When they were calmed, he undressed them and put them to bed, hardly aware of what he was doing. The presence in the upstairs room demanded all his attention. He went into the kitchen and sat at the table, his broad workman's knees bending with effort. He ached from balancing on a springy scaffold the whole day, all the while carrying a hawk of heavy plaster and reaching overhead to skim a finish coat on the ceiling. He felt too old to go on with the work. Tonight brought it to an end. No. There was book-work to do, orders to call in, material to get, his lunch to pack.

He wanted to go upstairs but wasn't sure it was the right thing to do. He didn't want his thoughts to focus. He was afraid of what he'd done. He started eating, but the food was chilly and he had no appetite.

He gathered up the dishes, carried them to the sink, shook detergent over them, adjusted the temperature of the water, and let it run while he took a rag from the S-trap under the sink and wiped off the table. Then he got down on his hands and knees, and as he was mopping up the milk and coffee his vision narrowed, the patch of linoleum he was staring at darkened, and he felt faint. He stood up and leaned against the table. An even, abrasive sound was travelling through his consciousness as though it meant to erode it. He hurried over to the sink and shut off the water. The sound stayed.

He dipped a plate in and out of the water, rinsing off the grease, and his sight fastened on the soapy rainbow sliding along the plate's rim. He let it slip beneath the suds. He had an image of her turning from the sink, inclining her head to one side and lifting the hair from her cheek with the back of her hand, her face flushed, her eyes travelling around the room restlessly, but with an abstract look, as though there was no name for what she was searching for.

He went up the steps. Kevin was lying face down on the unmade bed, his back heaving, his exclamations and sobs muted by a pillow he held clasped over his head. Stanion eased himself onto the edge of the bed and lifted the pillow away. "Listen. Listen, now. I've tried—"

The boy grabbed at the loose bedclothes and tucked them around his face.

"How many times have I told you—" Stanion began, then stopped. He couldn't stand being sanctimonious. He looked away and saw the bed— with Kevin's logs, Kevin's body half covered with a sheet stretched out on it—and part of his own shoulder enclosed in a mirror, and it was as though he were looking through to the past. The scene, scaled down, dimmer than in hospital light, was a scene he had lived through once, with her, and it was the same. Those close to you showed up well and were solid and understandable, were fixed for good in your mind—but only in your mind. Their real selves were at a distance, a part of the world, and the world opened up, took them without reason; was opening up just as before, the body beside him falling away, while he sat off to the side, his shoulder showing in the tilted mirror, helpless.

Then he felt himself being drawn down too. He searched for something outside him to hold to. Wadded socks lay on the floor, gathering tufts of dust. Tubes and coils of a dismantled radio were strewn in one corner along with a model pistol of plastic, model ships, and a Boy Scout neckerchief. Dirty clothes were spread over the top of the dresser, trailing down its front, and more clothes were draped over the back of a chair.

"If your mother—" Stanion stopped. The words only took him down deeper. He put his hands on the boy's shoulders and tried to lift him up, but Kevin struggled free and dropped back onto the mattress.

"Don't now," Stanion said. "Don't carry on so. Please. Sit up."

"I'm sorry!"

"I know. Now don't."

"I can't stop!"

"Try to look at it—"

"My head hurts! It feels like something wants to come out of it!"

Stanion passed his hand over Kevin's skull, and the sensation of stiff stubble rubbing across the palm of his hand—what led the boy to do this? what did this hark back to?—made him feel even more helpless and afraid. "Don't now," he said, and his being closed around the words. Father, mother, nurse, teacher, arbiter, guardian, judge—all the roles were too much. He no longer had the power to reach through to his children as the person he was, their father, the man who loved them, and let them know he loved them, and that inability, more than anything else, was the thing breaking him.

He heard a muffled sound, regular and tense, and at first he thought it was a summons, a last thing he would have to face up to, and when nothing came he believed it was the labored beating of his own heart. He turned. Kevin was lying in the same position, face down, but his hand was tapping over the covers in a widening arc, feeling its way toward Stanion; it touched him tentatively, backed away, and then came down, damp and hot with perspiration, on his thigh. Stanion took the hand in his and an order came over the room.

"I'm sorry," Kevin said in a muffled voice. "Forgive me."

"Did I hurt you?"

"No."

"Do you want to come downstairs?"

"No."

"Do you feel any better?"

"Yes."

"I've sent Jim and Carl outdoors. The girls are in bed. I'm sorry they had to see it."

"I didn't mean to do it. He wasn't playing right."

"I know. Here," he said, and raised Kevin and arranged him so they were sitting next to one another. "Let's go downstairs and do the dishes," Stanion said. "Then we'll both feel better." He put his arm around his son's waist. "Will you come downstairs and help me do the dishes?"

---

1. In order to be of value to another person, we must be able to identify with him sometimes, to get inside him and feel as he feels. In this story, we are never told how Kevin feels but only how he acts. Why does he behave as he does? Be specific. Try to account for each action by identifying with him and putting yourself in his situation.

2. At the beginning, Stanion is unable to identify with Kevin. Does he ever succeed?

3. Can you identify with Stanion? What is he looking for?

The Woman at the Washington Zoo

RANDALL JARRELL

The saris go by me from the embassies.

Cloth from the moon. Cloth from another planet.
They look back at the leopard like the leopard.

And I. . . .
        this print of mine, that has kept its color
Alive through so many cleanings, this dull null
Navy I wear to work, and wear from work, and so
To my bed, so to my grave, with no
Complaints, no comment: neither from my chief,
The Deputy Chief Assistant, nor his chief—
Only I complain. . . . this serviceable
Body that no sunlight dyes, no hand suffuses
But, dome-shadowed, withering among columns,
Wavy beneath fountains—small, far-off, shining
In the eyes of animals, these beings trapped
As I am trapped but not, themselves, the trap,
Aging, but without knowledge of their age,
Kept safe here, knowing not of death, for death—
Oh, bars of my own body, open, open!

The world goes by my cage and never sees me.
And there come not to me, as come to these,
The wild beasts, sparrows pecking the llamas' grain,
Pigeons settling on the bears' bread, buzzards
Tearing the meat the flies have clouded. . . .
                Vulture,
When you come for the white rat that the foxes left,
Take off the red helmet of your head, the black
Wings that have shadowed me, and step to me as man:
The wild brother at whose feet the white wolves fawn,

To whose hand of power the great lioness
Stalks, purring. . . .
You know what I was,
You see what I am: change me, change me!

---

1. This is a difficult poem: it must be read closely, with attention given to the meaning of each line in the context of the whole. For example, when you come to the line "The world goes by my cage and never sees me," you must have read the previous stanza carefully to know what the cage is. What is the cage in which the woman is trapped?
2. The poet has chosen to present the woman in terms of her own thoughts. What kind of person would she appear to be if you saw her on the street? Can you infer any parts of a physical description from the poem?
3. What is the woman like inside herself? What are her desires and dreams?
4. She says, "change me, change me!" Is there any reason she cannot change herself? Is the change she wants possible? Would it be possible in other surroundings?
5. Of course the language of the poem is not to be taken literally as the language of the woman's thoughts. The poet has taken what he supposes to be the imagery in the woman's mind and put it into his own words. Since he is not a mind reader, how does he go about figuring out what the woman's most secret thoughts are? Is he just making a wild guess?
6. Do you think the poet has succeeded in identifying with his subject? If not, what do you think he has succeeded in doing?

---

1. What is the first feeling you get when you see *Peasant Resting?*
2. What can you infer from the picture about what it is like to be a peasant? What does he think about? What is his home life like? What hopes does he have?
3. Where do you get the feelings that enable you to identify with the peasant?
4. The drawing is done with a minimum of detail. Why?
5. The few details that are drawn are emphasized. What are they? What do they mean?

PLATE VIII

PEASANT RESTING: Jean François Millet. Ashmolean Museum, Oxford, England

9

identifying
with a thing
or an animal

Identifying with a thing or an animal may be taken seriously or it may be regarded as a lighthearted exercise. In some mystical religions "getting outside yourself" is considered essential, and a first lesson in meditation may consist of concentrating on a stone, for example, until you feel you *are* that stone. On the other hand, student actors identify with chairs or mushrooms as an exercise in playing a part. Whether you take the exercise seriously or not, it is a way to stretch your imagination.

Identifying with a thing is really an exercise in sensory imagination, in feeling what it would be like to have a different form. If you imagine that you are a kitchen chair, you imagine what you would feel if you were that shape and made of wood, and people kicked you about and sat on you. The feelings you imagine will be projections of your own feelings as a human being experiencing the same things.

An animal is able to express some of its feelings, so you have a few clues as to what it might be like to be a dog, for example. You know that a dog depends heavily on its sense of smell, has a strong interest in food and strenuous activity, and enjoys company. When you imagine you are a dog, you can gain much from watching one closely.

class exercise

Assume that a tree has some tactile and kinesthetic awareness; do not assume that it can see, hear, or think, which is improbable. Imagine how it might feel to be a tree: the experiences you might have in your trunk, roots, and branches with the changing of the seasons; the movement of the wind; the absorbing of water by your roots; and so on. If it is practical, go outside and look at a tree while you do this; otherwise, use your memory of a tree. Try to describe the feelings you might have as things happen to you.

definition

We often think of *definition* as being an explanation of a word by other words, as in a dictionary. But this kind of dictionary definition is really a limited, substitute one we fall back on when we have no experience with the thing being defined. You probably know what soup or sandpaper is without ever having consulted a dictionary. The best definition of soup is in the eating of it. The most accurate way to define sandpaper is to look at it, feel it, handle it; then use it, observe what it does, what happens to it, and so on. The best definition is experience; the next best is a thorough description of that experience, like Orwell's of coal mining in Unit 3.

To define something is to say what it is like and what it is different from. Soup and sandpaper are both man-made things, but they are made with different ingredients for different purposes. Coal mining is one kind of work; Orwell, by describing it vividly, lets us see how it is like some other kinds of work and how it is different. All the exercises in this book help you to define yourself and the world around you by seeing more similarities and differences. Defining something is really becoming more aware of it, perceiving it better. As you identify with a thing or an animal, keep in the back of your mind that you are trying to become more conscious of your subject by thinking about how it is like you and how it is different from you and from other things.

writing assignment

1. Choose an object or animal in your immediate surroundings: a dog, a cat, a fly, a tree, a kitchen table, a chair, a stove. Avoid complex machines unless you understand their functioning perfectly. Examine your subject closely, so that you are much more familiar with it than you were before and so that you know how it is put together.
2. Sit in front of your subject and concentrate on projecting yourself into it, to the degree that you lose your identity for at least a short time and *become* the subject.
3. Take notes about how you feel being your subject. If you are an object,

where do you feel tensions and pressures? What changes are you aware of? If you are an animal, what sensations are important to you? What are you most keenly aware of?

4. Organize your notes into a narrative of a few minutes in the "life" of your subject, as felt from inside. If you wish, you may want to omit the name of your object or animal and try to make your description clear enough so that the reader will know what you are.

class exercise

It has been said that man is the measure of all things. Using the materials from the writing assignment, see if you can build a few satisfactory definitions of the subjects used in terms of how they are like a person and how they are different. You might begin something like this: "A chair is like a person in that it is a solid object with legs. . . ." Find as many points of likeness and difference as you can.

Hook

WALTER VAN TILBURG CLARK

Hook, the hawks' child, was hatched in a dry spring among the oaks beside the seasonal river, and was struck from the nest early. In the drouth his single-willed parents had to extend their hunting ground by more than twice, for the ground creatures upon which they fed died and dried by the hundreds. The range became too great for them to wish to return and feed Hook, and when they had lost interest in each other they drove Hook down into the sand and brush and went back to solitary courses over the bleaching hills.

Unable to fly yet, Hook crept over the ground, challenging all large movements with recoiled head, erected rudimentary wings and the small rasp of his clattering beak. It was during this time of abysmal ignorance and continual fear that his eyes took on the first quality of hawk, that of being wide, alert, and challenging. He dwelt, because of his helplessness, among the rattling brush which grew between the oaks and the river. Even in his

---

HOOK   From *The Watchful Gods and Other Stories* by Walter Van Tilburg Clark. Reprinted by permission of International Famous Agency. Copyright © 1940, 1968 by Walter Van Tilburg Clark.

thickets, and near the water, the white sun was the dominant presence. Except in the dawn, when the land wind stirred, or in the late afternoon, when the sea wind became strong enough to penetrate the half-mile inland to this turn in the river, the sun was the major force, and everything was dry and motionless under it. The brush, small plants and trees alike, husbanded the little moisture at their hearts; the moving creatures waited for dark, when sometimes the sea fog came over and made a fine, soundless rain which relieved them.

The two spacious sounds of his life environed Hook at this time. One was the great rustle of the slopes of yellowed wild wheat, with over it the chattering rustle of the leaves of the California oaks, already as harsh and individually tremulous as in autumn. The other was the distant whisper of the foaming edge of the Pacific, punctuated by the hollow shoring of the waves. But these Hook did not yet hear, for he was attuned by fear and hunger to the small, spasmodic rustlings of live things. Dry, shrunken, and nearly starved, and with his plumage delayed, he snatched at beetles, dragging in the sand to catch them. When swifter and stronger birds and animals did not reach them first, which was seldom, he ate the small silver fish left in the mud by the failing river. He watched, with nearly chattering beak, the quick, thin lizards pause, very alert, and raise and lower themselves, but could not catch them because he had to raise his wings to move rapidly, which startled them.

Only one sight and sound not of his world of microscopic necessity was forced upon Hook. That was the flight of the big gulls from the beaches, which sometimes, in quealing play, came spinning back over the foothills and the river bed. For some inherited reason the big, ship-bodied birds did not frighten Hook, but angered him. Small and chewed-looking, with his wide, already yellowing eyes glaring up at them, he would stand in an open place on the sand in the sun and spread his shaping wings and clatter his bill like shaken dice. Hook was furious about the swift, easy passage of gulls.

His first opportunity to leave off living like a ground owl came accidentally. He was standing in the late afternoon in the red light under the thicket, his eyes half-filmed with drowse and the stupefaction of starvation, when suddenly something beside him moved, and he struck, and killed a field mouse driven out of the wheat by thirst. It was a poor mouse, shriveled and lice-ridden, but in striking Hook had tasted blood, which raised nest memories and restored his nature. With started neck plumage and shining eyes he tore and fed. When the mouse was devoured Hook had entered hoarse adolescence. He began to seek with a conscious appetite, and move more readily out of shelter. Impelled by the blood appetite, so glorious after his long preservation upon the flaky and bitter stuff of bugs, he ventured even into the wheat in the open sun beyond the oaks, and discovered the small trails and holes among the roots. With his belly often partially filled with flesh he grew rapidly in strength and will. His eyes were taking on their final change, their yellow growing deeper and more opaque, their stare more constant, their challenge less desperate. Once during this transformation he surprised a ground squirrel, and although he was ripped and wing-bitten and could not hold his prey, he was not dismayed by the conflict, but exalted. Even while the wing was still drooping and the pinions not grown back he was excited by other ground squirrels and pursued them futilely, and was angered by their dusty escape. He realized that his world was a great arena for killing, and felt the magnificence of it.

The two major events of Hook's young life occurred in the same day. A little after dawn he made the customary essay and succeeded in flight. A little before sunset he made his first sustained flight of over two hundred yards, and at its termination struck and slew a great buck squirrel whose thrashing and terrified gnawing and squealing gave him a wild delight. When he had gorged on the strong meat, Hook stood upright, and in his eyes was the stare of the hawk, never flagging in intensity but never swelling beyond containment. After that the stare had only to grow more deeply challenging and more sternly controlled as his range and deadliness increased. There was no change in kind. Hook had mastered the first of the three hungers which are fused into the single flaming will of a hawk, and he had experienced the second.

The third and consummating hunger did not awaken in Hook until the following spring, when the exultation of space had grown slow and steady in him, so that he swept freely with the wind over the miles of the coastal foothills, circling, and ever in sight of the sea, and used without struggle the warm currents lifting from the slopes, and no longer desired to scream at the range of his vision, but intently sailed above his shadow swiftly climbing to meet him on the hillsides, sinking away and rippling across the brush-grown canyons.

That spring the rains were long, and Hook sat for hours, hunched and angry under their pelting, glaring into the fogs of the river valley, and killed only small, drenched things flooded up from their tunnels. But when the rains had dissipated, and there were sun and sea wind again, the game ran plentiful, the hills were thick and shining green, and the new river flooded about the boulders where battered turtles climbed up to shrink and sleep. Hook then was scorched by the third hunger. Ranging farther, often forgetting to kill and eat, he sailed for days with growing rage, and woke at night clattering on his dead tree limb, and struck and struck and struck at the porous wood of the trunk, tearing it away. After days, in the draft of a coastal canyon miles below his own hills, he came upon the acrid taint he did not know but had expected, and, sailing down it, felt his neck plumes rise and his wings quiver so that he swerved unsteadily. He saw the unmated female perched upon the tall and jagged stump of a tree that had been shorn by storm, and, as if upon game, he stooped. But she was older than he, and wary of the gripe of his importunity, and banked off screaming, and he screamed also at the intolerable delay.

At the head of the canyon the screaming pursuit was crossed by another male with a great wing spread and the light golden in the fringe of his plumage. But his more skillful opening played him false against the ferocity of the twice-balked Hook. His rising maneuver for position was cut short by Hook's wild upward stoop, and at the blow he raked wildly and tumbled off to the side. Dropping, Hook struck him again, struggled to clutch, but only raked and could not hold, and, diving, struck once more in passage, and then beat up, yelling triumph, and saw the crippled antagonist sideslip away, half-tumble once as the ripped wing failed to balance, then steady and glide obliquely into the cover of brush on the canyon side. Beating hard and stationary in the wind above the bush that covered his competitor, Hook waited an instant, but, when the bush was still, screamed again, and let himself go off with the current, reseeking, infuriated by the burn of his own wounds, the thin choke-thread of the acrid taint.

On a hilltop projection of stone two miles inland he struck her down, gripping her rustling body with his talons, beating her wings down with his wings, belting her head when she whimpered or thrashed, and at last clutching her neck with his hook, and, when her coy struggles had given way to stillness, succeeded.

In the early summer Hook drove the three young ones from their nest and went back to lone circling above his own range. He was complete.

II

Throughout that summer and the cool, growthless weather of the winter, when the gales blew in the river canyon and the ocean piled upon the shore, Hook was master of the sky and the hills of his range. His flight became a lovely and certain thing, so that he played with the treacherous currents of the air with a delicate ease surpassing that of the gulls. He could sail for hours searching the blanched grasses below him with telescopic eyes, gaining height against the wind, descending in mile-long, gently declining swoops when he curved and rode back, and never beating either wing. At the swift passage of his shadow within their vision gophers, ground squirrels, and rabbits froze, or plunged gibbering into their tunnels beneath matted turf. Now, when he struck, he killed easily in one hard-knuckled blow. Occasionally, in sport, he soared up over the river and drove the heavy and weaponless gulls downstream again, until they would no longer venture inland.

There was nothing which Hook feared now, and his spirit was wholly belligerent, swift, and sharp, like his gaze. Only the mixed smells and in-comprehensible activities of the people at the Japanese farmer's home, inland of the coastwise highway and south of the bridge across Hook's river, troubled him. The smells were strong, unsatisfactory, and never clear, and the people, though they behaved foolishly, constantly running in and out of their built-up holes, were large, and appeared capable, with fearless eyes looking up at him, so that he instinctively swerved aside from them. He cruised over their yard, their gardens, and their bean fields, but he would not alight close to their buildings.

But this one area of doubt did not interfere with his life. He ignored it, save to look upon it curiously as he crossed, his afternoon shadow sliding in an instant over the chicken- and crate-cluttered yard, up the side of the unpainted barn, and then out again smoothly, just faintly, liquidly rippling over the furrows and then the stubble of the grazing slopes. When the season was dry, and the dead earth blew on the fields, he extended his range to satisfy his great hunger, and again narrowed it when the fields were once more alive with the minute movements he could not only see but anticipate.

Four times in that year he was challenged by other hawks blowing up from behind the coastal hills to scud down his slopes, but two of these he slew in mid-air, and saw hurtle down to thump on the ground and lie still while he circled; and a third, whose wing he tore, he followed closely to earth and beat to death in the grass, making the crimson jet out from its breast and neck into the pale wheat. The fourth was a strong flier and experienced fighter, and theirs was a long, running battle, with brief, rising flurries of striking and screaming, from which down and plumage soared off.

Here, for the first time, Hook felt doubts, and at moments wanted to drop away from the scoring, burning talons and the twisted hammer strokes of the strong beak, drop away shrieking and take cover and be still. In the end, when Hook, having outmaneuvered his enemy and come above him, wholly in control and going with the wind, tilted and plunged for the death rap, the other, in desperation, threw over on his back and struck up. Talons locked, beaks raking, they dived earthward. The earth grew and spread under them amazingly, and they were not fifty feet above it when Hook, feeling himself turning toward the underside, tore free and beat up again on heavy, wrenched wings. The other, stroking swiftly, and so close to down that he lost wing plumes to a bush, righted himself and planed up, but flew on lumberingly between the hills and did not return. Hook screamed the triumph, and made a brief pretense of pursuit, but was glad to return, slow and victorious, to his dead tree.

In all of these encounters Hook was injured, but experienced only the fighter's pride and exultation from the sting of wounds received in successful combat. And in each of them he learned new skill. Each time the wounds healed quickly, and left him a more dangerous bird.

In the next spring, when the rains and the night chants of the little frogs were past, the third hunger returned upon Hook with a new violence. In this quest he came into the taint of a young hen. Others, too, were drawn by the unnerving perfume, but only one of them, the same with which Hook had fought his great battle, was a fit competitor. This hunter drove off two, while two others, game but neophytes, were glad enough that Hook's impatience would not permit him to follow and kill. Then the battle between the two champions fled inland and was a tactical marvel, but Hook lodged the neck-breaking blow, and struck again as they dropped past the treetops. The blood had already begun to pool on the gray, fallen foliage as Hook flapped up between branches, too spent to cry victory. Yet his hunger would not let him rest until, late in the second day, he drove the female to ground among the laurels of a strange river canyon.

When the two fledglings of this second brood had been driven from the nest, and Hook had returned to his own range, he was not only complete but supreme. He slept without concealment on his bare limb, and did not open his eyes when, in the night, the heavy-billed cranes coughed in the shallows below him.

III

The turning point of Hook's career came that autumn, when the brush in the canyons rustled dryly and the hills, mowed close by the cattle, smoked under the wind as if burning. One midafternoon, when the black clouds were torn on the rim of the sea and the surf flowered white and high on the rocks, raining in over the low cliffs, Hook rode the wind diagonally across the river mouth. His great eyes, focused for small things stirring in the dust and leaves, overlooked so large and slow a movement as that of the Japanese farmer rising from the brush and lifting the two black eyes of his shotgun. Too late Hook saw, and, startled, swerved, but wrongly. The surf muffled the reports, and nearly without sound Hook felt the minute whips of the first shot, and the astounding, breath-breaking blow of the second.

Beating his good wing, tasting the blood that quickly swelled into his beak, he tumbled off with the wind and struck into the thickets on the far side of the river mouth. The branches tore him. Wild with rage, he thrust up, clattered his beak, challenging, but, when he had twice fallen over, knew that the trailing wing would not carry, and then heard the boots of the hunter among the stones in the river bed, and, seeing him loom at the edge of the bushes, crept back amid the thickest brush, and was still. When he saw the boots stand before him he reared back, lifting his good wing and cocking his head for the serpent-like blow, his beak open but soundless, his great eyes hard and very shining. The boots passed on. The Japanese farmer, who believed that he had lost chickens, and who had cunningly observed Hook's flight for many afternoons until he could plot it, did not greatly want a dead hawk.

When Hook could hear nothing but the surf and the wind in the thicket he let the sickness and shock overcome him. The fine film of the inner lid dropped over his big eyes. His heart beat frantically, so that it made the plumage of his shot-aching breast throb. His own blood throttled his breathing.

But these things were nothing compared to the lightning of pain in his left shoulder where the shot had bunched, shattering the airy bones so the pinions trailed on the ground and could not be lifted. Yet when a sparrow lit in the bush over him Hook's eyes flew open again, hard and challenging, his good wing was lifted and his beak strained open. The startled sparrow darted piping out over the river.

Throughout that night, while the long clouds blew across the stars and the wind shook the bushes about him, and throughout the next day, while the clouds still blew and massed until there was no gleam of sunlight on the sand bar, Hook remained stationary, enduring his sickness. In the second evening the rains began. First there was a long, running patter of drops upon the beach and over the dry trees and bushes. At dusk there came a heavier squall, which did not die entirely, but slacked off to a continual, spaced splashing of big drops, and then returned with the front of the storm. In long, misty curtains, gust by gust, the rain swept over the sea, beating down its heaving, and coursed up the beach. The little jets of dust ceased to rise about the drops in the fields, and the mud began to gleam. Among the boulders of the river bed darkling pools grew slowly.

Still Hook stood behind his tree from the wind, only gentle drops reaching him, falling from the upper branches and then again from the brush. His eyes remained closed, and he could still taste his own blood in his mouth though it had ceased to come up freshly. Out beyond him he heard the storm changing. As rain conquered the sea the heave of the surf became a hushed sound, often lost in the crying of the wind. Then gradually, as the night turned toward morning, the wind also was broken by the rain. The crying became fainter, the rain settled toward steadiness, and the creep of the waves could be heard again, quiet and regular upon the beach.

At dawn there was no wind and no sun, but everywhere the roaring of the vertical, relentless rain. Hook then crept among the rapid drippings of the bushes, dragging his torn sail, seeking better shelter. He stopped often, and stood with the shutters of film drawn over his eyes. At midmorning he found a little cave under a ledge at the base of the sea cliff. Here, lost without branches and leaves about him, he settled to await improvement.

When, at midday of the third day, the rain stopped altogether and the sky opened before a small, fresh wind, letting light through to glitter upon a tremulous sea, Hook was so weak that his good wing also trailed to prop him upright, and his open eyes were lusterless. But his wounds were hardened and he felt the return of hunger. Beyond his shelter he heard the gulls flying in great numbers and crying their joy at the cleared air. He could even hear, from the fringe of the river, the ecstatic and unstinted bubblings and chirpings of the small birds. The grassland, he felt, would be full of the stirring anew of the close-bound life, the undrowned insects clicking as they dried out, the snakes slithering down, heads half erect, into the grasses where the mice, gophers, and ground squirrels ran and stopped and chewed and licked themselves smoother and drier.

With the aid of this hunger, and on the crutches of his wings, Hook came down to stand in the sun beside his cave, whence he could watch the beach. Before him, in ellipses on tilting planes, the gulls flew. The surf was rearing again and beginning to shelve and hiss on the sand. Through the white foam-writing it left the long-billed pipers twinkled in bevies, escaping each wave, then racing down after it to plunge their fine drills into the minute double holes where the sand crabs bubbled. In the third row of breakers two seals lifted sleek, streaming heads and barked, and over them, trailing his spider legs, a great crane flew south. Among the stones at the foot of the cliff small red and green crabs made a little, continuous rattling and knocking. The cliff swallows glittered and twanged on aerial forays.

The afternoon began auspiciously for Hook also. One of the two gulls which came squabbling above him dropped a freshly caught fish to the sand. Quickly Hook was upon it; gripping it, he raised his good wing and cocked his head with open beak at the many gulls which had circled and come down at once toward the fall of the fish. The gulls sheered off, cursing raucously. Left alone on the sand, Hook devoured the fish, and, after resting in the sun, withdrew again to his shelter.

IV

In the succeeding days, between rains, he foraged on the beach. He learned to kill and crack the small green crabs. Along the edge of the river mouth he found the drowned bodies of mice and squirrels and even sparrows. Twice he managed to drive feeding gulls from their catch, charging upon them with buffeting wing and clattering beak. He grew stronger slowly, but the shot sail continued to drag. Often, at the choking thought of soaring and striking and the good, hot-blood kill, he strove to take off, but only the one wing came up, winnowing with a hiss, and drove him over on to his side in the sand. After these futile trials he would rage and clatter. But gradually he learned to believe that he could not fly, that his life must now be that of the discharged nestling again. Denied the joy of space, without which the joy of loneliness was lost, the joy of battle and killing, the blood lust, became his whole concentration. It was his hope, as he charged feeding gulls, that they would turn and offer battle, but they never did. The sandpipers at his approach fled peeping, or, like a quiver of arrows shot together, streamed out over the surf in a long curve. Once, pent beyond bearing, he disgraced himself by shrieking challenge at the businesslike heron which flew south every evening at the same time. The heron did not even turn his head, but flapped and glided on.

Hook's shame and anger became such that he stood awake at night. Hunger kept him awake also, for these little leavings of the gulls could not sustain his great body in its renewed violence. He became aware that the gulls slept at night in flocks on the sand, each with one leg tucked under him. He discovered also that the curlews and the pipers, often mingling, likewise slept, on the higher remnant of the bar. A sensation of evil delight filled him in the consideration of protracted striking among them.

There was only half of a sick moon in a sky of running but far-separated clouds on the night when he managed to stalk into the center of the sleeping gulls. This was light enough, but so great was his vengeful pleasure that there broke from him a shrill scream of challenge as he first struck. Without the power of flight behind it the blow was not murderous, and this newly discovered impotence made Hook crazy, so that he screamed again and again as he struck and tore at the felled gull. He slew the one, but was twice knocked over by its heavy flounderings, and all the others rose above him, weaving and screaming, protesting in the thin moonlight. Wakened by their clamor, the wading birds also took wing, startled and plaintive. When the beach was quiet again the flocks had settled elsewhere, beyond his pitiful range, and he was left alone beside the single kill. It was a disappointing victory. He fed with lowering spirit.

Thereafter he stalked silently. At sunset he would watch where the gulls settled along the miles of beach, and after dark he would come like a sharp shadow among them, and drive with his hook on all sides of him, till the beatings of a poorly struck victim sent the flock up. Then he would turn vindictively upon the fallen and finish them. In his best night he killed five from one flock. But he ate only a little from one, for the vigor resulting from occasional repletion strengthened only his ire, which became so great at such a time that food revolted him. It was not the joyous, swift, controlled hunting anger of a sane hawk, but something quite different, which made him dizzy if it continued too long, and left him unsatisfied with any kill.

Then one day, when he had very nearly struck a gull while driving it from a gasping yellowfin, the gull's wing rapped against him as it broke for its running start, and, the trailing wing failing to support him, he was knocked over. He flurried awkwardly in the sand to regain his feet, but his mastery of the beach was ended. Seeing him, in clear sunlight, struggling after the chance blow, the gulls returned about him in a flashing cloud, circling and pecking on the wing. Hook's plumage showed quick little jets of irregularity here and there. He reared back, clattering and erecting the good wing, spreading the great, rusty tail for balance. His eyes shone with a little of the old pleasure. But it died, for he could reach none of them. He was forced to turn and dance awkwardly on the sand, trying to clash bills with each tormentor. They banked up quealing and returned, weaving about him in concentric and overlapping circles. His scream was lost in their clamor, and he appeared merely to be hopping clumsily with his mouth open. Again he fell sidewards. Before he could right himself he was bowled over, and a second time, and lay on his side, twisting his neck to reach them and clappering in blind fury, and was struck three times by three successive gulls, shrieking their flock triumph.

Finally he managed to roll to his breast, and to crouch with his good wing spread wide and the other stretched nearly as far, so that he extended like a gigantic moth, only his snake head, with its now silent scimitar, erect. One great eye blazed under its level brow, but where the other had been was a shallow hole from which thin blood trickled to his russet gap.

In this crouch, by short stages, stopping to turn and drive the gulls up repeatedly, Hook dragged into the river canyon and under the stiff cover of the bitter-leafed laurel. There the gulls left him, soaring up with great clatter of their valor. Till nearly sunset Hook, broken-spirited and enduring his hardening eye socket, heard them celebrating over the waves.

When his will was somewhat replenished, and his empty eye socket had stopped the twitching and vague aching which had forced him often to roll ignominiously to rub it in the dust, Hook ventured from the protective lacings of his thicket. He knew fear again, and the challenge of his remaining eye was once more strident, as in adolescence. He dared not return to the beaches, and with a new, weak hunger, the home hunger, enticing him, made his way by short hunting journeys back to the wild wheat slopes and the crisp oaks. There was in Hook an unwonted sensation now, that of the ever-neighboring possibility of death. This sensation was beginning, after his period as a mad bird on the beach, to solidify him into his last stage of life. When, during his slow homeward passage, the gulls wafted inland over him, watching the earth with curious, miserish eyes, he did not cower, but neither did he challenge, either by opened beak or by raised shoulder. He merely watched carefully, learning his first lesson in observing the world with one eye.

At first the familiar surroundings of the bend in the river and the tree with the dead limb to which he could not ascend aggravated his humiliation, but in time, forced to live cunningly and half-starved, he lost much of his savage pride. At the first flight of a strange hawk over his realm he was wild at his helplessness, and kept twisting his head like an owl, or spinning in the grass like a small and feathered dervish, to keep the hateful beauty of the wind rider in sight. But in the succeeding weeks, as one after another coasted his beat, his resentment declined, and when one of the raiders, a haughty yearling, sighted his up-staring eye and plunged and struck him dreadfully, and only failed to kill him because he dragged under a thicket in time, the second of his great hungers was gone. He had no longer the true lust to kill, no joy of battle, but only the poor desire to fill his belly.

Then truly he lived in the wheat and the brush like a ground owl, ridden with ground lice, dusty or muddy, ever half-starved, forced to sit hours by small holes for petty and unsatisfying kills. Only once during the final months before his end did he make a kill where the breath of danger recalled his valor, and then the danger was such as a hawk with wings and eyes would scorn. Waiting beside a gopher hole, surrounded by the high yellow grass, he saw the head emerge and struck, and was amazed that there writhed in his clutch the neck and dusty coffin-skull of a rattlesnake. Holding his grip, Hook saw the great thick body slither up after, the tip an erect, strident blur, and writhe on the dirt of the gopher's mound. The weight of the snake pushed Hook about, and once threw him down, and the rising and falling whine of the rattles made the moment terrible, but the vaulted mouth, gaping from the closeness of Hook's gripe, so that the pale, envenomed sabers stood out free, could not reach him. When Hook replaced the grip of his beak with the grip of his talons, and was free to strike again and again at the base of the head, the struggle was over. Hook tore and fed on the fine, watery flesh and left the tattered armor and the long, jointed bone for the marching ants.

When the heavy rains returned he ate well during the period of the first escapes from flooded burrows, and then well enough, in a vulture's way, on the drowned creatures. But as the rains lingered, and the burrows hung full of water, and there were no insects in the grass and no small birds sleeping in the thickets, he was constantly hungry, and finally unbearably hungry. His sodden and ground-broken plumage stood out raggedly about him, so that he looked fat, even bloated, but underneath it his skin clung to his bones. Save for his great talons and clappers, and the rain in his down, he would have been like a handful of air. He often stood for a long time under some bush or ledge, heedless of the drip, his one eye filmed over, his mind neither asleep nor awake, but between. The gurgle and swirl of the brimming river, and the sound of chunks of the bank cut away to splash and dissolve in the already muddy flood, became familiar to him, and yet a torment, as if that great, ceaselessly working power of water ridiculed his frailty, within which only the faintest spark of valor still glimmered. The last two nights before the rain ended he huddled under the floor of the bridge on the coastal highway and heard the palpitant thunder of motors swell and roar over him. The trucks shook the bridge so that Hook, even in his famished lassitude, would sometimes open his one great eye wide and startled.

v

After the rains, when things became full again, bursting with growth and sound, the trees swelling, the thickets full of song and chatter, the fields, turning green in the sun, alive with rustling passages, and the moonlit nights strained with the song of the peepers all up and down the river and in pools in the fields, Hook had to bear the return of the one hunger left him. At times this made him so wild that he forgot himself and screamed challenge from the open ground. The fretfulness of it spoiled his hunting, which was now entirely a matter of patience. Once he was in despair, and lashed himself through the grass and thickets trying to rise, when that virgin scent drifted for a few moments above the current of his own river. Then, breathless, his beak agape, he saw the strong suitor ride swiftly down on the wind over him, and heard afar the screaming fuss of the harsh wooing in the alders. For that moment even the battle heart beat in him again. The rim of his good eye was scarlet, and a little bead of new blood stood in the socket of the other. With beak and talon he ripped at a fallen log, made loam and leaves fly from above it.

But the season of love passed over to the nesting season, and Hook's love hunger, unused, shriveled in him with the others, and there remained in him only one stern quality befitting a hawk, and that the negative one, the remnant, the will to endure. He resumed his patient, plotted hunting, now along a field on the land of the Japanese farmer, but ever within reach of the river thickets.

Growing tough and dry again as the summer advanced, inured to the family of the farmer, whom he saw daily stooping and scraping with sticks in the ugly, open rows of their fields, where no lovely grass rustled and no life stirred save the shameless gulls which walked at the heels of the workers, gobbling the worms and grubs they turned up, Hook became nearly content with his shard of life. The only longing or resentment to pierce him was that he suffered occasionally when forced to hide at the edge of the mile-long bean field from the wafted cruising and the restive, down-bent gaze of one of his own kind. For the rest he was without flame, a snappish, dust-colored creature, fading into the grasses he trailed through and suited to his petty way.

At the end of that summer, for the second time in his four years, Hook underwent a drouth. The equinoctial period passed without a rain. The laurel and the rabbit brush dropped dry leaves. The foliage of the oaks shriveled and curled. Even the night fogs in the river canyon failed. The farmer's red cattle on the hillside lowed constantly, and could not feed on the dusty stubble. Grass fires broke out along the highway and ate fast in the wind, filling the hollows with the smell of smoke, and died in the dirt of the shorn hills. The river made no sound; scum grew on its vestigial pools, and turtles died and stank among the rocks. The dust rode before the wind, and ascended and flowered to nothing between the hills, and every sunset was red with the dust in the air. The people in the farmer's house quarreled, and even struck one another. Birds were silent, and only the hawks flew much. The animals lay breathing hard for very long spells, and ran and crept jerkily. Their flanks were fallen in, and their eyes were red.

At first Hook gorged at the fringe of the grass fires on the multitudes of tiny things that came running and squeaking. But thereafter there were the blackened strips on the hills, and little more in the thin, crackling grass. He found mice and rats, gophers and ground squirrels and even rabbits, dead in the stubble and under the thickets, but so dry and fleshless that only a faint smell rose from them, even on the sunny days. He starved on them. By early December he had wearily stalked the length of the eastern foothills, hunting at night to escape the voracity of his own kind, resting often upon his wings. The queer trail of his short steps and great horned toes zigzagged in the dust and was erased by the wind at dawn. He was nearly dead, and could make no sound through the horn funnels of his clappers.

Then one night the dry wind brought him, with the familiar, lifeless dust, another familiar scent, troublesome, mingled, and unclear. In his vision-dominated brain he remembered the swift circle of his flight a year past, crossing in one segment, his shadow beneath him, a yard cluttered with crates and chickens, a gray barn, and then again the plowed land and the stubble. Traveling faster than he had for days, impatient of his shrunken sweep, Hook came down to the farm. In the dark, wisps of cloud blown among the stars over him, but no moon, he stood outside the wire of the chicken run. The scent of fat and blooded birds reached him from the shelter, and also within the enclosure was water. At the breath of the water Hook's gorge contracted and his tongue quivered and clove in its groove of horn. But there was the wire. He stalked its perimeter and found no opening. He beat it with his good wing, and felt it cut but not give. He wrenched at it with his beak in many places, but could not tear it. Finally, in a fury which drove the thin blood through him, he leaped repeatedly against it, beating and clawing. He was thrown back from the last leap as from the first, but in it he had risen so high as to clutch with his beak at the top wire. While he lay on his breast on the ground the significance of this came upon him.

Again he leapt, clawed up the wire, and as he would have fallen, made even the dead wing bear a little. He grasped the top and tumbled within. There again he rested flat, searching the dark with quick-turning head. There was no sound or motion but the throb of his own body. First he drank at the chill metal trough hung for the chickens. The water was cold, and loosened his tongue and his tight throat, but it also made him drunk and dizzy, so that he had to rest again, his claws spread wide to brace him. Then he walked stiffly, to stalk down the scent. He trailed it up the runway. Then there was the stuffy, body-warm air, acrid with droppings, full of soft rustlings as his talons clicked on the board floor. The thick white shapes showed faintly in the darkness. Hook struck quickly, driving a hen to the floor with one blow, its neck broken and stretched out stringily. He leaped the still pulsing body and tore it. The rich, streaming blood was overpowering to his dried senses, his starved, leathery body. After a few swallows the flesh choked him. In his rage he struck down another hen. The urge to kill took him again, insanely, as in those nights on the beach. He could let nothing go; balked of feeding, he was compelled to slaughter. Clattering, he struck again and again. The henhouse was suddenly filled with the squawking and helpless rushing and buffeting of the terrified, brainless fowls.

Hook reveled in mastery. Here was game big enough to offer weight against a strike, and yet unable to soar away from his blows. Turning in the midst of the turmoil, cannily, his fury caught at the perfect pitch, he struck unceasingly. When the hens finally discovered the outlet and streamed into the yard to run around the fence, beating and squawking, Hook followed them, scraping down the incline, clumsy and joyous. In the yard the cock, a bird as large as he and much heavier, found him out and gave valiant battle. In the dark, and both earth-bound, there was little skill, but blow upon blow and only chance parry. The still squawking hens pressed into one corner of the yard. While the duel went on a dog, excited by the sustained scuffling, began to bark. He continued to bark, running back and forth along the fence on one side. A light flashed on in an uncurtained window of the farmhouse and streamed whitely over the crates littering the ground.

Enthralled by his old battle joy, Hook knew only the burly cock before him. Now in the farthest reach of the window light they could see each other dimly. The Japanese farmer, with his gun and his lantern, was already at the gate when the finish came. The great cock leapt to jab with his spurs, and, toppling forward with extended neck as he fell, was struck and extinguished. Blood had loosened Hook's throat. Shrilly he cried his triumph. It was a thin and exhausted cry, but within him as good as when he shrilled in mid-air over the plummeting descent of a fine foe in his best spring.

The light from the lantern partially blinded Hook. He first turned and ran directly from it, into the corner where the hens were huddled. They fled apart before his charge. He essayed the fence, and on the second try, in his desperation, was out. But in the open dust the dog was on him, circling, dashing in, snapping. The farmer, who at first had not fired because of the chickens, now did not fire because of the dog, and, when he saw that the hawk was unable to fly, relinquished the sport to the dog, holding the lantern up in order to see better. The light showed his own flat, broad, dark face as sunken also, the cheekbones very prominent, and showed the torn-off sleeves of his shirt and the holes in the knees of his overalls. His wife, in a stained wrapper and barefooted, heavy black hair hanging around a young, passionless face, joined him hesitantly, but watched, fascinated and a little horrified. His son joined them, too, encouraging the dog, but quickly grew silent. Courageous and cruel death, however it may afterward sicken the one who has watched it, is impossible to look away from.

In the circle of the light Hook turned to keep the dog in front of him. His one eye gleamed with malevolence. The dog was an Airedale, and large. Each time he pounced Hook stood ground, raising his good wing, the pinions torn by the fence, opening his beak soundlessly, and at the closest approach hissed furiously and at once struck. Hit and ripped twice by the whetted horn, the dog recoiled more quickly on several subsequent jumps, and, infuriated by his own cowardice, began to bark wildly. Hook maneuvered to watch him, keeping his head turned to avoid losing the foe on the blind side. When the dog paused, safely away, Hook watched him quietly, wing partially lowered, beak closed, but at the first move again lifted the wing and gaped. The dog whined, and the man spoke to him encouragingly. The awful sound of his voice made Hook for an instant twist his head to stare up at the immense figures behind the light. The dog again sallied, barking, and Hook's head spun back. His wing was bitten this time, and with a furious side blow he caught the dog's nose. The dog dropped him with a yelp, then, smarting, came on more warily as Hook propped himself up from the ground again between his wings. Hook's artificial strength was waning, but his heart still stood to the battle, sustained by a fear of such dimension as he had never known before, but only anticipated when the arrogant young hawk had driven him to cover. The dog, unable to find any point at which the merciless, unwinking eye was not watching him, the parted beak waiting, paused and whimpered again.

"Oh, kill the poor thing," the woman begged.

The man, though, encouraged the dog again, saying, "Sick him, sick him."

The dog rushed bodily. Unable to avoid him, Hook was bowled down, snapping and raking. He left long slashes, as from the blade of a knife, on the dog's flank, but before he could right himself and assume guard again was caught by the good wing and dragged, clattering and seeking to make a good stroke from his back. The man followed them to keep the light on them, and the boy went with him, wetting his lips with his tongue and keeping his fists closed tightly. The woman remained behind, but could not help watching the diminished conclusion.

In the little palely shining arena the dog repeated his successful maneuver three times, growling but not barking, and when Hook thrashed up from the third blow both wings were trailing and dark, shining streams crept on his black-fretted breast from the shoulders. The great eye flashed more furiously than it ever had in victorious battle, and the beak still gaped, but there was no more clatter. He faltered when turning to keep front; the broken wings played him false even as props. He could not rise to use his talons.

The man had tired of holding the lantern up, and put it down to rub his arm. In the low, horizontal light the dog charged again, this time throwing the weight on his fore-paws against Hook's shoulder, so that Hook was crushed as he struck. With his talons up, Hook raked at the dog's belly, but the dog conceived the finish, and furiously worried the feathered bulk. Hook's neck went limp, and between his gaping clappers came only a faint chittering, as from some small kill of his own in the grasses.

In this last conflict there had been some minutes of the supreme fire of the hawk whose three hungers are perfectly fused in the one will; enough to burn off a year of shame.

Between the great sails the light body lay caved and perfectly still. The dog, smarting from his cuts, came to the master and was praised. The woman, joining them slowly, looked at the great wingspread, her husband raising the lantern that she might see it better.

"Oh, the brave bird," she said.

---

1. The story "Hook" is an interesting experiment. The writer has had to move back and forth between identifying with the hawk and looking at him from the outside. If he identified completely with the hawk, we would not know what the story was about; if he described the hawk's actions objectively, we would not care. Can you find sentences written from Hook's point of view?

2. The writer attributes a number of feelings to Hook that are certainly human, but they may not be hawk feelings. Do you think he is justified, for example, in supposing that a hawk feels shame? What evidence is there to support your opinion?

3. Many facts are referred to that are not comprehensible to a hawk, such as the fact that the man who shoots him is a Japanese farmer. What are some others?

4. Since the writer's identification with the hawk is only partial and much of the story is about Hook's actions and the world around him, what do you conclude is Clark's purpose in writing the story?

A Deserted Barn

L. WOIWODE

I am a deserted barn—
my cattle robbed from me,

My horses gone,
Light leaking in my sides, sun piercing my tin roof
Where it's torn.
I am a deserted barn.

Dung's still in my gutter.
It shrinks each year as side planks shrink,
Letting in more of the elements,
                                   and flies.

Worried by termites, dung beetles,
        Maggots, and rats,
        Visited by pigeons and hawks,
No longer able to say what shall enter,
                                   or what shall not,
        I am a deserted barn.

        I stand in Michigan
A gray shape at the edge of a cedar swamp.
        Starlings come to my peak,
Dirty, and perch there;
                        swallows light on bent
        Lightning rods whose blue
        Globes have gone to

A tenant's son and his .22.
        My door is torn.
It sags from rusted rails it once rolled upon,
        Waiting for a wind to lift it loose;
Then a bigger wind will take out
        My back wall.

        But winter is what I fear,
                                 when swallows and hawks
Abandon me, when insects and rodents retreat,
        When starlings, like the last of bad thoughts, go off,
        And nothing is left to fill me
Except reflections—
                        reflections, at noon,
        From the cold cloak of snow, and
Reflections, at night, from the reflected light of the moon.

1. Try an experiment; read through the poem, substituting "it" for "I" and "me." Is the effect different? Has the poet accomplished anything by identifying with the barn, and if so, what?
2. Do you see any similarity between this poem and "The Snare" in Unit 4?
3. Can identifying with an object or animal help a writer express feelings that would be hard to express any other way? What kinds of feelings?

1. Again, as with *Secluded Fishermen on an Autumn River* in Unit 1, we have a Chinese painting meant to be participated in, not just looked at. The artist has participated in two important ways: he has contemplated his subject long and deeply, identifying with it; and he has followed the form of his subject with a minimum number of controlled brush strokes at a rapid, steady pace in order to keep his painting as spontaneous as nature, which he indentifies with. Each section of bamboo is a single stroke; each leaf is a single stroke. To enjoy the painting, we are expected to identify with both the subject and the artist, following their motions and feeling their unity. The painter holds his finely tapered brush vertically. How has he moved it to produce a bamboo section? A leaf?
2. The wind is as much a subject of the painting as the visible objects. Can you identify with it? What is happening to it in various parts of the picture?
3. Why has the artist included thorns, grass, and rock as well as bamboo?
4. The artist's movements are disciplined and structured in their spontaneity. Is this true of his subjects?

PLATE IX

BAMBOO IN THE WIND: P'u-ming. The Cleveland Museum of Art. John L. Severance Fund

1

4

2

5

3

6

Drawing by Giovannetti; © *Punch*, London

10

evaluating
a possession

To own something means to have exclusive rights to its use and to be able to keep others from using it if you wish. It may also mean that you accept responsibility for it: in the case of a dog, for example, it can become a question of who owns whom. Most people like to own things. There are a number of motives for this, of which the following are only a few:

1. Usefulness. A refrigerator and a milking machine are objects owned primarily for their practical functions.
2. Esthetic pleasure. A painting may be owned for the pleasure of looking at it; part of the motive for owning a sports car may be the pleasure offered by its superior handling qualities.
3. Prestige. Another aspect of owning a painting or a sports car may be pride in having something your neighbor can't afford or in displaying your own taste.

Many possessions are prized for all three qualities. The refrigerator may be decorated to make it more pleasing and to give it the appearance of being more expensive than the neighbors'; a car is often selected for usefulness, beauty, and prestige.

class exercise

Discuss the possible motives for wanting to own the following objects. Which motive dominates and under what circumstances? What would *your* motive be if you wanted one of the objects?

153

a diamond necklace
an athletic trophy
a pair of boots
a miniature railroad
a frisbee

Don't confine the discussion to the three motives listed above; there are many others.

argument

Argument is the art of getting others to agree with you. There are three good ways to do this: presenting evidence, reasoning, and persuading. Evidence consists of facts that support your view. Reasoning is giving reasons, or, in other words, theorizing about what advantages your view has. Persuading is enhancing your argument with appeals to emotion.

Evidence is by far the best technique in argument; if you have enough proven facts to support your view, and if the facts cannot be interpreted in a different way, then you have a sound argument. Reasoning is a weaker technique, but often effective. If you can demonstrate clearly, for example, just how the introduction of one-way streets will ease the flow of traffic, you may convince the city to adopt your plan. Persuasion is mainly useful in calling attention to the importance of your point. If you describe the horrors and frustrations of congested traffic, and then the delights of driving on unobstructed streets, you may get people to pay more attention to your one-way street plan. But nothing replaces evidence: if you can prove that several other cities have solved similar problems with one-way streets, you will probably win your argument.

In addition to presenting your own argument, you must always make allowance for any arguments that may be presented against you. If you fairly present and then dispose of opposing evidence, reasoning, and persuasion, you render your opponent defenseless. If you mean to win an argument, you must consider the other side fully in your own mind; if in doing so you find merit in that view and change your mind, you may have taken a step toward truth.

writing assignment

1. Choose your most valued material possession.
2. Write a full paragraph about how much this possession means to you, giving

many specific instances of enjoyment or benefit you have had from it. Let yourself go in expressing your pride in it.

3. Now—and this won't be easy—write a paragraph of equal length and persuasiveness expressing the opposite point of view toward the same possession. Pretend you despise it and give real, convincing reasons, so that your reader will think you are sincere. Do not make up qualities or events, just change your attitude. Write as though you are full of resentment toward this object.

class writing assignment

Write an essay of four paragraphs about the possession you examined in the previous assignment. It should include:

1. An introductory paragraph telling exactly what the possession is, where you got it, and how you use it.
2. A paragraph arguing the advantages of the possession. Use evidence, reasoning, and persuasion.
3. A paragraph arguing the disadvantages of the possession with equal enthusiasm.
4. A summary paragraph weighing these advantages and disadvantages and ending with a *qualified opinion* (see Unit 8) of the possession's worth to you.

The Road

T. E. LAWRENCE

The extravagance in which my surplus emotion expressed itself lay on the road. So long as roads were tarred blue and straight; not hedged; and empty and dry, so long I was rich.

Nightly I'd run up from the hangar, upon the last stroke of work, spurring my tired feet to be nimble. The very movement refreshed them, after the day-long restraint of service. In five minutes my bed would be down, ready for the night: in four more I was in breeches and puttees, pulling on my gauntlets as I walked over to my bike, which lived in a garage-hut, opposite. Its tyres never wanted air, its engine had a habit of starting at second kick: a good habit, for only by frantic plunges upon the starting pedal could my puny weight force the engine over the seven atmospheres of its compression.

Boanerges' first glad roar at being alive again nightly jarred the huts of Cadet College into life. 'There he goes, the noisy bugger,' someone would say enviously in every flight. It is part of an airman's profession to be knowing with engines: and a thoroughbred engine is our undying satisfaction. The camp wore the virtue of my Brough like a flower in its cap. Tonight Tug and Dusty came to the step of our hut to see me off. 'Running down to Smoke, perhaps?' jeered Dusty; hitting at my regular game of London and back for tea on fine Wednesday afternoons.

Boa is a top-gear machine, as sweet in that as most single-cylinders in middle. I chug lordly past the guard-room and through the speed limit at no more than sixteen. Round the bend, past the farm, and the way straightens. Now for it. The engine's final development is fifty-two horse-power. A miracle that all this docile strength waits behind one tiny lever for the pleasure of my hand.

Another bend: and I have the honour of one of England's straightest and fastest roads. The burble of my exhaust unwound like a long cord behind me. Soon my speed snapped it, and I heard only the cry of the wind which my battering head split and fended aside. The cry rose with my speed to a shriek: while the air's coldness streamed like two jets of iced water into my dissolving eyes. I screwed them to slits, and focused my sight two hundred yards ahead of me on the empty mosaic of the tar's gravelled undulations.

Like arrows the tiny flies pricked my cheeks: and sometimes a heavier body, some house-fly or beetle, would crash into face or lips like a spent bullet. A glance at the speedometer: seventy-eight. Boanerges is warming up. I pull

THE ROAD From *The Mint* by T. E. Lawrence. Reprinted by permission of Mr. A. W. Lawrence and the publishers, Jonathan Cape Ltd.

the throttle right open, on the top of the slope, and we swoop flying across the dip, and up-down up-down the switchback beyond: the weighty machine launching itself like a projectile with a whirr of wheels into the air at the take-off of each rise, to land lurchingly with such a snatch of the driving chain as jerks my spine like a rictus.

Once we so fled across the evening light, with the yellow sun on my left, when a huge shadow roared just overhead. A Bristol Fighter, from Whitewash Villas, our neighbour aerodrome, was banking sharply round. I checked speed an instant to wave: and the slip-stream of my impetus snapped my arm and elbow astern, like a raised flail. The pilot pointed down the road towards Lincoln. I sat hard in the saddle, folded back my ears and went away after him, like a dog after a hare. Quickly we drew abreast, as the impulse of his dive to my level exhausted itself.

The next mile of road was rough. I braced my feet into the rests, thrust with my arms, and clenched my knees on the tank till its rubber grips goggled under my thighs. Over the first pothole Boanerges screamed in surprise, its mud-guard bottoming with a yawp upon the tyre. Through the plunges of the next ten seconds I clung on, wedging my gloved hand in the throttle lever so that no bump should close it and spoil our speed. Then the bicycle wrenched sideways into three long ruts: it swayed dizzily, wagging its tail for thirty awful yards. Out came the clutch, the engine raced freely: Boa checked and straightened his head with a shake, as a Brough should.

The bad ground was passed and on the new road our flight became birdlike. My head was blown out with air so that my ears had failed and we seemed to whirl soundlessly between the sun-gilt stubble fields. I dared, on a rise, to slow imperceptibly and glance sideways into the sky. There the Bif was, two hundred yards and more back. Play with the fellow? Why not? I slowed to ninety: signalled with my hand for him to overtake. Slowed ten more: sat up. Over he rattled. His passenger, a helmeted and goggled grin, hung out of the cock-pit to pass me the 'Up yer' Raf randy greeting.

They were hoping I was a flash in the pan, giving them best. Open went my throttle again. Boa crept level, fifty feet below: held them: sailed ahead into the clean and lonely country. An approaching car pulled nearly into its ditch at the sight of our race. The Bif was zooming among the trees and telegraph poles, with my scurrying spot only eighty yards ahead. I gained though, gained steadily: was perhaps five miles an hour the faster. Down went my left hand to give the engine two extra dollops of oil, for fear that something was running hot: but an overhead Jap twin, super-tuned like this one, would carry on to the moon and back, unfaltering.

We drew near the settlement. A long mile before the first houses I closed down and coasted to the cross-roads by the hospital. Bif caught up, banked, climbed and turned for home, waving to me as long as he was in sight. Fourteen miles from camp, we are, here: and fifteen minutes since I left Tug and Dusty at the hut door.

I let in the clutch again, and eased Boanerges down the hill, along the tram-lines through the dirty streets and up-hill to the aloof cathedral, where it stood in frigid perfection above the cowering close. No message of mercy in Lincoln. Our God is a jealous God: and man's very best offering will fall disdainfully short of worthiness, in the sight of Saint Hugh and his angels.

Remigius, earthy old Remigius, looks with more charity on me and Boanerges. I stabled the steel magnificence of strength and speed at his west door and went in: to find the organist practising something slow and rhythmical, like a multiplication table in notes, on the organ. The fretted, unsatisfying and unsatisfied lace-work of choir screen and spandrels drank in the main sound. Its surplus spilled thoughtfully into my ears.

By then my belly had forgotten its lunch, my eyes smarted and streamed. Out again, to sluice my head under the White Hart's yard-pump. A cup of real chocolate and a muffin at the teashop: and Boa and I took the Newark road for the last hour of daylight. He ambles at forty-five and when roaring his utmost, surpasses the hundred. A skittish motor-bike with a touch of blood in it is better than all the riding animals on earth, because of its logical extension of our faculties, and the hint, the provocation, to excess conferred by its honeyed untiring smoothness. Because Boa loves me, he gives me five more miles of speed than a stranger would get from him.

At Nottingham I added sausages from my wholesaler to the bacon which I'd bought at Lincoln: bacon so nicely sliced that each rasher meant a penny. The solid pannier-bags behind the saddle took all this and at my next stop (a farm) took also a felt-hammocked box of fifteen eggs. Home by Sleaford, our squalid, purse-proud, local village. Its butcher had six penn'orth of dripping ready for me. For months have I been making my evening round a marketing, twice a week, riding a hundred miles for the joy of it and picking up the best food cheapest, over half the country side.

---

1. Lawrence has nothing but praise for his motorcycle; his evaluation is entirely on the positive side. Are all three reasons (suggested at the beginning of this unit) for wanting to own something included in Lawrence's evaluation? Find passages that indicate each reason.
2. Can you find evidence of any other reasons for his enjoyment?
3. He mentions no disadvantages in owning a motorcycle. Do you think there might be any?
4. Which technique of argument does Lawrence use most—evidence, reasoning, or persuasion? Point out examples.

Trespass

ROBERT FROST

No, I had set no prohibiting sign,
And yes, my land was hardly fenced.
Nevertheless the land was mine:
I was being trespassed on and against.

Whoever the surly freedom took
Of such an unaccountable stay
Busying by my woods and brook
Gave me strangely restless day.

He might be opening leaves of stone,
The picture-book of the trilobite,
For which the region round was known,
And in which there was little property right.

'Twas not the value I stood to lose
In specimen crab in specimen rock,
But his ignoring what was whose
That made me look again at the clock.

Then came his little acknowledgment:
He asked for a drink at the kitchen door,
An errand he may have had to invent,
But it made my property mine once more.

1. Robert Frost is describing a feeling many people have about property, especially land. What is this feeling?
2. If the poet is made uncomfortable by others using his property, why doesn't he drive them off?
3. Are such feelings an advantage or a disadvantage of owning property?

1. At the time of Mohandas Gandhi's death, this photograph of his possessions was published. Other than these items, he owned only the simple clothing he wore. What can you conclude about his evaluation of possessions?
2. Gandhi was one of the most successful political leaders of all time; his resistance movement forced Great Britain to free India with almost no violence. Would he have been able to be even more effective if he had owned property? Why or why not?
3. Most of us, even if we do not want luxury or prestige, feel it is necessary to own a number of "useful" things Gandhi did not own. What is the difference between our definition of "useful" and his?
4. In our own society, can you think of possible advantages of owning almost nothing?

PLATE X

MAHATMA GANDHI'S WORLDLY POSSESSIONS. Photo: Information Service of India, New York

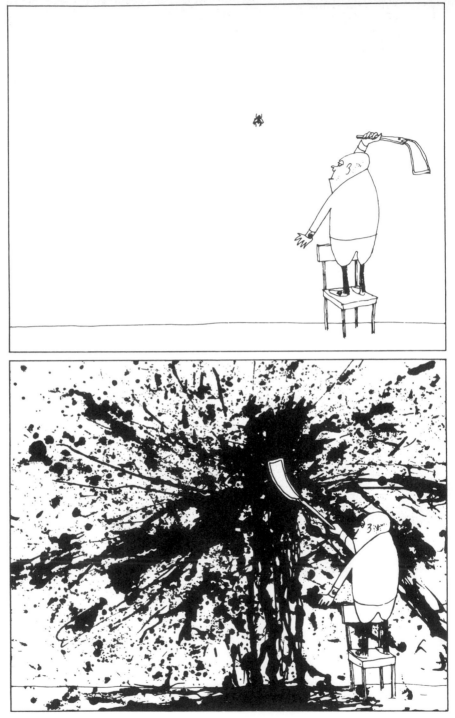

Drawing by Tony Munzlinger

11

examining
a desire

Like the man in the cartoon, we some-
times find that our desires lead us into making a mess of things. At best, what
we want may cost more than we figured.

Part of living in the present is examining our desires realistically. Most
of us think life will be much better after we get something we want: a new
car, a degree, a job, a wife or husband. Sometimes we become so absorbed
in dreaming of the future that we fail to take advantage of the present and
find that much of life has passed us by. Some Hindus and Buddhists believe
that instead of striving to fulfill desires, one should get rid of them. While
most of us do not feel ready for so difficult a psychological step, we may do
ourselves some good by analyzing our desires and determining which are the
most futile. We cannot deny that vain desires cloud our enjoyment of the
here and now.

class exercise

Think of something you desire that you do not have and submit this
desire for discussion. Let members of the class ask you reasons for wanting
this thing and suggest possible disadvantages. When you comment on another
person's desire, try identifying with him rather than using your own standards.

analysis

Analysis means examining something part by part in order
to understand or explain it. If we wanted to explain how a bicycle
works, we would describe each part and its function in relation to

the others: frame, wheels, handlebars, pedals, sprockets, and chain. We would use the same method to explain an atom or a government. You have already done some informal analysis in Units 1, 4, and 5 and have found that qualities such as emotions, as well as physical objects, can be analyzed.

writing assignment

1. Choose a real and practical desire that you hope to realize in the future, such as working in a certain profession, marrying and having a family, owning a farm, creating a great work of art, or something that you consider equally important.
2. Analyze this desire in terms of what you will gain by its realization and what it will cost. First, separate the gains into different kinds of advantages: practical advantages (financial security, sensory pleasure, health, convenience); social advantages (prestige, opportunity to make friends); emotional satisfactions (feeling useful, having pride in results, finding work activities varied and interesting); and any other categories that you find suit your material. Then do the same with the disadvantages or costs of realizing your desire. Sketch out these advantages and disadvantages in the form of a rough outline, so that you will have all your general material in categories under headings.
3. Now, write the rough draft of an essay, allowing a paragraph for each of your categories. Move from general to specific in each paragraph, describing in concrete detail just what form you expect your satisfactions and dissatisfactions to take. Write about them in terms of daily and hourly experience—what you expect to be doing and feeling at particular times and places.

class writing assignment

Rewrite your essay, with attention to completeness and coherence. Add an introductory paragraph explaining what your desire is and a conclusion in which you present a carefully qualified evaluation of your desire.

The Beach Umbrella

CYRUS COLTER

The Thirty-first Street beach lay dazzling under a sky so blue that Lake Michigan ran to the horizon like a sheet of sapphire silk, studded with little barbed white sequins for sails; and the heavy surface of the water lapped gently at the boulder "sea wall" which had been cut into, graded, and sanded to make the beach. Saturday afternoons were always frenzied: three black lifeguards, giants in sunglasses, preened in their towers and chaperoned the bathers—adults, teen-agers, and children—who were going through every physical gyration of which the human body is capable. Some dove, swam, some hollered, rode inner tubes, or merely stood waist-deep and pummeled the water; others—on the beach—sprinted, did handsprings and somersaults, sucked Eskimo pies, or just buried their children in the sand. Then there were the lollers—extended in their languor under a garish variety of beach umbrellas.

Elijah lolled too—on his stomach in the white sand, his chin cupped in his palm; but under no umbrella. He had none. By habit, though, he stared in awe at those who did, and sometimes meddled in their conversation: "It's gonna be gettin' hot pretty soon—if it ain't careful," he said to a Bantu-looking fellow and his girl sitting nearby with an older woman. The temperature was then in the nineties. The fellow managed a negligent smile. "Yeah," he said, and persisted in listening to the women. Buoyant still, Elijah watched them. But soon his gaze wavered, and then moved on to other lollers of interest. Finally he got up, stretched, brushed sand from his swimming trunks, and scanned the beach for a new spot. He started walking.

He was not tall. And he appeared to walk on his toes—his nut-colored legs were bowed and skinny and made him hobble like a jerky little spider. Next he plopped down near two men and two girls—they were hilarious about something—sitting beneath a big purple and white umbrella. The girls, chocolate brown and shapely, emitted squeals of laughter at the wisecracks of the men. Elijah was enchanted. All summer long the rambunctious gaiety of the beach had fastened on him a curious charm, a hex, that brought him gawking and twiddling to the lake each Saturday. The rest of the week, save Sunday, he worked. But Myrtle, his wife, detested the sport and stayed away. Randall, the boy, had been only twice and then without little Susan, who during the summer was her mother's own midget reflection. But Elijah came regularly, especially whenever Myrtle was being evil, which he felt now was almost always. She was getting worse, too—if that was possible. The woman was money-crazy.

"You gotta sharp-lookin' umbrella there!" he cut in on the two laughing couples. They studied him—the abruptly silent way. Then the big-shouldered fellow smiled and lifted his eyes to their spangled roof. "Yeah?. . . Thanks," he said. Elijah carried on: "I see a lot of 'em out here this summer—much more'n last year." The fellow meditated on this, but was noncommittal. The others went on gabbing, mostly with their hands. Elijah, squinting in the hot sun, watched them. He didn't see how they could be married; they cut the fool too much, acted like they'd itched to get together for weeks and just now made it. He pondered going back in the water, but he'd already had an hour of that. His eyes traveled the sweltering beach. Funny about his folks; they were every shape and color a God-made human could be. Here was a real sample of variety—pink white to jetty black. Could you any longer call that a race of people? It was a complicated complication—for some real educated guy to figure out. Then another thought slowly bore in on him: the beach umbrellas blooming across the sand attracted people—slews of friends, buddies; and gals, too. Wherever the loudest racket tore the air, a big red, or green, or yellowish umbrella—bordered with white fringe maybe—flowered in the middle of it all and gave shade to the happy good-timers.

Take, for instance, that tropical-looking pea-green umbrella over there, with the Bikinied brown chicks under it, and the portable radio jumping. A real beach party! He got up, stole over, and eased down in the sand at the fringe of the jubilation—two big thermos jugs sat in the shade and everybody had a paper cup in hand as the explosions of buffoonery carried out to the water. Chief provoker of mirth was a bulging-eyed old gal in a white bathing suit who, encumbered by big flabby overripe thighs, cavorted and pranced in the sand. When, perspiring from the heat, she finally fagged out, she flopped down almost on top of him. So far he had gone unnoticed. But now, as he craned in at closer range, she brought him up: "Whatta you want, Pops?" She grinned, but with a touch of hostility.

Pops! Where'd she get that stuff? He was only forty-one, not a day older than that boozy bag. But he smiled. "Nothin'," he said brightly, "but you sure got one goin' here." He turned and viewed the noise-makers.

"An' you wanta get in on it!" she wrangled.

"Oh, I was just lookin'—"

"—You was just lookin'. Yeah, you was just lookin' at them young chicks there!" She roared a laugh and pointed at the sexy-looking girls under the umbrella.

Elijah grinned weakly.

"Beat it!" she catcalled, and turned back to the party.

He sat like a rock—the hell with her. But soon he relented, and wandered down to the water's edge—remote now from all inhospitality—to sit in the sand and hug his raised knees. Far out, the sailboats were pinned to the horizon and, despite all the close-in fuss, the wide miles of lake lay impassive under a blazing calm; far south and east down the long curving lake shore, miles in the distance, the smoky haze of the Whiting plant of the Youngstown Sheet and Tube Company hung ominously in an otherwise bright sky. And so it was that he turned back and viewed the beach again—and suddenly caught his craving. Weren't they something—the umbrellas! The flashy colors of them! And the swank! No wonder folks ganged round them. Yes . . . yes, he too must have one. The thought came slow and final, and seared him. For there stood Myrtle in his mind. She nagged him now night and day, and it was always money that got her started; there was never enough—for Susan's shoes, Randy's overcoat, for new kitchen linoleum, Venetian blinds, for a better car than the old Chevy. "I just don't understand you!" she had said only night before last. "Have you got any plans at all for your family? You got a family, you know. If you could only bear to pull yourself away from that deaf old tightwad out at that warehouse, and go get yourself a real job . . . But no! Not you!"

She was talking about old man Schroeder, who owned the warehouse where he worked. Yes, the pay could be better, but it still wasn't as bad as she made out. Myrtle could be such a fool sometimes. He had been with the old man nine years now; had started out as a freight handler, but worked up to doing inventories and a little paper work. True, the business had been going down recently, for the old man's sight and hearing were failing and his key people had left him. Now he depended on him, Elijah—who of late wore a necktie on the job, and made his inventory rounds with a ball-point pen and clipboard. The old man was friendlier, too—almost "hat in hand" to him. He liked everything about the job now—except the pay. And that was only because of Myrtle. She just wanted so much; even talked of moving out of their rented apartment and buying out in the Chatham area. But one thing had to be said for her: she never griped about anything for herself; only for the family, the kids. Every payday he endorsed his check and handed it over to her, and got back in return only gasoline and cigarette money. And this could get pretty tiresome. About six weeks ago he'd gotten a ten-dollar-a-month raise out of the old man, but that had only made her madder than ever. He'd thought about looking for another job all right; but where would he go to get another white-collar job? There weren't many of them for him. She wouldn't care if he went back to the steel mills, back to pouring that white-hot ore out at Youngstown Sheet and Tube. It would be okay with her—so long as his paycheck was fat. But that kind of work was no good, undignified; coming home on the bus you were always so tired you went to sleep in your seat, with your lunch pail in your lap.

Just then two wet boys, chasing each other across the sand, raced by him into the water. The cold spray on his skin made him jump, jolting him out of his thoughts. He turned and slowly scanned the beach again. The umbrellas were brighter, gayer, bolder than ever—each a hiving center of playful people. He stood up finally, took a long last look, and then started back to the spot where he had parked the Chevy.

The following Monday evening was hot and humid as Elijah sat at home in their plain living room and pretended to read the newspaper; the windows were up, but not the slightest breeze came through the screens to stir Myrtle's fluffy curtains. At the moment she and nine-year-old Susan were in the kitchen finishing the dinner dishes. For twenty minutes now he had sat waiting for the furtive chance to speak to Randall. Randall, at twelve, was a serious, industrious boy, and did deliveries and odd jobs for the neighborhood grocer. Soon he came through—intent, absorbed—on his way back to the grocery for another hour's work.

"Gotta go back, eh, Randy?" Elijah said.

"Yes, sir." He was tall for his age, and wore glasses. He paused with his hand on the doorknob.

Elijah hesitated. Better wait, he thought—wait till he comes back. But Myrtle might be around then. Better ask him now. But Randall had opened the door. "See you later, Dad," he said—and left.

Elijah, shaken, again raised the newspaper and tried to read. He should have called him back, he knew, but he had lost his nerve—because he couldn't tell how Randy would take it. Fifteen dollars was nothing though, really— Randy probably had fifty or sixty stashed away somewhere in his room. Then he thought of Myrtle, and waves of fright went over him—to be even thinking about a beach umbrella was bad enough; and to buy one, especially now, would be to her some kind of crime; but to borrow even a part of the money for it from Randy . . . well, Myrtle would go out of her mind. He had never lied to his family before. This would be the first time. And he had thought about it all day long. During the morning, at the warehouse, he had gotten out the two big mail-order catalogues to look at the beach umbrellas; but the ones shown were all so small and dinky-looking he was contemptuous. So at noon he drove the Chevy out to a sporting-goods store on West Sixty-third Street. There he found a gorgeous assortment of yard and beach umbrellas. And there he found his prize. A beauty, a big beauty with wide red and white stripes, and a white fringe. But oh the price! Twenty-three dollars! And he with nine.

"What's the matter with you?" Myrtle had walked in the room. She was thin, and medium brown-skinned with a saddle of freckles across her nose, and looked harried in her sleeveless housedress with her hair unkempt.

Startled, he lowered the newspaper. "Nothing," he said.

"How can you read looking over the paper?"

"Was I?"

Not bothering to answer, she sank in a chair. "Susie," she called back into the kitchen, "bring my cigarettes in here, will you, baby?"

Soon Susan, chubby and solemn, with the mist of perspiration on her forehead, came in with the cigarettes. "Only three left, Mama," she said, peering into the pack.

"Okay," Myrtle sighed, taking the cigarettes. Susan started out. "Now, scour the sink good, honey—and then go take your bath. You'll feel cooler."

Before looking at him again, Myrtle lit a cigarette. "School starts in three weeks," she said, with a forlorn shake of her head. "Do you realize that?"

"Yeah? . . . Jesus, times flies." He could not look at her.

"Susie needs dresses, and a couple of pairs of good shoes—and she'll need a coat before it gets cold."

"Yeah, I know." He patted the arm of the chair.

"Randy bless his heart has already made enough to get most of his things. That boy's something; he's all business—I've never seen anything like it." She took a drag on her cigarette. "And old man Schroeder giving you a ten-dollar raise! What was you thinkin' about? What'd you say to him?"

He did not answer at first. Finally he said, "Ten dollars is ten dollars, Myrtle. You know business is slow."

"I'll say it is! And there won't be any business before long—and then where'll you be? I tell you over and over again, you better start looking for something now! I been preachin' it to you for a year."

He said nothing.

"Ford and International Harvester are hiring every man they can lay their hands on! And the mills out in Gary and Whiting are going full blast—you see the red sky every night. The men make good money."

"They earn every nickel of it, too," he said in gloom.

"But they get it! Bring it home! It spends! Does that mean anything to you? Do you know what some of them make? Well, ask Hawthorne—or ask Sonny Milton. Sonny's wife says his checks some weeks run as high as a hundred twenty, hundred thirty dollars. One week! Take-home pay!"

"Yeah? . . . And Sonny told me he wished he had a job like mine."

Myrtle threw back her head with a bitter gasp. "Oh-h-h, God! Did you tell him what you made? Did you tell him that?"

Suddenly Susan came back into the muggy living room. She went straight to her mother and stood as if expecting an award. Myrtle absently patted her on the side of the head. "Now, go and run your bath water, honey," she said.

Elijah smiled at Susan. "Susie," he said, "d'you know your tummy is stickin' way out—you didn't eat too much, did you?" He laughed.

Susan turned and observed him; then looked at her mother. "No," she finally said.

"Go on now, baby," Myrtle said. Susan left the room.

Myrtle resumed. "Well, there's no use going through all this again. It's plain as the nose on your face. You got a family—a good family, I think. The only question is, do you wanta get off your hind end and do somethin' for it. It's just that simple."

Elijah looked at her. "You can talk real crazy sometimes, Myrtle."

"I think it's that old man!" she cried, her freckles contorted. "He's got you answering the phone, and taking inventory—wearing a necktie and all that. You wearing a necktie and your son mopping in a grocery store, so he can buy his own clothes." She snatched up her cigarettes, and walked out of the room.

His eyes did not follow her, but remained off in space. Finally he got up and went into the kitchen. Over the stove the plaster was thinly cracked, and in spots the linoleum had worn through the pattern; but everything was immaculate. He opened the refrigerator, poured a glass of cold water, and sat down at the kitchen table. He felt strange and weak, and sat for a long time sipping the water.

Then after a while he heard Randall's key in the front door, sending tremors of dread through him. When Randall came into the kitchen, he seemed to him as tall as himself; his glasses were steamy from the humidity outside, and his hands were dirty.

"Hi, Dad," he said gravely without looking at him, and opened the refrigerator door.

Elijah chuckled. "Your mother'll get after you about going in there without washing your hands."

But Randall took out the water pitcher and closed the door.

Elijah watched him. Now was the time to ask him. His heart was hammering. Go on—now! But instead he heard his husky voice saying, "What'd they have you doing over at the grocery tonight?"

Randall was drinking the glass of water. When he finished, he said, "Refilling shelves."

"Pretty hot job tonight, eh?"

"It wasn't so bad." Randall was matter-of-fact as he set the empty glass over the sink, and paused before leaving.

"Well . . . you're doing fine, son. Fine. Your mother sure is proud of you . . ." Purpose had lodged in his throat.

The praise embarrassed Randall. "Okay, Dad," he said, and edged from the kitchen.

Elijah slumped back in his chair, near prostration. He tried to clear his mind of every particle of thought, but the images became only more jumbled, oppressive to the point of panic.

Then before long Myrtle came into the kitchen—ignoring him. But she seemed not so hostile now as coldly impassive, exhibiting a bravado he had not seen before. He got up and went back into the living room and turned on the television. As the TV-screen lawmen galloped before him, he sat oblivious, admitting the failure of his will. If only he could have gotten Randall to himself long enough—but everything had been so sudden, abrupt; he couldn't just ask him out of the clear blue. Besides, around him Randall always seemed so busy, too busy to talk. He couldn't understand that; he had never mistreated the boy, never whipped him in his life; had shaken him a time or two, but that was long ago, when he was little.

He sat and watched the finish of the half-hour TV show. Myrtle was in the bedroom now. He slouched in his chair, lacking the resolve to get up and turn off the television.

Suddenly he was on his feet.

Leaving the television on, he went back to Randall's room in the rear. The door was open and Randall was asleep, lying on his back on the bed, perspiring, still dressed except for his shoes and glasses. He stood over the bed and looked at him. He was a good boy; his own son. But how strange—he thought for the first time—there was no resemblance between them. None whatsoever. Randy had a few of his mother's freckles on his thin brown face, but he could see none of himself in the boy. Then his musings were scattered by the return of his fear. He dreaded waking him. And he might be cross. If he didn't hurry, though, Myrtle or Susie might come strolling out any minute. His bones seemed rubbery for the strain. Finally he bent down and touched Randall's shoulder. The boy did not move a muscle, except to open his eyes. Elijah smiled at him. And he slowly sat up.

"Sorry, Randy—to wake you up like this."

"What's the matter?" Randall rubbed his eyes.

Elijah bent down again, but did not whisper. "Say, can you let me have fifteen bucks—till I get my check? . . . I need to get some things—and I'm a little short this time." He could hardly bring the words up.

Randall gave him a slow, queer look.

"I'll get my check a week from Friday," Elijah said, ". . . and I'll give it back to you then—sure."

Now instinctively Randall glanced toward the door, and Elijah knew Myrtle had crossed his thoughts. "You don't have to mention anything to your mother," he said with casual suddenness.

Randall got up slowly off the bed, and in his socks walked to the little table where he did his homework. He pulled the drawer out, fished far in the back a moment, and brought out a white business envelope secured by a rubber band. Holding the envelope close to his stomach, he took out first a ten-dollar bill, and then a five, and, sighing, handed them over.

"Thanks, old man," Elijah quivered, folding the money. "You'll get this back the day I get my check. . . . That's for sure."

"Okay," Randall finally said.

Elijah started out. Then he could see Myrtle on payday—her hand extended for his check. He hesitated, and looked at Randall, as if to speak. But he slipped the money in his trousers pocket and hurried from the room.

The following Saturday at the beach did not begin bright and sunny. By noon it was hot, but the sky was overcast and angry, the air heavy. There was no certainty whatever of a crowd, raucous or otherwise, and this was Elijah's chief concern as, shortly before twelve o'clock, he drove up in the Chevy and parked in the bumpy, graveled stretch of high ground that looked down eastward over the lake and was used for a parking lot. He climbed out of the car, glancing at the lake and clouds, and prayed in his heart it would not rain—the water was murky and restless, and only a handful of bathers had showed. But it was early yet. He stood beside the car and watched a bulbous, brown-skinned woman, in bathing suit and enormous straw hat, lugging a lunch basket down toward the beach, followed by her brood of children. And a fellow in swimming trunks, apparently the father, took a towel and sandals from his new Buick and called petulantly to his family to "just wait a minute, please." In another car, two women sat waiting, as yet fully clothed and undecided about going swimming. While down at the water's edge there was the usual cluster of dripping boys who, brash and boisterous, swarmed to the beach every day in fair weather or foul.

Elijah took off his shirt, peeled his trousers from over his swimming trunks, and started collecting the paraphernalia from the back seat of the car: a frayed pink rug filched from the house, a towel, sunglasses, cigarettes, a thermos jug filled with cold lemonade he had made himself, and a dozen paper cups. All this he stacked on the front fender. Then he went around to the rear and opened the trunk. Ah, there it lay— encased in a long, slim package trussed with heavy twine, and barely fitting athwart the spare tire. He felt prickles of excitement as he took the knife from the tool bag, cut the twine, and pulled the wrapping paper away. Red and white stripes sprang at him. It was even more gorgeous than when it had first seduced him in the store. The white fringe gave it style; the wide red fillets were cardinal and stark, and the white stripes glared. Now he opened it over his head for the full thrill of its colors, and looked around to see if anyone else agreed. Finally after a while he gathered up all his equipment and headed down for the beach, his short, nubby legs seeming more bowed than ever under the weight of their cargo.

When he reached the sand, a choice of location became a pressing matter. That was why he had come early. From past observation it was clear that the center of gaiety shifted from day to day; last Saturday it might have been nearer the water, this Saturday, well back; or up, or down, the beach a ways. He must pick the site with care, for he could not move about the way he did when he had no umbrella; it was too noticeable. He finally took a spot as near the center of the beach as he could estimate, and dropped his gear in the sand. He knelt down and spread the pink rug, then moved the thermos jug over onto it, and folded the towel and placed it with the paper cups, sunglasses, and cigarettes down beside the jug. Now he went to find a heavy stone or brick to drive down the spike for the hollow umbrella stem to fit over. So it was not until the umbrella was finally up that he again had time for anxiety about the weather. His whole morning's effort had been an act of faith, for, as yet, there was no sun, although now and then a few azure breaks appeared in the thinning cloud mass. But before very long this brighter texture of the sky began to grow and spread by slow degrees, and his hopes quickened. Finally he sat down under the umbrella, lit a cigarette, and waited.

It was not long before two small boys came by—on their way to the water. He grinned, and called to them, "Hey, fellas, been in yet?"—their bathing suits were dry.

They stopped, and observed him. Then one of them smiled, and shook his head.

Elijah laughed. "Well, whatta you waitin' for? Go on in there and get them suits wet!" Both boys gave him silent smiles. And they lingered. He thought this a good omen—it had been different the Saturday before.

Once or twice the sun burst through the weakening clouds. He forgot the boys now in watching the skies, and soon they moved on. His anxiety was not detectable from his lazy posture under the umbrella, with his dwarfish, gnarled legs extended and his bare heels on the little rug. But then soon the clouds began to fade in earnest, seeming not to move away laterally, but slowly to recede into a lucent haze, until at last the sun came through hot and bright. He squinted at the sky and felt delivered. They would come, the folks would come!—were coming now; the beach would soon be swarming. Two other umbrellas were up already, and the diving board thronged with wet, acrobatic boys. The lifeguards were in their towers now, and still another launched his yellow rowboat. And up on the Outer Drive, the cars, one by one, were turning into the parking lot. The sun was bringing them out all right; soon he'd be in the middle of a field day. He felt a low-key, welling excitement, for the water was blue and far out the sails were starched and white.

Soon he saw the two little boys coming back. They were soaked. Their mother—a thin, brown girl in a yellow bathing suit—was with them now, and the boys were pointing to his umbrella. She seemed dignified for her youth, as she gave him a shy glance and then smiled at the boys.

"Ah, ha!" he cried to the boys. "You've been in now all right!" And then laughing to her, "I was kiddin' them awhile ago about their dry bathing suits."

She smiled at the boys again. "They like for me to be with them when they go in," she said.

"I got some lemonade here," he said abruptly, slapping the thermos jug. "Why don't you have some?" His voice was anxious.

She hesitated.

He jumped up. "Come on, sit down." He smiled at her and stepped aside.

Still she hesitated. But her eager boys pressed close behind her. Finally she smiled and sat down under the umbrella.

"You fellas can sit down under there too—in the shade," he said to the boys, and pointed under the umbrella. The boys flopped down quickly in the shady sand. He started at once serving them cold lemonade in the paper cups.

"Whew! I thought it was goin' to rain there for a while," he said, making conversation after passing out the lemonade. He had squatted on the sand and lit another cigarette. "Then there wouldn't a been much goin' on. But it turned out fine after all—there'll be a mob here before long."

She sipped the lemonade, but said little. He felt she had sat down only because of the boys, for she merely smiled and gave short answers to his questions. He learned the boys' names, Melvin and James; their ages, seven and nine; and that they were still frightened by the water. But he wanted to ask her name, and inquire about her husband. But he could not capture the courage.

Now the sun was hot and the sand was hot. And an orange and white umbrella was going up right beside them—two fellows and a girl. When the fellow who had been kneeling to drive the umbrella spike in the sand stood up, he was string-bean tall, and black, with his glistening hair freshly processed. The girl was a lighter brown, and wore a lilac bathing suit, and although her legs were thin, she was pleasant enough to look at. The second fellow was medium, really, in height, but short beside his tall, black friend. He was yellow-skinned, and fast getting bald, although still in his early thirties. Both men sported little shoestring moustaches.

Elijah watched them in silence as long as he could. "You picked the right spot all right!" he laughed at last, putting on his sunglasses.

"How come, man?" The tall, black fellow grinned, showing his mouthful of gold teeth.

"You see everybody here!" happily rejoined Elijah. "They all come here!"

"Man, I been coming here for years," the fellow reproved, and sat down in his khaki swimming trunks to take off his shoes. Then he stood up. "But right now, in the water I goes." He looked down at the girl. "How 'bout you, Lois, baby?"

"No, Caesar," she smiled, "not yet; I'm gonna sit here awhile and relax."

"Okay, then—you just sit right there and relax. And Little Joe"—he turned and grinned to his shorter friend—"you sit there an' relax right along with her. You all can talk with this gentleman here"—he nodded at Elijah—"an' his nice wife." Then, pleased with himself, he trotted off toward the water.

The young mother looked at Elijah, as if he should have hastened to correct him. But somehow he had not wanted to. Yet too, Caesar's remark seemed to amuse her, for she soon smiled. Elijah felt the pain of relief—he did not want her to go; he glanced at her with a furtive laugh, and then they both laughed. The boys had finished their lemonade now, and were digging in the sand. Lois and Little Joe were busy talking.

Elijah was not quite sure what he should say to the mother. He did not understand her, was afraid of boring her, was desperate to keep her interested. As she sat looking out over the lake, he watched her. She was not pretty; and she was too thin. But he thought she had poise; he liked the way she treated her boys—tender, but casual; how different from Myrtle's frantic herding.

Soon she turned to the boys. "Want to go back in the water?" she laughed.

The boys looked at each other, and then at her. "Okay," James said finally, in resignation.

"Here, have some more lemonade," Elijah cut in

The boys, rescued for the moment, quickly extended their cups. He poured them more lemonade, as she looked on smiling.

Now he turned to Lois and Little Joe sitting under their orange and white umbrella. "How 'bout some good ole cold lemonade?" he asked with a mushy smile. "I got plenty of cups." He felt he must get something going.

Lois smiled back. "No thanks," she said, fluttering her long eyelashes, "not right now."

He looked anxiously at Little Joe.

"I'll take a cup!" said Little Joe, and turned and laughed to Lois: "Hand me that bag there, will you?" He pointed to her beach bag in the sand. She passed it to him, and he reached in and pulled out a pint of gin. "We'll have some *real* lemonade," he vowed with a daredevilish grin.

Lois squealed with pretended embarrassment. "Oh, Joe!"

Elijah's eyes were big now; he was thinking of the police. But he handed Little Joe a cup and poured the lemonade, to which Joe added gin. Then Joe, grinning, thrust the bottle at Elijah. "How 'bout yourself, chief?" he said.

Elijah, shaking his head, leaned forward and whispered, "You ain't suppose to drink on the beach y'know."

"This ain't a drink, man—it's a taste!" said Little Joe, laughing and waving the bottle around toward the young mother. "How 'bout a little taste for your wife here?" he said to Elijah.

The mother laughed and threw up both hands. "No, not for me!"

Little Joe gave her a rakish grin. "What'sa matter? You 'fraid of that guy?" He jerked his thumb toward Elijah. "You 'fraid of gettin' a whippin', eh?"

"No, not exactly," she laughed.

Elijah was so elated with her his relief burst up in hysterical laughter. His laugh became strident and hoarse and he could not stop. The boys gaped at him, and then at their mother. When finally he recovered, Little Joe asked him, "Whut's so funny 'bout that?" Then Little Joe grinned at the mother. "You beat him up sometimes, eh?"

This started Elijah's hysterics all over again. The mother looked concerned now, and embarrassed; her laugh was nervous and shadowed. Little Joe glanced at Lois, laughed, and shrugged his shoulders. When Elijah finally got control of himself again he looked spent and demoralized.

Lois now tried to divert attention by starting a conversation with the boys. But the mother showed signs of restlessness and seemed ready to go. At this moment Caesar returned. Glistening beads of water ran off his long, black body; and his hair was unprocessed now. He surveyed the group and then flashed a wide, gold-toothed grin. "One big, happy family, like I said." Then he spied the paper cup in Little Joe's hand. "Whut you got there, man?"

Little Joe looked down into his cup with a playful smirk. "Lemonade, lover boy, lemonade."

"Don't hand me that jive, Joey. You ain't never had any straight lemonade in your life."

This again brought uproarious laughter from Elijah. "I got the straight lemonade here!" He beat the thermos jug with his hand. "Come on—have some!" He reached for a paper cup.

"Why, sure," said poised Caesar. He held out the cup and received the lemonade. "Now, gimme that gin," he said to Little Joe. Joe handed over the gin, and Caesar poured three fingers into the lemonade and sat down in the sand with his legs crossed under him. Soon he turned to the two boys, as their mother watched him with amusement. "Say, ain't you boys goin' in any more? Why don't you tell your daddy there to take you in?" He nodded toward Elijah.

Little Melvin frowned at him. "My daddy's workin'," he said.

Caesar's eyebrows shot up. "Oooh, la, la!" he crooned. "Hey, now!" And he turned and looked at the mother and then at Elijah, and gave a clownish little snigger.

Lois tittered before feigning exasperation at him. "There you go again," she said, "talkin' when you shoulda been listening."

Elijah laughed along with the rest. But he felt deflated. Then he glanced at the mother, who was laughing too. He could detect in her no sign of dismay. Why then had she gone along with the gag in the first place, he thought—if now she didn't hate to see it punctured?

"Hold the phone!" softly exclaimed Little Joe. "Whut is this?" He was staring over his shoulder. Three women, young, brown, and worldly looking, wandered toward them, carrying an assortment of beach paraphernalia and looking for a likely spot. They wore scant bathing suits, and were followed, but slowly, by an older woman with big, unsightly thighs. Elijah recognized her at once. She was the old gal who the Saturday before had chased him away from her beach party. She wore the same white bathing suit, and one of her girls carried the pea-green umbrella.

Caesar forgot his whereabouts ogling the girls. The older woman, observing this, paused to survey the situation. "How 'bout along in here?" she finally said to one of the girls. The girl carrying the thermos jug set it in the sand so close to Caesar it nearly touched him. He was rapturous. The girl with the umbrella had no chance to put it up, for Caesar and Little Joe instantly encumbered her with help. Another girl turned on a portable radio, and grinning, feverish Little Joe started snapping his fingers to the music's beat.

Within a half hour, a boisterous party was in progress. The little radio, perched on a hump of sand, blared out hot jazz, as the older woman—whose name turned out to be Hattie—passed around some cold, rum-spiked punch; and before long she went into her dancing-prancing act—to the riotous delight of all, especially Elijah. Hattie did not remember him from the Saturday past, and he was glad, for everything was so different today! As different as milk and ink. He knew no one realized it, but this was his party really—the wildest, craziest, funniest, and best he had ever seen or heard of. Nobody had been near the water—except Caesar, and the mother and boys much earlier. It appeared Lois was Caesar's girl friend, and she was hence more capable of reserve in face of the come-on antics of Opal, Billie, and Quanita—Hattie's girls. But Little Joe, to Caesar's tortured envy, was both free and aggressive. Even the young mother, who now volunteered her name to be Mrs. Green, got frolicsome, and twice jabbed Little Joe in the ribs.

Finally Caesar proposed they all go in the water. This met with instant, tipsy acclaim; and Little Joe, his yellow face contorted from laughing, jumped up, grabbed Billie's hand and made off with her across the sand. But Hattie would not budge. Full of rum, and stubborn, she sat sprawled with her flaccid thighs spread in an obscene V, and her eyes half shut. Now she yelled at her departing girls: "You all watch out, now! Don'tcha go in too far. . . . Just wade! None o'you can swim a lick!"

Elijah now was beyond happiness. He felt a floating, manic glee. He sprang up and jerked Mrs. Green splashing into the water, followed by her somewhat less ecstatic boys. Caesar had to paddle about with Lois and leave Little Joe unassisted to caper with Billie, Opal, and Quanita. Billie was the prettiest of the three, and despite Hattie's contrary statement, she could swim; and Little Joe, after taking her out in deeper water, waved back to Caesar in triumph. The sun was brazen now, and the beach and lake thronged with a variegated humanity. Elijah, a strong but awkward, country-style swimmer, gave Mrs. Green a lesson in floating on her back, and though she too could swim, he often felt obligated to place both his arms under her young body and buoy her up.

And sometimes he would purposely let her sink to her chin, whereupon she would feign a happy fright and utter faint simian screeches. Opal and Quanita sat in the shallows and kicked up their heels at Caesar, who, fully occupied with Lois, was a grinning, water-threshing study in frustration.

Thus the party went—on and on—till nearly four o'clock. Elijah had not known the world afforded such joy; his homely face was a wet festoon of beams and smiles. He went from girl to girl, insisting she learn to float on his outstretched arms. Once begrudging Caesar admonished him, "Man, you gonna drown one o' them pretty chicks." And Little Joe bestowed his highest accolade by calling him "lover boy," as Elijah nearly strangled from laughter.

At last they looked up to see old Hattie as she reeled down to the water's edge, coming to fetch her girls. Both Caesar and Little Joe ran out of the water to meet her, seized her by the wrists, and, despite her struggles and curses, dragged her in. "Turn me loose! You big galoots!" she yelled and gasped as the water hit her. She was in knee-deep before she wriggled and fought herself free, with such force she sat down in the wet sand with a thud. She roared a laugh now, and spread her arms for help, as her girls came sprinting and splashing out of the water and tugged her to her feet. Her eyes narrowed to vengeful, grinning slits as she turned on Caesar and Little Joe: "I know whut you two're up to!" She flashed a glance around toward her girls. "I been watchin' both o' you studs! Yeah, yeah, but your eyes may shine, an' your teeth may grit. . . ." She went limp in a sneering, raucous laugh. Everybody laughed now—except Lois and Mrs. Green.

They had all come out of the water now, and soon the whole group returned to their three beach umbrellas. Hattie's girls immediately prepared to break camp. They took down their pea-green umbrella, folded some wet towels, and donned their beach sandals, as Hattie still bantered Caesar and Little Joe.

"Well, you sure had yourself a ball today," she said to Little Joe, who was sitting in the sand.

"Coming back next Saturday?" asked grinning Little Joe.

"I jus' might at that," surmised Hattie. "We wuz here last Saturday."

"Good! Good!" Elijah broke in. "Let's all come back—next Saturday!" He searched every face.

"I'll be here," chimed Little Joe, grinning to Caesar. Captive Caesar glanced at Lois, and said nothing.

Lois and Mrs. Green were silent. Hattie, insulted, looked at them and started swelling up. "Never mind," she said pointedly to Elijah, "you jus' come on anyhow. You'll run into a slew o' folks lookin' for a good time. You don't need no certain people." But a little later, she and her girls all said friendly goodbyes and walked off across the sand.

The party now took a sudden downturn. All Elijah's efforts at resuscitation seemed unavailing. The westering sun was dipping toward the distant buildings of the city, and many of the bathers were leaving. Caesar and Little Joe had become bored; and Mrs. Green's boys, whining to go, kept a reproachful eye on their mother.

"Here, you boys, take some more lemonade," Elijah said quickly, reaching for the thermos jug. "Only got a little left—better get while gettin's good!" He laughed. The boys shook their heads.

On Lois he tried cajolery. Smiling and pointing to her wet, but trim bathing suit, he asked, "What color would you say that is?"

"Lilac," said Lois, now standing.

"It sure is pretty! Prettiest on the beach!" he whispered.

Lois gave him a weak smile. Then she reached down for her beach bag, and looked at Caesar.

Caesar stood up. "Let's cut," he turned and said to Little Joe, and began taking down their orange and white umbrella.

Elijah was desolate. "Whatta you goin' for? It's getting cooler! Now's the time to enjoy the beach!"

"I've got to go home," Lois said.

Mrs. Green got up now; her boys had started off already. "Just a minute, Melvin," she called, frowning. Then, smiling, she turned and thanked Elijah.

He whirled around to them all. "Are we comin' back next Saturday? Come on—let's all come back! Wasn't it great! It was great! Don't you think? Whatta you say?" He looked now at Lois and Mrs. Green.

"We'll see," Lois said, smiling. "Maybe."

"Can you come?" He turned to Mrs. Green.

"I'm not sure," she said. "I'll try."

"Fine! Oh, that's fine!" He turned on Caesar and Little Joe. "I'll be lookin' for you guys, hear?"

"Okay, chief," grinned Little Joe. "An' put somethin' in that lemonade, will ya?"

Everybody laughed . . . and soon they were gone.

Elijah slowly crawled back under his umbrella, although the sun's heat was almost spent. He looked about him. There was only one umbrella on the spot now, his own, where before there had been three. Cigarette butts and paper cups lay strewn where Hattie's girls had sat, and the sandy imprint of Caesar's enormous street shoes marked his site. Mrs. Green had dropped a bobby pin. He too was caught up now by a sudden urge to go. It was hard to bear much longer—the lonesomeness. And most of the people were leaving anyway. He stirred and fidgeted in the sand, and finally started an inventory of his belongings. . . . Then his thoughts flew home, and he reconsidered. Funny—he hadn't thought of home all afternoon. Where had the time gone anyhow? . . . It seemed he'd just pulled up in the Chevy and unloaded his gear; now it was time to go home again. Then the image of solemn Randy suddenly formed in his mind, sending waves of guilt through him. He forgot where he was as the duties of his existence leapt on his back—where would he ever get Randy's fifteen dollars? He felt squarely confronted by a great blank void. It was an awful thing he had done—all for a day at the beach . . . with some sporting girls. He thought of his family and felt tiny—and him itching to come back next Saturday! Maybe Myrtle was right about him after all. Lord, if she knew what he had done. . . .

He sat there for a long time. Most of the people were gone now. The lake was quiet save for a few boys still in the water. And the sun, red like blood, had settled on the dark silhouettes of the housetops across the city. He sat beneath the umbrella just as he had at one o'clock . . . and the thought smote him. He was jolted. Then dubious. But there it was—quivering, vital, swelling inside his skull like an unwanted fetus. So this was it! He mutinied inside. So he must sell it . . . his umbrella. Sell it for anything—only as long as it was enough to pay back Randy. For fifteen dollars even, if necessary. He was dogged; he couldn't do it; that wasn't the answer anyway. But the thought clawed and clung to him, rebuking and coaxing him by turns, until it finally became conviction. He must do it; it was the right thing to do; the only thing to do. Maybe then the awful weight would lift, the dull commotion in his stomach cease. He got up and started collecting his belongings; placed the thermos jug, sunglasses, towel, cigarettes, and little rug together in a neat pile, to be carried to the Chevy later. Then he turned to face his umbrella. Its red and white stripes stood defiant against the wide, churned-up sand. He stood for a moment mooning at it. Then he carefully let it down, and carrying it in his right hand, went off across the sand.

The sun now had gone down behind the vast city in a shower of crimson-golden glints, and on the beach only a few stragglers remained. For his first prospects he approached two teen-age boys, but suddenly realizing they had no money he turned away and went over to an old woman, squat and black, in street clothes—a spectator—who stood gazing eastward out across the lake. She held in her hand a little black book, with red-edged pages, which looked like the New Testament. He smiled at her. "Wanna buy a nice new beach umbrella?" He held out the collapsed umbrella toward her.

She gave him a beatific smile, but shook her head. "No, son," she said, "that ain't what I want." And she turned to gaze out on the lake again.

For a moment he still held the umbrella out, with a question mark on his face. "Okay, then," he finally said, and went on.

Next he hurried down to the water's edge, where he saw a man and two women preparing to leave. "Wanna buy a nice new beach umbrella?" His voice sounded high-pitched, as he opened the umbrella over his head. "It's brand-new. I'll sell it for fifteen dollars—it cost a lot more'n that."

The man was hostile, and glared. Finally he said, "Whatta you take me for—a fool?"

Elijah looked bewildered, and made no answer. He observed the man for a moment. Finally he let the umbrella down. As he moved away, he heard the man say to the women, "It's hot—he stole it somewhere."

Close by another man sat alone in the sand. Elijah started toward him. The man wore trousers, but was stripped to the waist, and bent over intent on some task in his lap. When Elijah reached him he looked up from half a hatful of cigarette butts he was breaking open for the tobacco he collected in a little paper bag. He grinned at Elijah, who meant now to pass on.

"No, I ain't interested either, buddy," the man insisted as Elijah passed him. "Not me. I jus' got outa jail las' week—an' ain't goin' back for no umbrella." He laughed, as Elijah kept on.

Now he saw three women, still in their bathing suits, sitting together near the diving board. They were the only people he had not yet tried—except the one lifeguard left. As he approached them, he saw that all three wore glasses and wore sedate. Some schoolteachers maybe, he thought, or office workers. They were talking—until they saw him coming; then they stopped. One of them was plump, but a smooth dark brown, and sat with a towel around her shoulders. Elijah addressed them through her: "Wanna buy a nice beach umbrella?" And again he opened the umbrella over his head.

"Gee! It's beautiful," the plump woman said to the others. "But where'd you get it?" she suddenly asked Elijah, polite mistrust entering her voice.

"I bought it—just this week."

The three women looked at each other. "Why do you want to sell it so soon then?" a second woman said.

Elijah grinned. "I need the money."

"Well!" The plump woman was exasperated. "No, we don't want it." And they turned from him. He stood for a while, watching them; finally he let the umbrella down and moved on.

Only the lifeguard was left. He was a huge youngster, not over twenty, and brawny and black as he bent over cleaning out his beached rowboat. Elijah approached him so suddenly he looked up startled.

"Would you be interested in this umbrella?" Elijah said, and proffered the umbrella. "It's brand-new—I just bought it Tuesday. I'll sell it cheap." There was urgency in his voice.

The lifeguard gave him a queer stare; and then peered off toward the Outer Drive, as if looking for help. "You're lucky as hell," he finally said. "The cops just now cruised by—up on the Drive. I'd have turned you in so quick it'd make your head swim. Now you get the hell outa here." He was menacing.

Elijah was angry. "Whatta you mean? I bought this umbrella—it's mine."

The lifeguard took a step toward him. "I said you better get the hell outa here! An' I mean it! You thievin' bastard, you!"

Elijah, frightened now, gave ground. He turned and walked away a few steps; and then slowed up, as if an adequate answer had hit him. He stood for a moment. But finally he walked on, the umbrella drooping in his hand.

He walked up the gravelly slope now toward the Chevy, forgetting his little pile of belongings left in the sand. When he reached the car, and opened the trunk, he remembered; and went back down and gathered them up. He returned, threw them in the trunk and, without dressing, went around and climbed under the steering wheel. He was scared, shaken; and before starting the motor sat looking out on the lake. It was seven o'clock; the sky was waning pale, the beach forsaken, leaving a sense of perfect stillness and approaching night; the only sound was a gentle lapping of the water against the sand—one moderate hallo-o-o-o would have carried across to Michigan. He looked down at the beach. Where were they all now—the funny, proud, laughing people? Eating their dinners, he supposed, in a variety of homes. And all the beautiful umbrellas—where were they? Without their colors the beach was so deserted. Ah, the beach . . . after pouring hot ore all week out at Youngstown Sheet and Tube, he would probably be too fagged out for the beach. But maybe he wouldn't—who knew? It was great while it lasted . . . great. And his umbrella . . . he didn't know what he'd do with that . . . he might never need it again. He'd keep it, though—and see. Ha! . . . hadn't he sweat to get it! . . . and they thought he had stolen it . . . stolen it . . . ah . . . and maybe they were right. He sat for a few moments longer. Finally he started the motor, and took the old Chevy out onto the Drive in the pink-hued twilight. But down on the beach the sun was still shining.

1. Like Mr. Martin in "The Catbird Seat," Elijah has a consuming desire, and like Mr. Martin, he realizes it. But his happiness is short-lived. Why?

2. Perhaps the theme of this story concerns pride and vanity. What do you feel Cyrus Colter is saying about these qualities? What is the difference between them?

3. If Elijah were rich and handsome, he might be happier. Since he cannot be either, is he doomed to unhappiness? Is there anything he could do to make his life better? Do you know of any poor, homely people who are happy and popular?

4. Sometimes a desire becomes an obsession and we are unable to evaluate it realistically. If Elijah had kept his head and thought about it, might he have changed his desire?

Drunken Lover

OWEN DODSON

This is the stagnant hour:
The dead communion between mouth and mouth,
The drunken kiss lingered,
The dreadful equator south.

This is the hour of impotence
When the unfulfilled is unfulfilled.
Only the stale breath is anxious
And warm. All else is stilled.

Why did I come to this reek,
This numb time, this level?
Only for you, my love, only for you
Could I endure this devil.

I dreamed when I was
A pimply and urgent adolescent
Of these hours when love would be fire
And you the steep descent.

My mouth's inside is like cotton,
Your arm is dead on my arm,
What I pictured so lovely and spring
Is August and fungus calm.

O lover, draw away, grow small, go magic,
O lover, disappear into the tick of this bed;
Open all the windows to the north
For the wind to cool my head.

---

1. What is the poet trying to tell us? How seriously does he intend us to take his message? What are some clues to his attitude?
2. If the man in bed had examined his desire when he was a "pimply and urgent adolescent," would he have avoided his present situation?
3. What do you think he means by "the windows to the north" in contrast to "the dreadful equator to the south"? Can you infer a generalization about desire and its satisfaction?
4. In order to make his state of emotion clear to us, the poet has analyzed the state of the man in bed. What are some of the parts of his experience that add up to the total situation?
5. Should he swear off liquor and women forever, or is a better answer implied?

1. What seem to be the desires of the woman in the fish bowl?
2. How is she different from "The Woman at the Washington Zoo" in Unit 8?
3. A fish bowl can be seen out of as well as into. Is this part of the woman's problem?
4. She is obviously unhappy. What might make her happy? Are her desires capable of fulfillment?
5. What kind of activity might make her at least partially happy?

PLATE XI

THE FISH BOWL: Pavel Tchelitchew. Collection of R. Kirk Askew, Jr.

The Law: William Gropper

12

analyzing an institution

An institution is a firmly established way of doing things. Marriage is an institution for dealing with the problems of sex and child-rearing; the school is an institution for learning. An institution exists as long as most people believe it is the best way of accomplishing its purpose. But institutions are changed from time to time or even eliminated. Monarchy was once an institution questioned by few; now there are few monarchies left.

In our society, institutions are constantly being questioned. War is no longer taken for granted as inevitable. The Electoral College and the makeup of congressional committees are being looked at closely. The efficacy of schools, prisons, and police is being examined, and these institutions are changing.

An important part of being aware of our surroundings is taking a hard look at some of the institutions that affect us, especially those with which we have had intimate experience. By analyzing these institutions, we may find points where they could be improved.

class discussion

The school is one institution with which you have had experience. In your experience, what parts of the school seem to function well and what parts less well? At what points in its contact with you has the school succeeded in its purpose, and at what points has it failed? What parts of the school would you change and what parts would you leave as they are? Exactly what changes or replacements would you like to see? Why?

writing assignment

1. Choose an institution that is familiar to you: the family, the church, the school, the retail business, the farm (if you have lived or worked on one), the city (if you grew up in one).
2. Define precisely the purposes of this institution in relation to you and others around you.
3. Analyze this institution. Exactly how, part by part, does it function to achieve the purposes you have defined? As you would describe how the parts of a bicycle serve the purpose of moving you around, describe clearly and step by step how the parts of the institution work together.
4. Select the part or parts that you find weakest in their function. Try to find the reason for this weakness and suggest, by reasoning, how the part could be strengthened or eliminated.

class writing assignment

Rewrite your analysis, improving clarity and coherence and adding a functional introduction and conclusion.

The Police Band

DONALD BARTHELME

It was kind of the Department to think up the Police Band. The original impulse, I believe, was creative and humanitarian. A better way of doing things. Unpleasant, bloody things required by the line of duty. Even if it didn't work out.

The Commissioner (the old Commissioner, not the one they have now) brought us up the river from Detroit. Where our members had been, typically, working the Sho Bar two nights a week. Sometimes the Glass Crutch. Friday and Saturday. And the rest of the time wandering the streets disguised as postal employees. Bitten by dogs and burdened with third-class mail.

What are our duties? we asked at the interview. Your duties are to wail, the Commissioner said. That only. We admired our new dark-blue uniforms as we came up the river in canoes like Indians. We plan to use you in certain situations, certain tense situations, to alleviate tension, the Commis-

---

sioner said. I can visualize great success with this new method. And would you play "Entropy." He was pale, with a bad liver.

We are subtle, the Commissioner said, never forget that. Subtlety is what has previously been lacking in our line. Some of the old ones, the Commissioner said, all they know is the club. He took a little pill from a little box and swallowed it with his Scotch.

When we got to town we looked at those Steve Canyon recruiting posters and wondered if we resembled them. Henry Wang, the bass man, looks like a Chinese Steve Canyon, right? The other cops were friendly in a suspicious way. They liked to hear us wail, however.

The Police Band is a very sensitive highly trained and ruggedly anti-Communist unit whose efficacy will be demonstrated in due time, the Commissioner said to the Mayor (the old Mayor). The Mayor took a little pill from a little box and said, We'll see. He could tell we were musicians because we were holding our instruments, right? Emptying spit valves, giving the horn that little shake. Or coming in at letter E with some sly emotion stolen from another life.

The old Commissioner's idea was essentially that if there was a disturbance on the city's streets—some ethnic group cutting up some other ethnic group on a warm August evening—the Police Band would be sent in. The handsome dark-green band bus arriving with sirens singing, red lights whirling. Hard-pressed men on the beat in their white hats raising a grateful cheer. We stream out of the vehicle holding our instruments at high port. A skirmish line fronting the angry crowd. And play "Perdido." The crowd washed with new and true emotion. Startled, they listen. Our emotion stronger than their emotion. A triumph of art over good sense.

That was the idea. The old Commissioner's *musical* ideas were not very interesting, because after all he was a cop, right? But his police ideas were interesting.

We had drills. Poured out of that mother-loving bus onto vacant lots holding our instruments at high port like John Wayne. Felt we were heroes already. Playing "Perdido," "Stumblin'," "Gin Song," "Feebles." Laving the terrain with emotion stolen from old busted-up loves, broken marriages, the needle, economic deprivation. A few old ladies leaning out of high windows. Our emotion washing rusty Rheingold cans and parts of old doors.

This city is too much! We'd be walking down the street talking about our techniques and we'd see out of our eyes a woman standing in the gutter screaming to herself about what we could not imagine. A drunk trying to strangle a dog somebody'd left leashed to a parking meter. The drunk and the dog screaming at each other. This city is too much!

We had drills and drills. It is true that the best musicians come from Detroit but there is something here that you have to get in your playing and that is simply the scream. We got that. The Commissioner, a sixty-three-year-old hippie with no doubt many graft qualities and unpleasant qualities, nevertheless understood that. When we'd play "ugly," he understood that. He understood the rising expectations of the world's peoples also. That our black members didn't feel like toting junk mail around Detroit forever until the ends of their lives. For some strange reason.

He said one of our functions would be to be sent out to play in places where people were trembling with fear inside their houses, right? To inspirit them in difficult times. This was the plan. We set up in the street. Henry Wang grabs hold of his instrument. He has a four-bar lead-in all by himself. Then the whole group. The iron shutters raised a few inches. Shorty Alanio holding his horn at his characteristic angle (sideways). The reeds dropping lacy little fill-ins behind him. We're cooking. The crowd roars.

The Police Band was an idea of a very romantic kind. The Police Band was an idea that didn't work. When they retired the old Commissioner (our Commissioner), who it turned out had a little drug problem of his own, they didn't let us even drill anymore. We have never been used. His idea was a romantic idea, they said (right?), which was not adequate to the rage currently around in the world. Rage must be met with rage, they said. (Not in so many words.) We sit around the precinct houses, under the filthy lights, talking about our techniques. But I thought it might be good if you knew that the Department still has us. We have a good group. We still have emotion to be used. We're still here.

---

1. "The Police Band" is a complex satire that deserves a leisurely reading or two. Is its target police methods, or is its aim broader than that?
2. The old Commissioner is said to have a "drug problem of his own." What is his real problem?
3. Why is the duty of the Police Band to "wail"?
4. Why is the Police Band never used? What comment about our society is implied?

Hawk Roosting

TED HUGHES

I sit in the top of the wood, my eyes closed.
Inaction, no falsifying dream
Between my hooked head and hooked feet:
Or in sleep rehearse perfect kills and eat.

The convenience of the high trees!
The air's buoyancy and the sun's ray
Are of advantage to me;
And the earth's face upward for my inspection.

My feet are locked upon the rough bark.
It took the whole of Creation
To produce my foot, my each feather:
Now I hold Creation in my foot

Or fly up, and revolve it all slowly—
I kill where I please because it is all mine.
There is no sophistry in my body:
My manners are tearing off heads—

The allotment of death.
For the one path of my flight is direct
Through the bones of the living.
No arguments assert my right:

The sun is behind me.
Nothing has changed since I began.
My eye has permitted no change.
I am going to keep things like this.

1. What is the hawk's attitude toward the world? What does he conceive the purpose of the universe to be?
2. What is the hawk's philosophy based on?
3. In order to surprise his victim, the hawk keeps the sun behind him as he descends. What is another meaning of the line "The sun is behind me"?
4. The last five lines indicate that the poem may not be simply about a hawk. Are there people who embody these attitudes? What kinds of people do not use argument to assert their rights and refuse to permit change?
5. Though the poet may not have had this in mind, the line "The sun is behind me" might remind us of the Aztec priesthood of Mexico, which sacrificed to the sun thousands of people a year. The Aztecs believed that the immense power of the sun demanded their blood and that the sun would go out if it was not given. Are there any parallels to the power of the Aztec priests in the modern world? What gives people such power?
6. Is it possible for a person without courage to be a hawk? How?

1. No one could prove that the trinity shown here is anything but noble, even heroic, and worthy of the honor being given and received; but somehow we feel that this is not what the artist intended. Can you point out some proportions, analogies, and details that indicate the artist is being satirical?
2. One art critic has said of the picture, "Grant Wood has caricatured a disagreeable American vice: glorification of the second-rate by mumbo-jumbo." What comment might he be making about institutions?

PLATE XII

HONORARY DEGREE: Grant Wood. Prints Division, The New York Public Library,
Astor Lenox and Tilden Foundations

13

looking
back

Recalling pleasant scenes from childhood is not only enjoyable in itself, but may remind us of simple pleasures we have forgotten. Because children are less preoccupied with study, work, and future goals, they experience more keenly the here and now of the senses. Reliving a childhood episode can help us "get ourselves together" and bring some of the vividness of the past into the present.

class discussion

What are some of the things you enjoyed doing as a child? Let as many members of the class as possible describe different activities. Do you still do any of these things and enjoy them as much? Do you have other activities you enjoy as much? How and why does an adult seem to be different in this respect from a child? Is it possible to be an adult and still hold on to the pleasures of childhood?

narration

Narration is the art of telling a story. Most of us take to it pretty naturally, since we all have listened to stories and told them. Whenever you tell somebody what happened at the drive-in last night, you are narrating. When you are writing, there are a few easy rules to observe. First, you should keep your story unified; it should be about one happening or a series of closely related happenings. Second, it should follow a time sequence and not jump back and forth; you don't want to be one of those storytellers who is always saying, "Oh, I forgot to tell you. . . ." Third, it should begin and end with the beginning and end of the action you are telling about. A story about the night the dinner table collapsed should not begin with your getting up in the morning.

writing assignment

1. Choose the most pleasant childhood experience you can recall.
2. Spend an hour or so in a quiet place writing down all the details you can remember about this experience. Concentrate on sensory data: colors, textures, sounds, smells, bodily sensations. Don't worry about order at this stage.
3. Put everything in the present tense, as though it were happening to you now. Begin each sentence with an expression such as "I feel," "I smell," and so on.
4. Exhaust your memory of the experience. Don't be satisfied until you have thought of many details you haven't recalled in years. You should have several pages when you are through.

class writing assignment

Look over the material you have gathered for the writing assignment and see if you can discover a *thesis*, or generalization, about what was most impressive about the experience. As you rewrite your notes into a narration, emphasize those aspects of the experience.

Village School

LAURIE LEE

The village to which our family had come was a scattering of some twenty to thirty houses down the southeast slope of a valley. The valley was narrow, steep and almost entirely cut off; it was also a funnel for winds, a channel for the floods, and a jungly, bird-crammed, insect-hopping sun trap whenever there happened to be any sun. It was not high and open like the Windrush country, but had secret origins, having been gouged from the escarpment by the melting ice caps some time before we got there. The old flood-terraces still showed on the slopes, along which the cows walked sideways. Like an island, it was possessed of curious survivals—rare orchids and Roman snails; and there were chemical qualities in the limestone springs which gave the women pre-Raphaelite goitres. The sides of the valley were rich in pasture and the crests heavily covered in beech woods.

Living down there was like living in a bean pod; one could see nothing but the bed one lay in. Our horizon of woods was the limit of our world. For weeks on end the trees moved in the wind with a dry roaring that seemed a natural utterance of the landscape. In winter they ringed us with frozen spikes, and in summer they oozed over the lips of the hills like layers of thick green lava. Mornings, they steamed with mist or sunshine, and almost every evening threw streamers above us, reflecting sunsets we were too hidden to see.

Water was the most active thing in the valley, arriving in the long rains from Wales. It would drip all day from clouds and trees, from roofs and eaves and noses. It broke open roads, carved its way through gardens, and filled the ditches with sucking noises. Men and horses walked about in wet sacking, birds shook rainbows from sodden branches, and streams ran from holes, and back into holes, like noisy underground trains.

I remember, too, the light on the slopes, long shadows in tufts and hollows, with cattle, brilliant as painted china, treading their echoing shapes. Bees blew like cake crumbs through the golden air, white butterflies like sugared wafers, and when it wasn't raining a diamond dust took over, which veiled and yet magnified all things.

Most of the cottages were built of Cotswold stone and were roofed by split-stone tiles. The tiles grew a kind of golden moss which sparkled like crystallized honey. Behind the cottages: fruit bushes, roses, rabbit hutches, earth closets, bicycles, and pigeon lofts. In the very sump of the valley wallowed the Squire's Big House—once a fine, though modest, sixteenth-century manor, to which a Georgian façade had been added.

The villagers themselves had three ways of living: working for the Squire, or on the farms, or down in the cloth mills at Stroud. Apart from the Manor, and the ample cottage gardens—which were an insurance against hard times—all other needs were supplied by a church, a chapel, a vicarage, a manse, a wooden hut, a pub—and the village school.

The village school at that time provided all the instruction we were likely to ask for. It was a small stone barn divided by a wooden partition into two rooms—the Infants and the Big Ones. There was one dame teacher, and perhaps a young girl assistant. Every child in the valley came crowding there, remained till he was fourteen years old, then was presented to the working field or factory with nothing in his head more burdensome than a few mnemonics, a jumbled list of wars, and a dreamy image of the world's geography. It seemed enough to get by with, in any case; and was one up on our poor old grandparents.

This school, when I came to it, was at its peak. Universal education and unusual fertility had packed it to the walls with pupils. Wild boys and girls from miles around—from the outlying farms and half-hidden hovels way up at the ends of the valley—swept down each day to add to our numbers, bringing with them strange oaths and odours, quaint garments, and curious pies. They were my first amazed vision of any world outside the womanly warmth of my family; I didn't expect to survive it for long, and I was confronted with it at the age of four.

The morning came, without any warning, when my sisters surrounded me, wrapped me in scarves, tied up my boot laces, thrust a cap on my head, and stuffed a baked potato in my pocket.

"What's this?" I said.

"You're starting school today."

"I ain't. I'm stopping 'ome."

"Now, come on, Loll. You're a big boy now."

"I ain't."

"You are."

"Boo-hoo."

They picked me up bodily, kicking and bawling, and carried me up to the road.

"Boys who don't go to school get put into boxes, and turn into rabbits, and get chopped up Sundays."

I felt this was overdoing it rather, but I said no more after that. I arrived at the school just three feet tall and fatly wrapped in my scarves. The playground roared like a rodeo, and the potato burned through my thigh. Old boots, ragged stockings, torn trousers and skirts, went skating and skidding round me. The rabble closed in; I was encircled; grit flew in my face like shrapnel. Tall girls with frizzled hair, and huge boys with sharp elbows, began to prod me with hideous interest. They plucked at my scarves, spun me round like a top, screwed my nose, and stole my potato.

I was rescued at last by a gracious lady—the sixteen-year-old junior teacher—who boxed a few ears and dried my face and led me off to the Infants. I spent that first day picking holes in paper, then went home in a smouldering temper.

"What's the matter, Loll? Didn't he like it at school, then?"

"They never give me the present!"

"Present? What present?"

"They said they'd give me a present."

"Well, now, I'm sure they didn't."

"They did! They said: 'You're Laurie Lee, ain't you? Well, just you sit there for the present.' I sat there all day but I never got it I ain't going back there again!"

But after a week I felt like a veteran and grew as ruthless as anyone else. Somebody had stolen my baked potato, so I swiped somebody else's apple. The Infant Room was packed with toys such as I'd never seen before— coloured shapes and rolls of clay, stuffed birds and men to paint. Also a frame of counting beads which our young teacher played like a harp, leaning her bosom against our faces and guiding our wandering fingers. . . .

The beautiful assistant left us at last, and was replaced by an opulent widow. She was tall, and smelt like a cartload of lavender; and wore a hair net, which I thought was a wig. I remember going close up and having a good look—it was clearly too square to be hair.

"What are you staring at?" the widow enquired.

I was much too soft-hearted to answer.

"Go on. Do tell. You needn't be shy."

"You're wearing a wig," I said.

"I can assure you I'm not!" She went very red.

"You are. I seen it." I said.

The new teacher grew flustered and curiously cross. She took me upon her knee.

"Now look very close. Is that really a wig?"

I looked hard, saw the net, and said, "Yes."

"Well, really!" she said, while the Infants gaped. "I can assure you it's *not* a wig! And if only you could watch me getting dressed in the morning you'd know it wasn't one either."

She shook me from her knee like a sodden cat, but she'd stirred my imagination. To suggest I might watch her getting dressed in the morning seemed to me both outrageous and wonderful.

This tiny, white-washed Infants' Room was a brief but cozy anarchy. In that short time allowed us we played and wept, broke things, fell asleep, cheeked the teacher, discovered the things we could do to each other, and exhaled our last guiltless days.

My desk companions were those two blond girls, already puppyishly pretty, whose names and bodies were to distract and haunt me for the next fifteen years of my life. Rosie and Jo were limpet chums; they sat holding hands all day; and there was a female self-possession about their pink sticky faces that made me shout angrily at them.

Vera was another I studied and liked; she was lonely, fuzzy and short. I felt a curious compassion for stumpy Vera; and it was through her, and no beauty, that I got into trouble and received the first public shock of my life. How it happened was simple, and I was innocent, so it seemed. She came up to me in the playground one morning and held her face close to mine. I had a stick in my hand, so I hit her on the head with it. Her hair was springy, so I hit her again and watched her mouth open with a yell.

To my surprise a commotion broke out around me, cries of scandal from the older girls, exclamations of horror and heavy censure mixed with Vera's sobbing wails. I was intrigued, not alarmed, that by wielding a beech stick I was able to cause such a stir. So I hit her again, without spite or passion, then walked off to try something else.

The experiment might have ended there and, having ended, would have been forgotten. But no; angry faces surrounded me, very red, all spitting and scolding.

"Horrid boy! Poor Vera! Little monster! Urgh! We're going to tell teacher about you!"

Something was wrong, the world seemed upset; I began to feel vaguely uneasy. I had only hit Vera on her wiry black hair, and now everybody was shouting at me. I ran and hid, feeling sure it would pass, but they hunted me down in the end. Two big righteous girls hauled me out by the ears.

"You're wanted in the Big Room, for 'itting Vera. You're 'alf going to cop it!" they said.

So I was dragged to that Room, where I'd never been before and, under the savage eyes of the older children, Teacher gave me a scalding lecture. I was confused by now and shaking with guilt. At last I smirked and ran out of the room. I had learnt my first lesson, that I could not hit Vera, no matter how fuzzy her hair. And something else too: that the summons to the Big Room, the policeman's hand on the shoulder, comes almost always as a complete surprise, and for the crime that one has forgotten.

My brother Jack, who was with me in the Infants, was too clever to stay there long. Indeed, he was so bright he made us uncomfortable, and we were all of us glad to get rid of him. Sitting pale in his pinafore, gravely studying, commanding the teacher to bring him fresh books, or to sharpen his pencils, or to make less noise, he was an Infant freak from the start. So he was promoted to the Big Room with unprecedented promptness, given a desk and a dozen atlases to sit on, from which he continued to bully the teachers in that cold clear voice of his.

But I, myself, was a natural Infant, content to serve out my time, to slop around and whine and idle; and no one suggested I shouldn't. So I remained long after bright Jack had moved on, the fat lord of my nursery life, skilled at cutting out men from paper, chalking suns on the walls, making snakes from clay, idling voluptuously through the milky days with a new young teacher to feed on. But my time was slowly running out; my Big Room bumps were growing. Suddenly, almost to my dismay, I found that I could count up to a hundred, could write my name in both large and small letters, and subtract certain numbers from each other. I had even just succeeded in subtracting Rosie from Jo, when the call came down from on high. Infant no longer, I was being moved up—the Big Room was ready for me.

I found there a world both adult and tough, with long desks and inkwells, strange maps on the walls, huge boys, heavy boots, scratching pens, groans of labour, and sharp and sudden persecutions. Gone for ever were the infant excuses, the sanctuary of lisping charms. Now I was alone and unprotected, faced by a struggle which required new techniques, where one made pacts and split them, made friends and betrayed them, and fought for one's place near the stove.

The stove was a symbol of caste among us, the tub of warmth to which we cleaved during the long seven months of winter. It was made of cast-iron and had a noisy mouth which rattled coke and breathed out fumes. It was decorated by a tortoise labelled "Slow But Sure," and in winter it turned red hot. If you pressed a pencil against it the wood burst into flames; and if you spat on the top the spit hopped and gambolled like tiny ping-pong balls.

My first days in the Big Room were spent in regret for the young teacher I'd left in the Infants, for her braided breasts and unbuttoning hands and her voice of sleepy love. Quite clearly the Big Room boasted no such comforts; Miss B., the Head Teacher, to whom I was now delivered, being about as physically soothing as a rake.

She was a bunched and punitive little body and the school had christened her Crabby; she had a sour yellow look, lank hair coiled in earphones, and the skin and voice of a turkey. We were all afraid of the gobbling Miss B.; she spied, she pried, she crouched, she crept, she pounced—she was a terror.

Each morning was war without declaration; no one knew who would catch it next. We stood to attention, half-crippled in our desks, till Miss B. walked in, whacked the walls with a ruler, and fixed us with her squinting eye. "Good a-morning, children!" "Good morning, Teacher!" The greeting was like a rattling of swords. Then she would scowl at the floor and begin to growl "Ar Farther . . ."; at which we said the Lord's Prayer, praised all good things, and thanked God for the health of our King. But scarcely had we bellowed the last Amen than Crabby coiled, uncoiled and sprang, and knocked some poor boy sideways.

One seldom knew why; one was always off guard, for the punishment preceded the charge. The charge, however, followed hard upon it, to a light shower of angry spitting.

"Shuffling your feet! Playing with the desk! A-smirking at that miserable Betty! I will not have it. I'll not, I say. I repeat—I will not have it!"

Many a punch-drunk boy in a playground battle, out-numbered and beaten to his knees, would be heard to cry: "I will not have it! I'll not, I say! I repeats I will not have it." It was an appeal to the code of our common suffering, and called for immediate mercy.

So we did not much approve of Crabby—though she was responsible for our excellent reflexes. Apart from this, her teaching was not memorable. She appears in my recollection as merely a militant figure, a hunched-up little creature all spring-coils and slaps—not a monster by any means, but a natural manifestation of what we expected of school.

For school in my day, that day, Crabby's day, seemed to be designed simply to keep us out of the air and from following the normal pursuits of the fields. Crabby's science of dates and sums and writing seemed a typical invention of her own, a sour form of fiddling or prison labour like picking oakum or sewing sacks.

So while the bright times passed, we sat locked in our stocks, our bent backs turned on the valley. The June air infected us with primitive hungers, grass seed and thistledown idled through the windows, we smelt the fields and were tormented by cuckoos, while every out-of-door sound that came drifting in was a sharp nudge in the solar plexus. The creaking of wagons going past the school, harness-jingle and the cries of the carters, the calling of cows from the seventeen-acre, Fletcher's chattering mower, gunshots from the warrens—all tugged and pulled at our active wishes till we could have done Miss B. a murder.

And indeed there came the inevitable day when rebellion raised its standard, when the tension was broken and a hero emerged whom we would willingly have named streets after. At least, from that day his name was honoured, though we gave him little support at the time. . . .

Spadge Hopkins it was, and I must say we were surprised. He was one of those heavy, full-grown boys, thick-legged, red-fisted, bursting with flesh, designed for the great outdoors. He was nearly fourteen by then, and physically out of scale—at least so far as our school was concerned. The sight of him squeezed into his tiny desk was worse than a bullock in ballet shoes. He wasn't much of a scholar; he groaned as he worked, or hacked at his desk with a jackknife. Miss B. took her pleasure in goading him, in forcing him to read out loud; or in asking him sudden unintelligible questions which made him flush and stumble.

The great day came; a day of shimmering summer, with the valley outside in a state of leafy levitation. Crabby B. was at her sourest, and Spadge Hopkins had had enough. He began to writhe in his desk, and roll his eyes, and kick with his boots, and mutter: "She'd better look out. 'Er—Crabby B. She'd better, that's all. I can tell you . . ."

We didn't quite know what the matter was, in spite of his meaning looks. Then he threw down his pen, said: "Sod it all," got up and walked to the door.

"And where are you going, young man, may I ask?" said Crabby with her awful leer.

Spadge paused and looked her straight in the eye.

"If it's any business of yourn."

We shivered with pleasure at this defiance. Spadge leisurely made for the door.

"Ta-ta," said Spadge.

"Sit down this instant!" Crabby suddenly screamed. "I won't have it!"

Then Crabby sprang like a yellow cat, spitting and clawing with rage. She caught Spadge in the doorway and fell upon him. There was a shameful moment of heavy breathing and scuffling, while the teacher tore at his clothes. Spadge caught her hands in his great red fists and held her at arm's length, struggling.

"Come and help me, someone!" wailed Crabby, demented. But nobody moved; we just watched. We saw Spadge lift her up and place her on the top of the cupboard, then walk out of the door and away. There was a moment of silence, then we all laid down our pens and began to stamp on the floor in unison. Crabby stayed where she was, on top of the cupboard, drumming her heels and weeping.

We expected some terrible retribution to follow, but nothing happened at all. Not even the trouble-spark, Spadge, was called to account—he was simply left alone. From that day Crabby never spoke to him, or crossed his path, or denied him anything at all. He perched idly in his desk, his knees up to his chin, whistling in a world of his own. Sometimes Miss B. would consider him narrowly, and if he caught her glance he just winked. Otherwise he was free to come and go, and to take time off as he pleased.

But we never revelled again; things changed. Crabby B. was replaced by a new Head Teacher—a certain Miss Wardley from Birmingham. This lady was something quite new in our lives. She wore sharp glass jewellery which winked as she walked, and she sounded her "gees" like gongs. But she was fond of singing and she was fond of birds, and she encouraged us in the study of both. She was more sober than Crabby, her reins looser but stronger; and after the first hilarity of her arrival and strangeness, we accepted her proper authority.

Not that she approved very much of me. "Fat-and-Lazy," was the name she called me. After my midday dinner of baked cabbage and bread I would often nod off in my desk. "Wake up!" she would cry, cracking my head with a ruler. "You and your little red eyes!" She also took exception to my steady sniff, which to me came as natural as breathing. "Go out into the road and have a good blow, and don't come back in till you're clear." But I wouldn't blow, not for anyone on earth, especially if ordered to do so; so I'd sit out on the wall, indignant and thunderous, and sniff away louder than ever. I wouldn't budge either, or come back in, till a boy was sent to fetch me. Miss Wardley would greet me with freezing brightness. "A little less beastly now? How about bringing a hanky tomorrow? I'm sure we'd all be grateful." I'd sit and scowl, then forget to scowl, and would soon be asleep again. . . .

My brothers, by this time, were all with me at school. Jack, already the accepted genius, was long past our scope or help. It was agreed that his brains were of such distinction that they absolved him from mortal contacts. So he was left in a corner where his flashes of brilliance kept him twinkling away like a pin-table. Young Tony came last, but he again was different, being impervious either to learning or authority, importing moreover a kind of outrageous cheekiness so inspired that it remained unanswerable. He would sit all day picking holes in blotting paper, his large eyes deep and knowing, his quick tongue scandalous, his wit defiant, his will set against all instruction. There was nothing anyone could do about him, except to yelp at the things he said.

I alone, the drowsy middleman of these two, found it hard to win Miss Wardley's approval. I achieved this in the end by writing long faked essays on the lives and habits of otters. I'd never seen an otter, or even gone to look for one, but the essays took her in. They were read out aloud, and even earned me medals, but that's nothing to boast about.

Our village school was poor and crowded, but in the end I relished it. It had a lively reek of steaming life: boys' boots, girls' hair, stoves and sweat, blue ink, white chalk and shavings. We learnt nothing abstract or tenuous there—just simple patterns of facts and letters, portable tricks of calculation, no more than was needed to measure a shed, write out a bill, read a swine-disease warning. Through the dead hours of the morning, through the long afternoons, we chanted away at our tables. Passers-by could hear our rising voices in our bottled-up room on the bank: "Twelve-inches-one-foot. Three-feet-make-a-yard. Fourteen-pounds-make-a-stone. Twelve-stone-a-hundred-weight." We absorbed these figures as primal truths declared by some ultimate power. Unhearing, unquestioning, we rocked to our chanting, hammering the gold nails home. "Twice-two-are-four. One-God-is-Love. One-Lord-is-King. One-King-is-George. One-George-is-Fifth . . ." So it was always, had been, would be for ever; we asked no questions; we didn't hear what we said; yet neither did we ever forget it.

So do I now, through the reiterations of those days, recall that school-room which I scarcely noticed—Miss Wardley in glory on her high desk throne, her long throat tinkling with glass. The bubbling stove with its chink of red fire; the old world map as dark as tea; dead field-flowers in jars on the windowsills; the cupboard yawning with dog-eared books. Then the boys and the girls, the dwarfs and the cripples; the slow fat ones and the quick bony ones; giants and louts, angels and squinters—Walt Kerry, Bill Timbrell, Spadge Hopkins, Clergy Green, the Ballingers and Browns, Betty Gleed, Clarry Hogg, Sam and Sixpence, Rosie and Jo—were ugly and beautiful, scrofulous, warted, ringwormed and scabbed at the knees; we were noisy, crude, intoler ant, cruel, stupid and superstitious. But we moved together out of the clutch of the fates, inhabitors of a world without doom; with a scratching, licking and chewing of pens, a whisper and passing of jokes, a titter of tickling, a grumble of labour, a vague stare at the wall in a dream. . . .

"Oh, miss, please miss, can I go round the back?"

An unwilling nod permits me. I stamp out noisily into a swoop of fresh air and a musical surge of birds. All around me now is the free green world, with Mrs. Birt hanging out her washing. I take stock of myself for a moment, alone. I hear the schoolroom's beehive hum. Of course I don't really belong to that lot at all; I know I'm something special, a young king perhaps placed secretly here in order to mix with the commoners. There is clearly a mystery about my birth, I feel so unique and majestic. One day, I know, the secret will be told. A coach with footmen will appear suddenly at our cottage, and Mother (my mother?) will weep. The family will stand very solemn and respectful, and I shall drive off to take up my throne. I'll be generous, of course, not proud at all; for my brothers there shall be no dungeons. Rather will I feed them on cakes and jellies, and I'll provide all my sisters with princes. Sovereign mercy shall be their portion, little though they deserve it. . . .

I return to the schoolroom and Miss Wardley scowls (she shall curtsy when I am king). But all this is forgotten when Walt Kerry leans over and demands the results of my sums. "Yes, Walt. Of course, Walt. Here, copy them out. They ain't hard; I done 'em all." He takes them, the bully, as his tributary right, and I'm proud enough to give them. Then little Jim Fern, sitting beside me, looks up from his ruined pages. "Ain't you a good scholar! You and your Jack. I wish I was a good scholar like thee!" He gives me a sad, adoring look, and I begin to feel much better.

Playtime comes and we charge outdoors, releasing our steamed-up cries. Somebody punches a head. Somebody bloodies their knees. Boys cluster together like bees. "Let's go round the back then, shall us, eh?" To the dark narrow alley, rich with our mysteries, we make our clattering way. Over the wall is the girls' own place, quite close, and we shout them greetings.

"I 'eard you, Bill Timbrell! I 'eard what you said! You be careful, I'll tell our teacher!"

Flushed and refreshed, we stream back to the playground, whistling, indivisibly male.

"D'you 'ear what I said then? Did you then, eh? *I* told 'em! They 'alf didn't squeal!"

We all double up; we can't speak for laughing, we can't laugh without hitting each other.

Miss Wardley was patient, but we weren't very bright. Our books showed a squalor of blots and scratches as though monkeys were being taught to write. We sang in sweet choirs, and drew like cave-men, but most other faculties escaped us—apart from poetry, of course, which gave no trouble at all. I can remember Miss Wardley, with her squeaking chalk, scrawling the blackboard like a shopping list:

"Write a poem—which *must* scan— on one or more of the following: A Kitten. Fairies. My Holidays. An Old Tinker. Charity. Sea Wreck . . ." ("What's that, miss?")

But it was easy in those days; one wrote a dozen an hour, one simply didn't hesitate, just began at the beginning and worked steadily through the subjects, ticking them off with indefatigable rhymes.

Sometimes there was a beating, which nobody minded—except an occasional red-faced mother. Sometimes a man came and took out our teeth. ("My mum says you ain't to take out any double-'uns. . . ." ". . . Fourteen, fifteen, sixteen, seventeen . . ." "Is they all double-'uns?" "Shut up, you little horror.") Sometimes the Squire would pay us a visit, hand out prizes and make a misty-eyed speech. Sometimes an Inspector arrived on a bicycle and counted our heads and departed. Meanwhile Miss Wardley moved jingling amongst us, instructing, appealing, despairing:

"You're a grub, Walter Kerry. You have the wits of a hen. You're a great hulking lout of an oaf. You can just stay behind and do it over again. You can all stay behind, the lot of you."

When lessons grew too tiresome, or too insoluble, we had our traditional ways of avoiding them.

"Please, miss, I got to stay 'ome tomorrow, to 'elp with the washing— the pigs—me dad's sick."

"I dunno, miss; you never learned us that."

"I 'ad me book stole, miss. Carry Burdock pinched it."

"Please, miss, I got a gurt 'eadache."

Sometimes these worked, sometimes they didn't. But once, when some tests hung over our heads, a group of us boys evaded them entirely by stinging our hands with horseflies. The task took all day, but the results were spectacular—our hands swelled like elephants' trunks. "'Twas a swarm, please, miss. They set on us. We run, but they stung us awful." I remember how we groaned, and that we couldn't hold our pens, but I don't remember the pain.

At other times, of course, we forged notes from our mothers, or made ourselves sick with berries, or claimed to be relations of the corpse at funerals (the churchyard lay only next door). It was easy to start wailing when the hearse passed by. "It's my auntie, miss—it's my cousin Wolf—can I go miss, please miss, can I?" Many a lone coffin was followed to its grave by a straggle of long-faced children, pinched, solemn, raggedly dressed, all strangers to the astonished bereaved.

So our schoolwork was done—or where would we be today? We would be as we are: watching a loom or driving a tractor, and counting in images of fives and tens. This was as much as we seemed to need, and Miss Wardley did not add to the burden. What we learned in her care were the less formal truths—the names of flowers, the habits of birds, the intimacy of objects in being set to draw them, the treacherous innocence of boys, the sly charm of girls, the idiot's soaring fancies, and the tongue-tied dunce's informed authority when it came to talking about stoats. We were as merciless and cruel as most primitives are. But we learnt at that school the private nature of cruelty; and our inborn hatred for freaks and outcasts was tempered by meeting them daily.

There was Nick and Edna from up near the Cross, the children of that brother and sister—the boy was strong and the girl was beautiful, and it was not at school that we learned to condemn them. And there was the gypsy boy, Rosso, who lived up the quarry where his tribe had encamped for the summer. He had a chocolate-smooth face and crisp black curls, and at first we cold-shouldered him. He was a real outsider (they ate snails, it was said) and his slant Indian eyes repelled us. Then one day, out of hunger, he stole some sandwiches and was given the cane by Miss Wardley. Whatever the rights and wrongs of the case, that made him one of us.

We saw him run out of school, grizzling from the beating, and kneel down to tie up his boots. The shopkeeper's wife, passing by at that moment, stopped to preach him a little sermon. "You didn't have to steal, even if you was that hungry. Why didn't you come to me?" The boy gave her a look, picked himself up, and ran off without a word. He knew, as we did, the answer to that one: we set our dogs on the gypsies here. As we walked back home to our cabbage dinners we were all of us filled with compassion. We pictured poor Rosso climbing back to his quarry, hungry to his miserable tents, with nothing but mud and puddles to sit in and the sour banks to scavenge for food. Gypsies no longer seemed either sinister or strange. No wonder they eat snails, we thought.

The narrow school was just a conveyor belt along which the short years drew us. We entered the door marked "Infants," moved gradually to the other, and were then handed back to the world. Lucky, lucky point of time; our eyes were on it always. Meanwhile we had moved to grander desks, saw our juniors multiplying in number; Miss Wardley suddenly began to ask our advice and to spoil us as though we were dying. There was no more to be done, no more to be learned. We began to look round the schoolroom with nostalgia and impatience. During playtime in the road we walked about gravely, patronizing the younger creatures. No longer the trembling, white-faced battles, the flights, the buttering-up of bullies; just a punch here and there to show our authority, then a sober stroll with our peers.

At last Miss Wardley was wringing our hands, tender and deferential. "Good-bye, old chaps, and jolly good luck! Don't forget to come back and see me." She gave each one of us a coy sad glance. She knew that we never would.

---

1. Being an Englishman, Laurie Lee uses terms you may not be familiar with, such as "earth closets" and "picking oakum." However, you can enjoy his vivid childhood memories without understanding every word. What kinds of things does he remember especially? Try to put them into two or three categories.
2. Do you remember the same kinds of things from your early childhood, or do your memories fall into different categories?
3. Has your consciousness changed since you were a small child? In what ways? What are you less aware of now and what are you more aware of?
4. How has Laurie Lee unified his narration?
5. Which senses does he use most? Point out a number of examples.

Eleven

ARCHIBALD MACLEISH

And summer mornings the mute child, rebellious,
Stupid, hating the words, the meanings, hating
The Think now, Think, the Oh but Think! would leave
On tiptoe the three chairs on the verandah
And crossing tree by tree the empty lawn
Push back the shed door and upon the sill
Stand pressing out the sunlight from his eyes
And enter and with outstretched fingers feel
The grindstone and behind it the bare wall
And turn and in the corner on the cool
Hard earth sit listening. And one by one,
Out of the dazzled shadow in the room,
The shapes would gather, the brown plowshare, spades,
Mattocks, the polished helves of picks, a scythe
Hung from the rafters, shovels, slender tines
Glinting across the curve of sickles—shapes
Older than men were, the wise tools, the iron
Friendly with earth. And sit there, quiet, breathing
The harsh dry smell of withered bulbs, the faint
Odor of dung, the silence. And outside
Beyond the half-shut door the blind leaves
And the corn moving. And at noon would come,
Up from the garden, his hard crooked hands
Gentle with earth, his knees still earth-stained, smelling
Of sun, of summer, the old gardener, like
A priest, like an interpreter, and bend
Over his baskets.
                And they would not speak:
They would say nothing. And the child would sit there
Happy as though he had no name, as though
He had been no one: like a leaf, a stem,
Like a root growing—

ELEVEN   from *Collected Poems 1917–1952*. Copyright, 1952, by Archibald MacLeish. Reprinted by permission of the publisher, Houghton Mifflin Company.

1. Why does the child retreat to the shed?
2. Why does he like the company of the gardener at this time, in preference to his parents?
3. Some people believe children should be brought up; others feel they should be allowed to grow up. What is MacLeish saying on this subject?
4. Most children, if they can, find a private place where they can be alone now and then. Can you remember having such a place? If so, can you clearly define why you needed to be alone?

1. Dali has his own way of presenting a childhood memory, using symbols rather than literal images. In general, how would you say the child feels about sex? What are some aspects of the painting that convey this feeling?
2. From the child's sailor suit, we might guess that he belongs to a conservative, middle- or upper-class family where sex is not discussed with children. Where is he likely to have gotten his impressions?
3. Can you remember what your own earliest impressions of sex were like? Do you find any reflection of your feelings in Dali's painting, or were yours entirely different?
4. Using your own experiences as a guide, what kind of sex education do you think children should have?

PLATE XIII

SPECTRE OF SEX APPEAL: Salvador Dali. Private Collection Courtesy, M. Knoedler & Co., Inc., New York, Paris, London

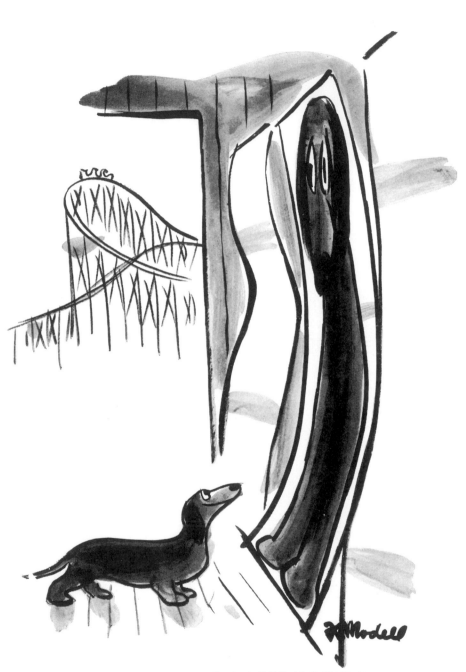

14

taking

a new

perspective

Sometimes when we become too absorbed in looking at the problems of the world around us in conventional ways, it helps to employ fantasy and try a far-out, "just-for-fun" approach. Writers of science fiction make a profession out of such approaches.

There are many ways in which we can take a new perspective by using the imagination: some are being a visitor from another planet, a ghost from the past, or an animal; introducing an event that our world is unprepared for; going to visit a different kind of society; or simply withdrawing to a distance from which we can observe without being involved. By these means, and others, we can look at the foibles of mankind as the entomologist looks at the peculiar customs of ants.

class writing assignment

Imagine that you are an intelligent creature, about the size of a cockroach, green, and shaped like an eggbeater. You have just found your way by accident into this classroom. Describe what you see. (After twenty minutes or so of writing, it might be fun to read some examples aloud.)

writing assignment

1. Imagine that you are a highly intelligent being from a planet unlike the earth, and that you are visiting the area where you live in real life.
2. Narrate your tour of the local area, describing the objects and activities

you see, as a scientist might describe the activities of a newly discovered species.

alternate writing assignment

1. Imagine that a common element in your environment disappears: all the steel around you melts into thin air; or all the money (including substitutes such as checks and credit cards) ceases to exist; or all the trees, plants, and grass are entirely gone.
2. Narrate in concrete detail what happens around you, in your family and community, after this event. How do various people react? What problems arise and how do people try to solve them? How is daily life different and how do you adjust yourself to changes? What is the final outcome?

The Supremacy of Uruguay

E. B. WHITE

Fifteen years after the peace had been made at Versailles, Uruguay came into possession of a very fine military secret. It was an invention, in effect so simple, in construction so cheap, that there was not the slightest doubt that it would enable Uruguay to subdue any or all of the other nations of the earth. Naturally the two or three statesmen who knew about it saw visions of aggrandizement; and although there was nothing in history to indicate that a large country was any happier than a small one, they were very anxious to get going.

The inventor of the device was a Montevideo hotel clerk named Martín Casablanca. He had got the idea for the thing during the 1933 mayoralty campaign in New York City, where he was attending a hotel men's convention. One November evening, shortly before election, he was wandering in the Broadway district and came upon a street rally. A platform had been erected on the marquee of one of the theatres, and in an interval between speeches a cold young man in an overcoat was singing into a microphone. "Thanks," he crooned, "for all the lovely deelight I found in your embrace . . ." The inflection of the love words was that of a murmurous voice, but the volume of the amplified sound was enormous; it carried for blocks, deep into the ranks of the electorate. The Uruguayan paused. He was not unfamiliar with the delight of a lovely embrace, but in his experience it had been pitched lower— more intimate, concentrated. This sprawling, public sound had a curious effect on him. "And thanks for unforgettable nights I never can replace . . ." People swayed against him. In the so bright corner in the too crowded press of bodies, the dominant and searching booming of the love singer struck sharp into him and he became for a few seconds, as he later realized, a loony man. The faces, the mask-faces, the chill air, the advertising lights, the steam rising from the jumbo cup of A. & P. Coffee high over Forty-seventh Street, these added to his enchantment and his unbalance. At any rate, when he left and walked away from Times Square and the great slimy sounds of the love embrace, this was the thought that was in his head:

> If it unhinged me to hear such a soft crooning sound slightly amplified, what might it not do to me to hear a far greater sound greatlier amplified?

Mr. Casablanca stopped. "Good Christ!" he whispered to himself; and his own whisper frightened him, as though it, too, had been amplified.

Chucking his convention, he sailed for Uruguay the following after-noon. Ten months later he had perfected and turned over to his government a war machine unique in military history—a radio-controlled plane carrying an electric phonograph with a retractable streamlined horn. Casablanca had got hold of Uruguay's loudest tenor, and had recorded the bar of music he had heard in Times Square. "Thanks," screamed the tenor, "for unforgettable nights I never can replace . . ." Casablanca prepared to step it up a hundred and fifty thousand times, and grooved the record so it would repeat the phrase endlessly. His theory was that a squadron of pilotless planes scattering this unendurable sound over foreign territories would immediately reduce the populace to insanity. Then Uruguay, at her leisure, could send in her armies, subdue the idiots, and annex the land. It was a most engaging prospect.

The world at this time was drifting rapidly into a nationalistic phase. The incredible cancers of the World War had been forgotten, armaments were being rebuilt, hate and fear sat in every citadel. The Geneva gesture had been prolonged, but only by dint of removing the seat of disarmament to a walled city on a neutral island and quartering the delegates in the waiting destroyers of their respective countries. The Congress of the United States had appro-priated another hundred million dollars for her naval program; Germany had expelled the Jews and recast the steel of her helmets in a firmer mold; and the world was re-living the 1914 prologue. Uruguay waited till she thought the moment was at hand, and then struck. Over the slumbrous hemispheres by night sped swift gleaming planes, and there fell upon all the world, except Uruguay, a sound the equal of which had never been heard before on land or sea.

The effect was as Casablanca had predicted. In forty-eight hours the peoples were hopelessly mad, ravaged by an ineradicable noise, ears shattered, minds unseated. No defence had been possible because the minute anyone came within range of the sound, he lost his sanity and, being daft, proved ineffectual in a military way. After the planes had passed over, life went on much as before, except that it was more secure, sanity being gone. No one could hear anything except the noise in his own head. At the actual moment when people had been smitten with the noise, there had been, of course, some rather amusing incidents. A lady in West Philadelphia happened to be talking to her butcher on the phone. "Thanks," she had just said, "for taking back that tough steak yesterday. And thanks," she added, as the plane passed over, "for unforgettable nights I never can replace." Linotype operators in compos-ing-rooms chopped off in the middle of sentences, like the one who was setting a story about an admiral in San Pedro:

> I am tremendously grateful to all the ladies of San Pedro for the wonderful hospitality they have shown the men of the fleet during our recent

maneuvers and thanks for unforgettable nights I never can replace and thanks
for unforgettable nights I nev-

To all appearances Uruguay's conquest of the earth was complete.
There remained, of course, the formal occupation by her armed forces. That
her troops, being in possession of all their faculties, could establish her
supremacy among idiots, she never for a moment doubted. She assumed that
with nothing but lunacy to combat, the occupation would be mildly stimu-
lating and enjoyable. She supposed her crazy foes would do a few rather funny,
picturesque things with their battleships and their tanks, and then surrender.
What she failed to anticipate was that her foes, being mad, had no intention
of making war at all. The occupation proved bloodless and singularly un-
impressive. A detachment of her troops landed in New York, for example,
and took up quarters in the RKO Building, which was fairly empty at the
time; and they were no more conspicuous around town than the Knights of
Pythias. One of her battleships steamed for England, and the commanding
officer grew so enraged when no hostile ship came out to engage him that
he sent a wireless (which of course nobody in England heard): "Come on out,
you yellow-bellied rats!"

It was the same story everywhere. Uruguay's supremacy was never
challenged by her silly subjects, and she was very little noticed. Territorially
her conquest was magnificent; politically it was a fiasco. The people of the
world paid slight attention to the Uruguayans, and the Uruguayans, for their
part, were bored by many of their territorials—in particular by the
Lithuanians, whom they couldn't stand. Everywhere crazy people lived
happily as children, in their heads the old refrain: "And thanks for unforgettable nights . . ." Billions dwelt contentedly in a fool's paradise. The earth
was bountiful and there was peace and plenty. Uruguay gazed at her vast
domain and saw the whole incident lacked authenticity.

It wasn't till years later, when the descendants of some early American
idiots grew up and regained their senses, that there was a wholesale return
of sanity to the world, land and sea forces were restored to fighting strength,
and the avenging struggle was begun that eventually involved all the races
of the earth, crushed Uruguay, and destroyed mankind without a trace.

1. This fantasy was written in 1933. Since then music amplified to high volume has become a reality, at least at rock concerts, and is usually associated, along with other aids, with a peaceful state of mind. Do you think there is any grain of truth in the story? What is it?
2. Why do the military forces of Uruguay find their victory disappointing? According to the author's implication, what motivates military conquest?
3. Like "The Police Band," this new perspective might stimulate fresh thinking about a stale problem. Discuss.

Southbound on the Freeway

MAY SWENSON

A tourist came in from Orbitville,
parked in the air, and said:

The creatures of this star
are made of metal and glass.

Through the transparent parts
you can see their guts.

Their feet are round and roll
on diagrams or long

measuring tapes, dark
with white lines.

They have four eyes.
The two in back are red.

Sometimes you can see a five-eyed
one, with a red eye turning

on the top of his head.
He must be special—

the others respect him
and go slow

when he passes, winding
among them from behind.

They all hiss as they glide,
like inches, down the marked

tapes. Those soft shapes,
shadowy inside

the hard bodies—are they
their guts or their brains?

---

1. The poet assumes a pose of ignorance and distance to show us what
   a part of our world really looks like. Is there any truth to be found
   in this new perspective?
2. The tourist from Orbitville partially analyzes what he observes. What
   kinds of objects does he see and what qualities of theirs? What are
   some things he fails to see?
3. If the tourist found out more, which of his conclusions would he
   change? Would he still find any of them right?
4. How would you answer the question posed in the last four lines?

1. What things in the painting are not seen in a new way?
2. Try answering the question above with the answer "Nothing." Explain.
3. In this new way of seeing, what are mountains? What is the moon? What are clouds?

PLATE XIV

THE SENSE OF REALITIES: René Magritte. Collection, Oonagh, Lady Oranmore and Browne, Co. Wicklow, Ireland

Index of Authors and Titles

Index of Artists and Plates

A   2
B   3
C   4
D   5
E   6
F   7
G   8
H   9
I   0
J   1